Our/
Courage/ Jews
in Europe
1945–48

With contributions by

Natalia Aleksiun
Moritz Bauerfeind
Kata Bohus
Katharina Friedla
Elisabeth Gallas
Philipp Graf
Atina Grossmann
Werner Hanak
Laura Hobson Faure
Lena Inowlocki
Kamil Kijek
Tamar Lewinsky
Avinoam Patt
Katarzyna Person
Erik Riedel
Joanna Tokarska-Bakir
Mirjam Wenzel

Edited by

Kata Bohus
Atina Grossmann
Werner Hanak
Mirjam Wenzel

This publication was made possible through a generous
donation by Christiane und Nicolaus Weickart.

It is published in conjunction with the exhibition
Our Courage: Jews in Europe 1945–48
Jewish Museum Frankfurt
March 24 – August 22, 2021

JÜDISCHES
MUSEUM
FRANKFURT

Our
Courage / Jews
in Europe
1945–48

DE GRUYTER
OLDENBOURG

TABLE OF CONTENTS

FOREWORD

Werner Hanak
Mirjam Wenzel

Our Courage: Jews in Europe 1945–48 looks at the time immediately after the Holocaust: the days in 1945 when in many parts of Europe it was not the rule of law that prevailed but hunger and violence, and millions of displaced or fleeing persons on the move. It was a time just after the war when many surviving Jews returning to their home towns realized that they had escaped with their lives but had lost everything else. It was a time for taking their destiny into their own hands. In the year 1948 the State of Israel was founded and the United Nations Organization established a new international order and, taking the atrocities in Auschwitz into consideration, new legal norms: the Universal Declaration of Human Rights ("All human beings are born free and equal in dignity and rights") and the Convention on the Prevention and Punishment of the Crime of Genocide.

In recent years, historians have been taking a closer look at the immediate post-war period, particularly the situation of European Jews. The exhibition *Our Courage: Jews in Europe 1945–48* follows up this research and adds to it through specific studies of seven selected places in Europe. It is the first exhibition to look at the situation of Jews in a pan-European perspective. In some places, a new Jewish life was established, only to disappear again in many cases after 1948. All of these places were marked by the Shoah.

The exhibition connects the places with Jewish biographies. It considers transnational and shared features and highlights the attempt by survivors and returnees to take their lives into their own hands again—by reinventing and re-orienting themselves after the brutal dehumanization, and also the search for surviving relatives, the founding of new families, the struggle for support from Allied and Jewish aid organizations to survive, the recording of personal recollections and the associated documentation of Nazi crimes, cultural and artistic activities, a reinterpretation of Jewish holiday traditions, and finally the often desperate attempts to reconstruct destroyed communities or to organize emigration away from Europe.

The life of Jews after World War II was not only marked by the traumatic memory of what had happened just before. It also produced new, sometimes surprising, sometimes distressing moments: Jews who had survived the Shoah in

Eleanor Roosevelt, chairwoman of the UN Human
Rights Commission, in front of the memorial to the
victims of the Shoah at the Zeilsheim DP camp,
surrounded by bodyguards and survivors, 1946.
Beit Hatfutsot, Tel Aviv, courtesy of Stephan Cohen

David Ben-Gurion, chairman of the Jewish Agency
Executive, gives a speech at a public forum during
an official visit to the Zeilsheim DP camp, 1946.
United States Holocaust Memorial Museum, Washington D.C., courtesy of Alice Lev

concentration and extermination camps, in hiding, or in the resistance meeting Jewish soldiers in the Soviet, US, and British armies, or returnees who had fled to the Soviet Union and were repatriated after the war. In Central and Eastern Europe Jewish survivors discovered that their belongings had been looted and that their former neighbors wanted nothing to do with them. The antisemitism still rife in Eastern Europe prompted many to flee again–most to the West, to the DP camps in the American zone. Many were aware that they were living in the proximity of people who had recently espoused Nazi values.

The exhibition title, *Our Courage*, expresses the will to self-assertion and survival after the Shoah. The Yiddish partisan song *Zog nit keyn mol* from 1943 already acknowledged this courage:

> And where a drop of our blood has been spilled,
> Our heroism will grow, our courage.

Undzer Mut is also the name of the first newspaper published in the DP camp at Zeilsheim near Frankfurt. It reported on the latest developments in Europe and the American zone of occupation. The promise expressed in the fight against an overpowering enemy spurred the members of the postwar community to take courage and to concentrate on their own lives, despite the strange and hostile environment.

Our Courage: Jews in Europe 1945–48 is the second temporary exhibition since the reopening of the Jewish Museum Frankfurt in 2020. It underscores the museum's philosophy of looking at the European dimension of Frankfurt's Jewish history and also the history of Judaism and its present-day status. As a decidedly European exhibition, it will travel through Europe after its presentation in Frankfurt. We are pleased that the Foundation for Displacement, Expulsion, and Reconciliation in Berlin will be taking over the exhibition in early 2022, and that there are also plans for it to be shown at the Joods Historisch Museum in Amsterdam and the POLIN – Museum for the History of Polish Jews in Warsaw, two museums that have supported this project through consultation and loans.

The exhibition is based on a four-year research project begun in 2016 by the Jewish Museum Frankfurt in cooperation with the Leibniz Institute for Jewish History and Culture–Simon Dubnow. Under the guidance of Atina Grossmann from the Cooper Union, New York, the main themes were delineated and the research into the situation in different places in Europe, including Poland, Hungary, Germany, Italy, the Netherlands, Sweden, and France, was commissioned and undertaken. The first results of this research project and its network were presented in December 2017 at the international conference "Building from Ashes: Jews in Postwar Europe 1945–1950" at the University of Frankfurt, organized by the Jewish Museum Frankfurt in cooperation with the Seminar for Jewish Studies at the University of Frankfurt, the Fritz Bauer Institute, and the Leibniz Institute for Jewish History and Culture – Simon Dubnow. Many of the papers given at that conference by academics from Europe, the USA, and Israel formed the basis for essays in this publication. They are supplemented by the results of further research to provide a novel insight into and summary of Jewish history in immediate postwar Europe.

The exhibition is an extended work in progress combining museological and academic perspectives. We are particularly grateful to Kata Bohus, who devised the framework for the exhibition on the basis of her research, held the different academic threads together, and designed the curatorial concept, supported by the head of the Ludwig Meidner archive, the experienced exhibition curator Erik Riedel, and the research intern Moritz Bauerfeind. We also thank Atina Grossmann and Elisabeth Gallas for their scholarly consultancy. The exhibition administration was coordinated by Sabine Paukner, and the project was directed by Werner Hanak. The form of the exhibition was the result of creative discussion with the Berlin exhibition specialists gewerkdesign, who were also responsible for the book layout. We should like to express our particular thanks to Jens Imig, Bianca Mohr, Birgit Schlegel, and Franziska Schuh for their inspiring contributions.

Both the exhibition and the pan-European research were made possible thanks to the generous financial support of several donors. We are grateful to the Federal Cultural Foundation, Daimler, and the Hannelore Krempa Foundation, who contributed equally to the financing of the research and curatorial work. The conference "Building from Ashes: Jews in Postwar Europe 1945–1950" was subsidized by the European Association for Jewish Studies. The Hessian Cultural Foundation assisted in the production of the exhibition, and further research was carried out with the support of the Polytechnic Foundation of Frankfurt am Main and the Hertie Foundation. We are very grateful to them all. We also sincerely thank Christiane and Nicolaus Weickart for generously subsidizing this exhibition catalogue.

Any international project relies on a large number of people. Apart from those already mentioned, they include many others who were involved in the project at different stages in its development. We should like in particular to thank Nick Somers for the English translation of the exhibition, Julia Brauch for the publication of this catalogue, De Gruyter Verlag for its expert assistance, and David Brenner for copy editing. We were particularly pleased that lenders entrusted us with their objects. We should like to express our appreciation and heartfelt gratitude to all of the named and unnamed persons whom we have met and whose history we have learned during this project.

Frankfurt am Main, June 15, 2020

[1] The song was written by the 22-year-old lyricist and partisan Hirsch Glick, who died near Vilna (Vilnius) fighting the German Wehrmacht. The original Yiddish lyrics are:
Un vu gefaln s'iz a shprots fun undzer blut,
Shprotsn vet dort undzer gvure undzer mut.

INTRODUCTION

ATINA GROSSMANN

KATA BOHUS

The small remnant of European Jews who managed to survive the Holocaust did so under highly varied circumstances. The present catalogue and the exhibit it accompanies reflect on this wide spectrum of survival experiences–from Amsterdam through Dachau to Samarkand–and the multifaceted history of Jewish survivors in Europe during the years that followed the war.

During the immediate postwar period, Europe was a "savage continent,"[1] trying to cope with one of the most lethal moments in human history.[2] More than 30 million people died during the Second World War and millions were deported by the Nazis: foreign slave laborers to Germany, Jews to ghettos and camps in Eastern Europe. Seven to eight million of those uprooted by war remained as officially classified displaced persons after the war ended.[3] The postwar years were a period of uncertainty, scarcity, violence, and poverty but also an era of possibilities and a threshold for new beginnings. What was to come–the forty years of European division known as the Cold War–was not yet determined.

For the surviving Jews of Europe, the postwar experience was influenced by how they had experienced the war itself. Some managed to stay alive in German-occupied Europe, whether in labor or death camps, with fake "Aryan" identities, in hiding, or with partisan units. Others had spent the war quite differently, in exile abroad, in diverse political and personal contexts. Moreover, the beginning of the postwar period varied greatly from place to place. Although the Red Army liberated the few Jewish survivors in and around the Polish town of Białystok at the end of July 1944, the mass extermination of Hungarian Jews would continue in Auschwitz until the following January. Liberation itself had different implications as well. For many, it did not mean survival: tens of thousands died soon after liberation as a result of exhaustion, malnutrition, or disease. Nor did liberation always signal freedom. Many of those who had survived in labor and death camps were only free to stay where they were, behind barbed wire, under Allied jurisdiction. For others, liberation meant a joyless return home, where they found their families gone and encountered the indifference or even hostility

Demonstration in the Poppendorf DP camp, after
Jewish DPs trying to get to Palestine were refused
entry by the British authorities there, 1947.
Mémorial de la Shoah, Paris

of the local population.[4] For a great many survivors, the end of the war meant the beginning of a long period of migration and displacement. Postwar Europe was also home to Jews—in Great Britain, Sweden, and Switzerland for instance—who had experienced neither occupation nor exile.

Just as survival and liberation were experienced in a variety of ways, so too was Jewish life imagined and (re)constructed in diverse forms. There was, however, one important feature that characterized most of European Jewry during these early years: survivors across the continent reclaimed their agency, seeking to determine their fates and to assure that Jewish life and memory continued. They reconnected the remnants of family networks and established new ones. They created their own political organizations, cultural products, welfare networks, jurisdictional capacities and, in many locations, initiatives to document and commemorate the recent destruction. The stories of Jewish reconstruction in seven different European towns and cities included in this volume and exhibit (Amsterdam, Bari, Berlin (East), Białystok, Budapest, Dzierżoniów, and Frankfurt am Main) offer some examples of both the diversity and the similarities found throughout the continent. The examples showcase the range of experience from busy DP camps, to small towns with a mere handful of survivors, to the temporary and long-term (re)construction of Jewish communities in Central and Western Europe.[5]

A comprehensive transnational history of the postwar years is difficult to present given how vague and inaccurate our basic data still is. We know that European Jewry was reduced from 7.3 million in 1933 to 1.7 million by 1946.[6] But we do not know exactly how many of the survivors ended up as displaced persons or for how long. Fearing continued persecution, they were often reluctant to register with Jewish organizations and aid providers who might have been able to determine their numbers. Moreover, academic research has only recently begun to address the vast topic of Jewish survival in the Soviet Union[7] and statistics for this critical but still marginalized story are particularly imprecise.[8] Similarly, it is virtually impossible to determine the number of Jewish survivors who were included in the massive forced migrations and population transfers during the postwar years.[9] Finally, the long-held belief that Jewish survivors were mostly silent about their wartime experiences has been energetically challenged in the past decade,[10] but some areas of Europe, in particular the Soviet Union, still remain uncharted. This volume and exhibit highlight—and aim to stimulate—new research on transnational aspects of European Jewish (re)construction efforts in the immediate postwar years.

Though there was not an exact moment when the war ended for the survivors on the European continent, there were nevertheless significant key events which would affect their fates. After receiving unsettling accounts about deplorable conditions in DP camps, particularly from American Jewish GIs and

chaplains, President Truman ordered an investigation, with particular regard
to Jewish survivors. The resulting Harrison Report, dated August 24, 1945,
presented a scathing critique of American policies and their effects in the DP
camps of Germany and Austria. It recommended, first and foremost, that Jews
be recognized and managed by the American military government as a distinct group, separate from other displaced national groups who, mere months
before, might have collaborated with the Nazis and indeed had wished death
upon them. The report was an acknowledgement of the Jews' distinct experience of genocide during the war and their emerging nationalization, which
would have far-reaching consequences for the future of Jewish DPs, the Zionist
movement, and the drive to establish the new State of Israel. The Harrison
Report and, eight months later, the Anglo-American Committee of Inquiry both
recommended (unsuccessfully) that 100,000 immigration certificates to British
Mandate Palestine be granted to Jewish DPs. The combined effects of American
Jewish pressure, the Harrison Report, and the continued restriction of immigration to the United States and Palestine resulted in a significant improvement of
conditions for Jewish DPs trapped in the U.S. occupation zone.[11]

Meanwhile, at the Potsdam Conference of the victorious Allied powers
in August 1945, Poland's new borders were ratified, bringing a large number
of Polish nationals, including Jews, under Soviet rule. These, and many other
Polish Jewish survivors from the Soviet interior, were subsequently repatriated
to Poland, in particular to formerly German Lower Silesia,[12] an area which the
Polish government called "Recovered Territories." Jewish repatriates developed
a new center for postwar Jewish life in this strange borderland. It had previously
served as a home to many German Jews, who were now almost all gone or dead.
Now it was populated by Polish Jews who had never lived there but whose homes
and families in other parts of Poland had been destroyed during the war. The
postwar Jewish community in Poland's Lower Silesia was thus a center of Jewish
survivor culture at the same time as the much better known story of "life reborn"
associated with the DP camps.[13] A major contribution of the present volume, in
the texts by Katharina Friedla and Kamil Kijek, to postwar Jewish history in
Europe is that they reveal this lesser known dimension of a vibrant, if temporary,
Jewish life in postwar Poland.

In the "Recovered Territories," Jewish survivors could feel safer than in
other areas of Poland. With the German minority expelled, there was less competition over resources and housing, thus reducing tension between Jews and
non-Jews. In other parts of Poland, however, Jews experienced various forms
of violence. Rzeszów, Lublin, Radom, Częchowa and Kraków were all sites of
pogroms in the summer of 1945.[14] As Joanna Tokarska-Bakir points out, a particularly toxic mix of traditional antisemitic beliefs (i.e., blood-libel accusations),
racial ideas perpetrated by Nazi ideology, resentment at efforts by survivors to re-

claim property, and the policies instituted by the liberating Soviets all led to these anti-Jewish excesses, culminating in the Kielce pogrom in July 1946, leaving 42 Jews dead and many more injured.[15] The events in Kielce triggered a huge migration wave of Jewish survivors out of Poland towards the DP camps in the American occupation zone of Germany.[16] As a result, Bavaria (especially the three exclusively Jewish DP camps of Feldafing, Föhrenwald and Landsberg) became the other center for Jewish survivor culture in postwar Europe.[17]

The swelling number of Jews in the DP camps helped strengthen arguments that envisioned a Jewish state as the best solution for the DP problem. When the United Nations voted for the partition of Palestine on November 29, 1947 and when the foundation of the State of Israel was proclaimed on May 14, 1948, Jews across Europe greeted the news with great enthusiasm and many left or made plans to leave for the new Jewish state. An estimated two-thirds of the Jewish DPs went to Israel,[18] constituting some 70 percent of the 244,000 immigrants who arrived there in 1948 and 1949.[19] However, as Avinoam Patt clearly shows in his article, displaced Jews' enthusiasm for Zionism was not necessarily ideological, nor did it mean that they all wanted to emigrate to Palestine, and later Israel. Zionism, in the DP camps and elsewhere in postwar Europe, instead filled a symbolic and emotional need for a positive vision of the future for the Jewish people. It also provided some much-needed practical solutions to many everyday problems. Young survivors especially, lacking training and missing community and family ties, found a home in Zionist peer-culture. Moreover, American officials, unlike the British, were willing to support the Zionist dream at least partly because it provided a viable and compelling alternative destination to the U.S. As such, Zionism emerged as the dominant political and ideological trend among Jews in postwar Europe, even as many survivors still pursued the goal of eventually settling in the United States.

At the same time, emigration–to Israel or elsewhere–was simply not an option for all survivors. Some were too sick or felt they were too old to start their lives anew. Others had established small businesses or settled down with non-Jewish partners. Some were determined to amass some savings or complete professional training before leaving. There were other obstacles as well. Some desirable overseas destination countries–the United States, Australia, and Canada for example–were very reluctant to open their borders to the influx of survivors for at least some time after the war. As the communists tightened their grip on power in Soviet-occupied Eastern Europe, emigration from these countries became increasingly difficult. After the drawing of the Iron Curtain and the onset of the Cold War at the end of the 1940s, it was practically impossible.

Thus, between the end of the war and the end of the 1940s, Jewish survivors who had voluntarily or involuntarily remained in Europe established their lives anew. The immense help from world Jewry, transmitted to them through

Jewish repatriates from the Soviet Union in Wrocław, 1946. Emanuel Ringelblum Jewish Historical Institute, Warsaw

Jewish aid organizations, especially the American Jewish Joint Distribution Committee (JDC, also referred to as the "Joint"), facilitated these endeavors. As Laura Hobson Faure argues, the close to 200 million dollars[20] that Jewish Americans sent to Europe through the JDC between 1945 and 1948 ultimately made the rebirth of European Jewish life feasible. The JDC provided much needed emergency relief to vulnerable populations, yet it also helped establish long-term structures to administer Jewish communal life.

Foreign aid notwithstanding, the task of restarting their lives was a formidable project for survivors. Their efforts ranged widely, from the personal to the political. The remarkable boom in marriages and births among Jewish DPs is probably the most noted evidence of "Life Reborn."[21] Yet, Jews throughout Europe also engaged in multiple other activities which similarly indicated their commitment to "redeeming the future." They demanded justice from the perpetrators and meted out justice among themselves. They created new rituals, salvaged old documents, and recorded the recent destruction to ensure that Jews, and not their perpetrators, would tell their story.

Natalia Aleksiun's article about postwar Holocaust testimonies in Eastern Europe carefully delineates the differences between testimonies that were intended for Jewish and non-Jewish contexts. In postwar Poland, survivors tried to evaluate their audiences–whether the Polish and Soviet administrations or their Jewish contemporaries–in order to present their stories of survival in ways that helped to safeguard the memory of destruction, to prosecute the perpetrators, and to create a historical record. Meanwhile, Jewish survivors in the DP camps established hundreds of "honor courts" where they confronted possible Jewish collaborators (frequently former members of the wartime Jewish Councils, members of the ghetto police or informants) among their ranks.[22] Katarzyna Person shows that, by setting up their own courts, Jewish survivors refused to accept imposed, non-Jewish interpretations of their experience of persecution. In the DP camps of Western Europe or in the courtrooms of Soviet-dominated Poland, Jewish survivors faced up to and owned the debate on Jewish responsibility during the war, a key (if fraught and painful) way of reclaiming agency. This form of self-determination was powerful in the immediate postwar period but often silenced in later historical narratives and memoirs.

Related to the need to confront wartime responsibility was the drive to comprehend the enormity of the catastrophe. A poem by Shloyme Vorzoger from 1948 demonstrates this struggle:

"Too soon–to forget this shock,
Too deep–to close, mend, and heal,

Earl G. Harrison (right) with Dr. Joseph Schwartz,
JDC's Director of Overseas Operations, 1945. Harrison
arrived in Germany in the summer of 1945 to inspect
conditions in the U.S.-administered displaced persons
camps. JDC Archives, New York

Zionist youth in Budapest celebrate the proclamation
of the State of Israel, 1948. Magyar Zsidó Múzeum és
Levéltár, Budapest

Celebratory gathering of the Dutch Zionist Union
in the Concertgebouw in Amsterdam after the
proclamation of the State of Israel, 1948. Photo: Boris
Kowadlo, Nederlands Fotomuseum, Rotterdam

There's no language–for this ordeal,
No apt measure–to take stock.
Nor is there–a name…"[23]

The distinct iconography of the *Khurbn* (Yiddish for "destruction," because
the terms "Holocaust" and "Shoah" were only popularized decades later)
demonstrated by the works of art featured in this volume started to develop in the
hands of Jewish survivors during the immediate postwar years. And, despite the
lack of adequate words, survivors did speak. Tamar Lewinsky's text sheds light on
the processing of wartime experiences in cultural expression. Yiddish-language
poetry and prose were published in more than one hundred journals in DP
camps, and later in some thirty bound volumes. This literature treated all
aspects of Eastern European Jewry's experiences from the interwar period to
the postwar years, and across a wide geography. Theatre groups and orchestras
in DP camps–among them the Katset Theater in Bergen-Belsen featured in this
volume–performed scenes from the ghettos and camps while dressed in striped
uniforms. As Philipp Graf's contribution demonstrates, these attempts were not
exclusive to DPs. Despite the marginalization of Jewish suffering in communist
anti-fascist narratives in what would soon be declared the German Democratic
Republic, Jewish survivors in and outside the communist party made great
efforts to provide legal, political, and intellectual interpretations of what they
saw as a specifically Jewish experience of the Second World War.

The destruction of the war was also remembered through the handling
of objects, especially those which remained without owners. Varied attempts to
rescue what remained of European Jewish cultural heritage reflect the
participants' differing visions of the future of Jews in Europe, particularly about
reconstruction in a new Jewish homeland or in newly vital diaspora communities,
especially in the United States. Elisabeth Gallas discusses the postwar rescue
of Jewish books in the parallel histories of book depots in Offenbach am
Main, Germany and Prague, Czechoslovakia. The American Jewish Cultural
Reconstruction, Inc. (JCR) played a key role in transferring most of the books
found in Offenbach, looted by Nazis from Jewish libraries and communities
all over Europe, to the United States and Israel. Given the decimated population
of European Jews, JCR representatives, together with envoys of the *Yishuv*,
believed that the safe survival of these precious assets could only be guaranteed
if they were sent to Jewish communities in the U.S. or the new State of Israel.

In contrast, the Budapest Jewish Museum considered it a new postwar
mission to collect the remnants of Hungarian Jewish cultural heritage in
Hungary in order to protect the collective memory of destroyed communities.
The community *Pinkas* (ledger book) from the town of Kaba, presented in this
volume, is only one example of their efforts. These different approaches to

protecting European Jewish cultural heritage reflect fundamental dilemmas that the postwar European Jewish community had to face. Would the center of postwar Jewish culture become the United States, Israel, or Europe? If rebuilt, should postwar European Jewish communal life be based on the American model, prewar European institutional structures, or something completely new? Should the entire Jewish collective be considered a single non-territorial entity to be eventually gathered in a Jewish national state, or should each national Jewish community be separately recognized?

The concluding text by Lena Inowlocki reflects on one particular dilemma: how could and should Jewish religious traditions be modified in the postwar context? Concentrating on several generations of women in the families of former DP Jews, Inowlocki highlights the emergence of a new kind of Orthodoxy among a minority of these survivor families in the 1990s as a way of reclaiming lost families, communities, and traditions. At the same time, globalization has helped produce the growing multiculturalism of Jewish communities. These parallel, if divergent processes have led, in some cases, to a surprisingly lively Jewish presence even in those parts of Europe where, in the immediate postwar years, hardly anyone foresaw a Jewish future.

Though this volume attempts to raise and connect issues rarely discussed in a trans-European context, there are topics that are still missing. A social-historical perspective and the gender aspects of postwar Jewish history–for example the role of women in the family (re)construction processes, in memoir writing, and in providing aid–remain areas for future research. We could not present a comprehensive history of all postwar European Jewry, and we are of course aware that important centers of Jewish reconstruction such as London or Paris are missing from this account. Nevertheless, we hope that at a time when the future of European Jewry is once again the subject of intense concern and debate, we have managed to highlight issues in a trans-European context that will provide food for thought for future researchers and exhibitors of these critical yet understudied interim years wedged between destruction and the Cold War.

[1] Keith Lowe, *Savage Continent. Europe in the Aftermath of World War Two* (London: Viking, 2012).

[2] Tony Judt, *Postwar. A History of Europe since 1945* (New York: Penguin, 2005).

[3] Judt, *Postwar*, 14.

[4] *The Jews are Coming Back. The return of the Jews to their countries of origin after WWII*, ed. David Bankier (Jerusalem: Yad Vashem, 2005).

[5] In the museum field, this history has only been partially explored, with a predominant focus on the DP experience. In Germany, several museums have staged temporary exhibits concentrating on DP camps, for example, the Jewish Museum in Munich in 2011/2012 (*Juden 45/90. Von Da und Dort – Überlebende aus Osteuropa*), the Jewish Museum in Berlin in 2015 (*Im fremden Land/In a Foreign Country*), the Anne Frank Education Center in

Frankfurt am Main in 2014/2015 *("Wohin sollten wir nach der Befreiung?" Zwischenstationen: Displaced Persons nach 1945).* Other exhibits have focused on only a few locations. The Jewish Historical Museum in Amsterdam exhibited in 2015/2016 the photographs Leonard Freed made of the postwar Jewish community in the Dutch capital. The most recent exhibit, in 2016, at the Mémorial de la Shoah in Paris, mostly focused on survivor experiences in France, Poland, and Germany *(After the Holocaust/Après la Shoah).*

[6] "Statistics of Jews," *American Jewish Year Book* 48 (1946/47), 606. These numbers do not include Jews in the Soviet Union.

[7] Eliyana R. Adler, "Hrubieszów at the Crossroads: Polish Jews Navigate the German and Soviet Occupations," *Holocaust and Genocide Studies* 28, no. 1 (2014), 1-30. Mark Edele, Sheila Fitzpatrick and Atina Grossmann (eds.), *Shelter from the Holocaust. Rethinking Jewish Survival in the Soviet Union* (Detroit: Wayne State University Press, 2017). Eliyana R. Adler, and Natalia Aleksiun, "Seeking Relative Safety. The Flight of Polish Jews to the East in the Autumn of 1939," *Yad Vashem Studies* 46, (2018), 41–71. Markus Nesselrodt, *Dem Holocaust Entkommen: Polnische Juden in der Sowjetunion 1939-1946* (Berlin/Boston: De Gruyter, 2019).

[8] After the invasion of Poland by Nazi Germany and the Soviet Union in September 1939, between 150,000 and 350,000 Polish Jews fled from German-occupied areas to those invaded by the Soviets. It is not known how many Jews fled "voluntarily," or were deported by the Soviet authorities as suspect foreigners, or joined the general evacuation of Soviet citizens. According to the most recent research, about 230,000 Jews from Poland survived in the Soviet Union, first in Stalinist special settlements and then often in Central Asia after an "amnesty" had released them from harsh labor camps in 1941. Among numerous sources in Polish, Hebrew, German and English see especially: Andrzej Żbikowski, (ed.): *Archiwum Ringelbluma. Konspiracyjne Archiwum Getta Warszawy*, Bd. 3, Relacje z Kresów. (Warszawa: Żydowski Instytut Historyczny, 2000), 13. Eliyana R. Adler and Natalia Aleksiun, "Seeking Relative Safety," 41–71. Mark Edele and Wanda Warlik, "Saved by Stalin?", 95–131.

[9] Tara Zahra, *The Great Departure: Mass Migration from Eastern Europe and the Making of the Free World* (New York: Norton, 2016); Katerina Capkova, "Between Expulsion and Rescue: The Transports for German-speaking Jews of Czechoslovakia in 1946," *Holocaust and Genocide Studies* 32.1 (2018), 66–92.

[10] Laura Jockusch, *Collect and Record! Jewish Holocaust Documentation in Early Postwar Europe* (Oxford: Oxford University Press, 2012). Regarding the population transfer between the Soviet Union and Poland after the war, research is ongoing and numbers are vague. According to the most recent estimates, the total number of Polish Jews who returned to Poland, either with the Berling Army, on their own, or as part of official repatriation schemes, was ca. 175,000 between 1944/45 and 1947, and rose to 200,000 to 230,000 by 1949. See Lucjan Dobroszycki, *Survivors of the Holocaust in Poland. A Portrait Based on Jewish Community Records 1944–1947* (London: Routledge, 2015); Nesselrodt, *Dem Holocaust entkommen,* 323; Edele and Warlik, "Saved by Stalin?", 121.

[11] Angelika Königseder and Juliane Wetzel, *Lebensmut im Wartesaal. Die jüdischen DPs (Displaced Persons) im Nachkriegsdeutschland* (Frankfurt a. M.: Fischer, 1994).

[12] Kamil Kijek, "Aliens in the Land of the Piasts: The Polonization of Lower Silesia and Its Jewish Community in the Years 1945–1950," in *Jews and Germans in Eastern Europe. Shared and Comparative Histories,* ed. Tobias Grill (Berlin: DeGruyter, 2018), 234–255; Bożena Szaynok, "The Beginnings of Jewish Settlement in Lower Silesia after World War II (May 1945–January 1946)," *Acta Poloniae Historica* 76 (1997), 171–195.

[13] *Life Reborn: Jewish Displaced Persons, 1945–1951: Conference Proceedings, Washington D.C. January 14-17, 2000,* ed. Menachem Z. Rosensaft (Washington, DC: United States Holocaust Memorial Museum, 2001).

[14] Joanna Tokarska-Bakir, "Cries of the Mob in the Pogroms of Rzeszów (June 1945), Cracow (August 1945), and Kielce (July 1946) as a Source for the State of Mind of the Participants," *East European Politics and Societies* 25.3 (2011), 553–574; Barbara Engelking, *Unbequeme Wahrheiten. Polen und sein Verhältnis zu den Juden* (Frankfurt a. M.:

15 Suhrkamp Verlag, 2009). Jan T. Gross, *Fear. Anti-Semitism in Poland after Auschwitz* (Princeton: Princeton University Press, 2007).

15 For a detailed description of the Kielce pogrom, see Joanna Tokarska-Bakir, *Pod klątwą. Społeczny portret pogromu kieleckiego* 2 vols. (Warsaw: Czarna Owca, 2018).

16 It is estimated that some 150,000 Jews fled at this point. See Piotr Wróbel, "Double Memory. Poles and Jews after the Holocaust," *East European Politics and Societies* 11.3 (1997), 560–574.

17 Most recent estimates put the number of Jewish DPs in allied-occupied Germay, Austria, and Italy in 1947/1948 at around 300,000. See Atina Grossmann, *Jews, Germans, and Allies: Close Encounters in Occupied Germany* (Princeton: Princeton University Press, 2007), 132. Ze'ev W. Mankowitz, *Life between Memory and Hope. The Survivors of the Holocaust in Occupied Germany* (Cambridge: Cambridge University Press, 2002), 2.

18 Sharon Kangisser Cohen, "Choosing a Heim: Survivors of the Holocaust and Post-war Immigration," *European Judaism* 46.2 (2013), 33.

19 Hanna Yablonka, *Survivors of the Holocaust: Israel after the War* (New York: New York University Press, 1999), 9.

20 On the figures, see Yehuda Bauer, *Out of the Ashes. The Impact of American Jews on Post-Holocaust European Jewry* (Oxford: Pergamon Press, 1989), xviii.

21 See: Grossmann, *Jews, Germans and Allies*, chapter 5.

22 *Jewish Honor Courts: Revenge, Retribution, and Reconciliation in Europe and Israel after the Holocaust*, ed. Laura Jockusch and Gabriel N. Finder (Detroit: Wayne State University Press, 2015).

23 Shloyme Vorzoger, *Zayn. Lider* (Munich: Nayvelt, 1948), 35.

BIBLIOGRAPHY

Adler, Eliyana R. "Hrubieszów at the Crossroads: Polish Jews Navigate the German and Soviet Occupations." *Holocaust and Genocide Studies* 28.1 (2014), 1–30. / **Adler, Eliyana R.** and **Natalia Aleksiun**, "Seeking Relative Safety. The Flight of Polish Jews to the East in the Autumn of 1939." *Yad Vashem Studies* 46 (2018), 41–71. / **Bankier, David**, ed. *The Jews are Coming Back. The return of the Jews to their countries of origin after WWII*. Jerusalem: Yad Vashem, 2005. / **Bauer, Yehuda**. *Out of the Ashes. The Impact of American Jews on Post-Holocaust European Jewry*. Oxford: Pergamon Press, 1989. / **Capkova, Katerina**. "Between Expulsion and Rescue: The Transports for German-speaking Jews of Czechoslovakia in 1946." *Holocaust and Genocide Studies* 32.1 (2018), 66–92. / **Cohen, Sharon Kangisser**. "Choosing a Heim: Survivors of the Holocaust and Post-war Immigration." *European Judaism* 46.2 (2013), 32–54. / **Dobroszycki, Lucjan**. *Survivors of the Holocaust in Poland. A Portrait Based on Jewish Community Records 1944–1947*. London: Routledge, 2015. / **Edele, Mark** and **Wanda Warlik**, "Saved by Stalin?" In *Shelter from the Holocaust. Rethinking Jewish Survival in the Soviet Union*, edited by Mark Edele, Sheila Fitzpatrick, and Atina Grossmann, 95–131. Detroit: Wayne State University Press, 2017. / **Edele, Mark, Sheila Fitzpatrick**, and **Atina Grossmann**, eds. *Shelter from the Holocaust. Rethinking Jewish Survival in the Soviet Union*. Detroit: Wayne State University Press, 2017. / **Engelking, Barbara**. *Unbequeme Wahrheiten. Polen und sein Verhältnis zu den Juden*. Frankfurt a. M.: Suhrkamp Verlag, 2009. / **Gross, Jan T**. *Fear. Anti-Semitism in Poland after Auschwitz*. Princeton: Princeton University Press, 2007. / **Grossmann, Atina**. *Jews, Germans, and Allies: Close Encounters in Occupied Germany*. Princeton: Princeton University Press, 2007. / **Jockusch, Laura**. *Collect and Record! Jewish Holocaust Documentation in Early Postwar Europe*. Oxford: Oxford University Press, 2012. / **Jockusch, Laura** and **Gabriel N. Finder**, eds. *Jewish Honor Courts: Revenge, Retribution, and Reconciliation in Europe and Israel after the Holocaust*. Detroit: Wayne State University Press, 2015. / **Judt, Tony**. *Postwar. A History of Europe since 1945*. New York: Penguin, 2005. / **Kijek, Kamil**. "Aliens in the Land of the Piasts: The Polonization of Lower Silesia and Its Jewish Community in the Years 1945–1950." In *Jews and Germans in Eastern Europe. Shared and Comparative Histories*, edited by Tobias Grill,

234–255. Berlin: De Gruyter, 2018. / **Königseder, Angelika** and **Juliane Wetzel**, *Lebensmut im Wartesaal. Die jüdischen DPs (Displaced Persons) im Nachkriegsdeutschland*. Frankfurt a. M.: Fischer, 1994. / **Lowe, Keith**. *Savage Continent. Europe in the Aftermath of World War Two*. London: Viking, 2012. / **Mankowitz, Ze'ev W**. *Life between Memory and Hope. The Survivors of the Holocaust in Occupied Germany*. Cambridge: Cambridge University Press, 2002. / **Nesselrodt, Markus**. *Dem Holocaust Entkommen: Polnische Juden in der Sowjetunion 1939–1946*. Berlin: De Gruyter, 2019. / **Rosensaft, Menachem Z.**, ed. *Life Reborn: Jewish Displaced Persons, 1945–1951: Conference Proceedings, Washington D.C. January 14–17, 2000*. Washington, DC: United States Holocaust Memorial Museum, 2001. / "Statistics of Jews." *American Jewish Year Book* 48 (1946/47), 599–618. / **Szaynok, Bożena**. "The Beginnings of Jewish Settlement in Lower Silesia after World War II (May 1945–January 1946)." *Acta Poloniae Historica* 76 (1997), 171–195. / **Tokarska-Bakir, Joanna**. "Cries of the Mob in the Pogroms of Rzeszów (June 1945), Cracow (August 1945), and Kielce (July 1946) as a Source of the State for the State of Mind of the Participants." *East European Politics and Societies* 25.3 (2011), 553–574. / **Tokarska-Bakir, Joanna**. *Pod klątwą. Społeczny portret pogromu kieleckiego* 2 vols. Warsaw: Czarna Owca, 2018. / **Vorzoger, Shloyme**. *Zayn. Lider*. Munich: Nayvelt, 1948. / **Wróbel, Piotr**. "Double Memory. Poles and Jews after the Holocaust." *East European Politics and Societies* 11.3 (1997), 560–574. / **Yablonka, Hanna**. *Survivors of the Holocaust: Israel after the War*. New York: New York University Press, 1999. / **Zahra, Tara**. *The Great Departure: Mass Migration from Eastern Europe and the Making of the Free World*. New York: Norton, 2016. / **Żbikowski, Andrzej**, ed. *Archiwum Ringelbluma. Konspiracyjne Archiwum Getta Warszawy* vol. 3: *Relacje z Kresów*. Warsaw: Żydowski Instytut Historyczny, 2000.

Young mothers take their babies for a stroll in the
Landsberg DP camp, ca. 1948. United States Holocaust
Memorial Museum, Washington D.C., courtesy of Dorit
Mandelbaum

HOLOCAUST TESTIMONIES
IN EASTERN EUROPE IN THE IMMEDIATE POSTWAR PERIOD

NATALIA ALEKSIUN

In January 1946, the historian and Holocaust survivor Philip Friedman (1901–1960) gave an account to the Commission for the Great Patriotic War of the Ukrainian Soviet Academy of Sciences detailing the destruction of the Jewish community in Lwów (Lemberg, today Lviv, Ukraine).[1] Recalling the pogroms that took place shortly after the entrance of the German troops, Friedman reported:

> Elimination of Jews in the city of Lviv started from the first day of the German arrival, i.e., from 30 June, 1941. However, at first the Germans conducted this elimination in a provocative way. Taking advantage of the Soviet Army's retreat, the Germans took a part of the Jewish population to prisons and shot them there; the shootings were accompanied by torture so that the victims could not be identified. At the same time, they pursued another purpose: to present this as an example of the "atrocities" committed by the NKVD [the People's Commissariat for Internal Affairs] who allegedly shot political prisoners before leaving Lviv. So, to clear the bodies (which in fact were the bodies of the Jews killed by Germans) immediately on arrival, Germans started seizing Jews in their homes and in the street to clear the bodies; but the ones who survived, later said that they had not cleared any bodies but that they had recognized many local Jews who had just been murdered.[2]

In his testimony, Friedman obscured the NKVD murders committed in the prisons shortly before the arrival of the German troops.[3] He incorporated them seamlessly into the background of the first wave of violence against the Jews in his city on July 3 and 4, 1941. Moreover, while Friedman described the death of several prominent Jews at that time, he made no mention of the participation

Meeting of the Jewish Historical Commission in Łódź.
Philip Friedman is sitting at the end of the table with
his eyes closed, 1946. Emanuel Ringelblum Jewish
Historical Institute, Warsaw

of the local population in the public humiliation, rape, torture, and killing. Rather, in his testimony, the pogrom appeared as planned and carried out solely by the Germans.[4] Recalling the so-called Petliura Days, the second wave of anti-Jewish violence which engulfed Lwów on July 25–27, 1941, Friedman linked the role of the Ukrainians with the Germans' encouragement of the pogrom: "The Germans allowed the Ukrainian police to select a certain number of Jews and to do whatever they wanted with them, as a way to get their revenge."[5] As to the "revenge" exacted for the atrocities in Lwów prisons that had allegedly been committed by Jewish Bolsheviks, Friedman's testimony did not elaborate on its immediate background or on its interwar context.[6] On the other hand, Friedman stressed that "it is telling that the civilian population of Lviv took no part in this brutalization of the Jews and that the Germans' attempts to set the Ukrainians and the Polish upon the Jews failed."[7] Thus, in his testimony to the Soviet Ukrainian body in Soviet Ukraine, Friedman chose to obscure the NKVD crimes on the eve of the German occupation of Lwów and to downplay the local population's participation in the atrocities against Jews.

A native of Lwów who had received his doctoral degree from the University of Vienna, Friedman taught history at a prestigious Jewish secondary school for boys in Łódź. With the outbreak of war in 1939, he returned to his home-town and found employment at the Institute of Economics of the Academy of Sciences of the Ukrainian Soviet Socialist Republic. During the German occupation, he worked in a bread shop from June 1941 until August 1942. Captured in the ghetto during the round up (*Aktion*), he was taken to the noto-rious Janowska camp. Friedman managed to escape and hid in Lwów and its vicinity until the arrival of the Soviet Army in the summer of 1944.[8] Before the war, this seasoned historian had collaborated with the YIVO in Wilno (Vilna, today Vilnius, Lithuania), which carried out pioneering scholarship in Yiddish and about the history and culture of East European Jews. He collected material about local history in Łódź while working there, and published scholarly books and articles. So why did he state what he must have known not to be true?

In newly liberated Lwów, Friedman recalled the destruction of his com-munity, deliberately avoiding statements that could jeopardize his relationship not only with the Soviet authorities but also with the local Ukrainian population. Perhaps he was determined to exact vengeance on the Germans or had made a tactical decision motivated by self-preservation and fear of the Soviets. However, his written statement shows that Friedman understood the limits of narrating the Holocaust in the postwar political context of Eastern Europe. From Lwów, he moved back west, first to Lublin and then to Łódź, where he found a more conducive environment for recounting the destruction of his community. His multiple accounts recorded under the aegis of different institutions in the immediate postwar period help us examine the role of historical documentation for Jewish survivors and their active role in highlighting various aspects in different circumstances. How did Polish Jewish survivors outside the Soviet Union address issues that constituted political taboos in Friedman's testimony to Soviet institutions? And more broadly, what do we make of the role played by self-censorship in the body of early Holocaust documentation created by traumatized and vulnerable Holocaust survivors as they addressed both Jewish and non-Jewish institutions and audiences? The question of contextually shaped testimonies will be discussed in relation to three issues: neighbors' collaboration in the Holocaust, the fraught role of Jewish functionaries and, more generally, the impact of communal taboos in post-genocidal societies.

NEIGHBORS' COLLABORATION

Already in Lwów, right after liberation in 1944, Friedman began working on a monograph documenting the almost complete destruction of the Jewish community there. His booklet was published in 1945 under the auspices of the Central Jewish Historical Commission in Poland which he headed first in Lublin and then, until his departure from Poland in the summer of 1946, in Łódź.[9] On the subject of local participation in anti-Jewish violence and persecutions, this historical account struck a very different note from that of his testimony to the Soviet authorities. Friedman underlined that "the Germans were received with cheers by the Ukrainian masses who hoped, with German assistance, to detach eastern Ukraine from the Soviet Union, and unite the two parts of the Ukraine into one independent country."[10] In this account of the first wave of violence, from June 30 to July 3, we read: "German soldiers spread through the streets of the city in the company of Ukrainian nationalists and an unruly mob of the local population. They fell upon Jews in the streets, beat them murderously, and dragged them away for 'work'—especially for cleansing of prisons filled with corpses and blood."[11]

Furthermore, Friedman stressed the role of the newly organized Ukrainian militia in capturing Jewish men and women who were then forced to wash the corpses of the victims found in the prisons in Lwów and in other locations throughout eastern Galicia.[12] Writing for a Polish Jewish audience in Polish, Friedman described the second wave of violence, mentioning the role of the Ukrainian population much more clearly:

> Thousands of Jewish men and women were seized by Ukrainian militiamen, ostensibly for "work." The unfortunate were for the most part brought to the prison in Łąckiego Street; intermittently, Ukrainian mobs would burst in, howling "revenge for Petliura," and would beat many Jews to death. [...]

Rumors spread through the city that the Germans had given the Ukrainian nationalists "three days" to do with the Jews as they saw fit to avenge the death of Semyon Petliura.[13]

Friedman framed the issue of local collaboration differently in his accounts for the Polish and primarily Jewish audience in Poland and the Ukrainian institution in Soviet Lviv, respectively. The stark contrast between these two accounts given by this historian and witness underscores the unique position of the Central Jewish Historical Commission in Poland which allowed survivors to discuss their politically sensitive experiences.

The Commission operated during a brief yet important liminal period following the liberation from Nazi occupation and before the consolidation of the Soviet-sponsored communist regime. The status of the commission as a Jewish communal organization, which did not need to satisfy a Polish audience, allowed it to be less concerned with the emerging Polish narrative of competitive victimhood. In her comparative monograph on survivors' efforts at documenting the Holocaust, Laura Jockusch stresses that this institution brought together a number of individuals who had been involved with the project of collecting historical and communal documents before the war. They recognized the centrality of testimonies for future historical accounts of the Holocaust and for punishing all those who had participated in the destruction of Jewish communities.[14] The closing of the commission in the autumn of 1947 coincided with the increase in communist control over Jewish autonomous institutions and efforts that led, by 1950, to their being dismantled.

Still, the Central Jewish Historical Commission in Poland recognized how explosive the subject of local collaboration could have been. In 1945, in a first brochure, the commission published methodological instructions for collecting historical material. It stressed the aid non-Jewish Poles had given to Jews and downplayed their complicity. Thus, it instructed the activists gathering survivor testimonies to proceed with caution with regard to "the attitude of the local population towards the Jews during the occupation."[15] For all the complexity of wartime interethnic relations, the activists or *zamlers* were to encourage testimonies that would document the assistance and empathy of those non-Jews referred to as "friends of humanity."[16] Evidence about "the criminal elements" among the non-Jewish population appeared only as an apparent afterthought.[17] Some survivors, like Friedman, moved west from what became part of the Soviet Union and then submitted their testimonies in local branches of the Central Jewish Historical Commission in Poland. Only then did they map out interethnic relations during the war and the thorny question of local collaboration.

For example, in his testimony recorded in Polish by the commission in the fall of 1944, Ryszard Ryndner, who had lived in Lwów before and during the

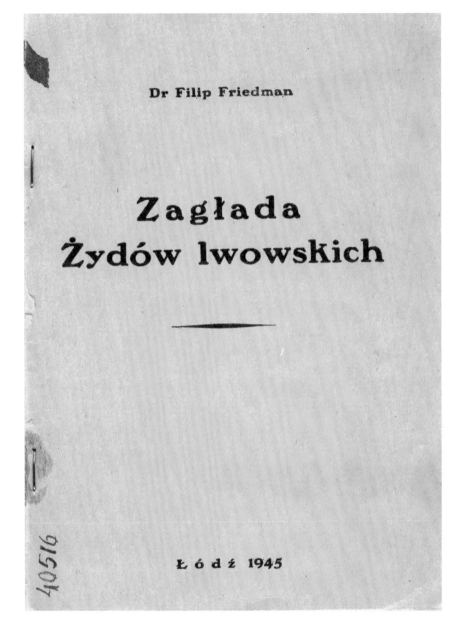

Dr Filip Friedman

Zagłada
Żydów lwowskich

Łódź 1945

Philip Friedman's account of Jewish persecution in
Lwów was published under the title *Zagłada Żydów
lwowskich* (*The Extermination of Lwów Jews*) by the
Central Jewish Historical Commission in Poland in
1945. Emanuel Ringelblum Jewish Historical Institute,
Warsaw

DOKUMENTY

ZBRODNI I MĘCZEŃSTWA

1945

Three books of testimonies about the persecution of Jews in Poland during the Shoah, published under the auspices of the Central Jewish Historical Commission in Poland between 1945 and 1947.

Dokumenty Zbrodni i męczeństwa (*Documents of Crime and Martyrdom*) contains numerous testimonies of survivors. It was edited by Michał Borwicz, Nella Rost, and Józef Wulf and published in 1945. Emanuel Ringelblum Jewish Historical Institute, Warsaw

Dzieci oskarżają (*The Children Accuse*) contains 55 testimonies by child survivors who were between the ages of seven and seventeen at the end of the war. It was published in 1947. Emanuel Ringelblum Jewish Historical Institute, Warsaw

Janina Hescheles' memoir about the persecution of Jews in Lwów was published under the title *Oczyma 12 letniej dziewczyny* (*Through the Eyes of a 12 Year-Old Girl*) in 1946. Emanuel Ringelblum Jewish Historical Institute, Warsaw

German occupation, recalled the German arrival in the city on June 30, 1941 and the immediate beginning of "agitation (*nagonka*)" against Jews on July 1: "The Ukrainian militia captured Jews in the streets and delivered them to various collection points where they were mercilessly beaten. While returning home, a rabbi was attacked by the Ukrainians, dragged to Brygidki [prison] and murdered there."[18] Although Ryndner had survived in hiding with the support of his former maid, he remarked that, in general, "the attitude of the local population was indifferent."[19] In his Yiddish testimony, Pesach Herzog stated that Ukrainian participation in the pogrom on July 4–5, 1941 in Tarnopol (today Ternopil, Ukraine) was "very substantial."[20] Mendel Ruder testified that on July 2, 1941, a day after the German units had marched into Złoczów (today Zolotchiv, Ukraine), a local meeting decided to carry out a pogrom in which Ukrainians assisted the Germans in killing Jews.[21] When Jews living in the vicinity of Złoczów were forced into the ghetto there in the fall of 1942, they arrived "naked and barefoot. Ukrainians did not allow them to take anything with them."[22] The survivors not only alleged or recounted initial local support for German atrocities in general. Some also directly identified their persecutors; Rudolf Reder named a Ukrainian family who–he believed–had betrayed him when he hid with them in August 1942 in Lwów.[23]

Jews liberated in the territories that became part of the Soviet Union seem to have had no qualms about reporting local collaboration in their testimonies once they had arrived or been repatriated to Poland. In the early survivors' testimonies from eastern Galicia and Volhynia, local collaboration was primarily blamed on Ukrainians collectively, while ethnic Poles were singled out for assisting Jews.[24] Still, the testimonies accuse numerous non-Jewish neighbors of collective crimes of collaboration, or at the very least, of appalling indifference (as described in Ryndner's testimony above).[25] Also, testimonies of survivors from other regions, where ethnic Poles constituted the majority, reported instances of local collaboration and identified those who were held responsible for betraying or even murdering Jews. For example, Alter Ogień, a tailor who survived in hiding in the vicinity of his hometown Łączna near Lublin, testified in the fall of 1944 that when he escaped from the Warsaw ghetto, he was recognized as a Jew by Polish passengers and thrown off the train.[26] He also mentioned two brothers who had been murdered in the village next to the one where he hid, and named the local perpetrator. While neither of these facts was mentioned in the Polish summary of the testimony, the account in Yiddish named both the village and the perpetrator.[27] This linguistic distinction underscores the difference between testimonies given to Jewish institutions and those given to non-Jewish ones. Possibly the best known case of this kind of testimony naming Polish neighbors guilty of killing Jews is Szmul Wasersztejn's account of the events in Jedwabne.[28]

The willingness of survivors to discuss their betrayal by other Polish citizens suggests that they did not fear revealing these details and indeed may have hoped for official and symbolic retribution. The new Polish government initially extended moral and financial support to Jewish institutions. In its Manifesto of July 22, 1944, the Polish Committee of National Liberation acknowledged the brutal murder of Jews by the German occupiers, announced the return to equal rights, and promised survivors that their communities would be rebuilt. Moreover, Jewish vigilante actions that intended to punish collaborators resonated with the spirit of the so-called *sierpniówki* or trials that were based on the decree issued by the Polish Committee of National Liberation on August 31, 1944, providing for the punishment of collaboration with the German occupation authorities.[29] In this climate, some survivors sought to testify about their experiences during the Holocaust without any concerns about discussing local collaboration.

THE QUESTION OF JEWISH FUNCTIONARIES

Another subject that early Jewish testimonies confronted is the contentious role of the *Judenräte*. Writing about the *Judenrat* in Lwów in his later accounts, Friedman did not need to change the original version of his Soviet testimony. In his account for the Soviet commission, Friedman was critical of the first *Judenrat* in Lwów but pointed to mitigating historical circumstances because the decisions of the German-appointed Jewish community leaders in July 1941 were still informed by their experiences of German occupation during the First World War. He divided members of the *Judenrat* into two categories: "the naïve ones and the scoundrels."[30] As for the scoundrels, Friedman opined–along the lines of the Soviet language of class conflict–that they had no illusions about the Germans' intentions and "wanted to save themselves and to profit somehow."[31] The aforementioned instructions for collecting historical material of 1945 suggested that "most attention needs to be paid to collecting material that would shed light on the dignified behavior of the Jewish population, its particular groups or even individuals." But testimonies also needed to confront the "debasement and betrayal, cowardice and lack of personal dignity, which unfortunately did take place in almost all Jewish communities."[32] It was precisely the willingness to call out the questionable behavior of some Jews and their lack of personal dignity that afforded survivors a sense of agency.

Many Polish Jewish survivors recalled the role of the members of the *Judenräte* and the Jewish police in harsh terms. Testifying about events in Tarnopol, Pesach Herzog wrote that the *Judenrat* handed over hundreds of poor Jews, including orphans, when the Germans demanded a "Death List" in the spring of 1942.[33] The young male survivor Ogień blamed the *Judenrat* and the Jewish police in Warsaw for participating in the round ups of Jews for forced labor, "dragging Jews from their homes and delivering them to the Germans, and therefore making the work easier for the latter."[34] Ryndner stated that, in their decrees, "the [Jewish] administration tried to outdo the Germans in their zeal."[35] Following another round up on January 5–6, 1943, the Germans murdered the members of the final *Judenrat*, and the SS took direct control of the Lwów ghetto. Stressing the role of the Jewish police, which followed German orders, Ryndner noted that at this point, "The Jewish militia took power, replacing the *Judenrat*. Thereafter, the population was constantly harassed–and those who did not work were constantly removed [from the ghetto]."[36]

One could argue that these testimonies about Jews who supposedly betrayed their communities in an attempt to secure survival for themselves and their families were collected primarily for internal consumption and the historical record. However, records of the Polish courts show that, in some cases at least, survivors were willing to discuss the subject in a more public context. Survivors turned to Polish courts to sue Jewish functionaries, testifying during investigations and in court, as in the summer of 1946, when the Special Criminal Court in Lublin tried and sentenced Maks Heimberg, a Jewish policeman from Borysław (today Boryslav, Ukraine), to death.[37] While a Polish court adjudicated the case, the investigation and the conviction relied on the testimonies of several Jewish survivors, all natives of Borysław, who pressured the authorities into bringing Heimberg to justice. Three Jewish survivors testified at the trial: Dawid Kestenbaum, Maks Doner, and Matys Heilig.[38] Kestenbaum made a statement as the Investigative Department of the Militia in Lublin began its work in April 1945. He informed the authorities that Maks Heimberg had served in the Jewish police in Borysław during the German occupation. Heimberg had "distinguished himself with particular fury and sadism vis-à-vis the Jews in Borysław, beating them mercilessly." He accused Heimberg of "participation in killing 13,000 Jews in Borysław,"[39] arguing that

> Such a bandit at large ought to be subjected to the most awful punishment–this is the demand of the 13,000 dead Jews of Borysław. I demand in the name of the perished that the above-mentioned bandit be put on trial at the site of his crimes, according to the International Committee for Punishing Hitlerite Criminals.[40]

Kestenbaum was one of several witnesses who came forward to testify at Heimberg's trial in June 1946. News about the investigation and the trial evidently circulated among the survivors. Sworn testimonies were sent from different parts of Poland: Łódź, Kraków, and Dzierżoniów (Reichenbach). The second witness who testified against Heimberg–Maks Donner–accused him of assisting the Germans in finding Jewish hideouts, stealing provisions from inmates in the local labor camp, and brutalizing Jews with his whip.[41] Those survivors who either intended to settle in Poland or to move further westwards appeared to adopt a common project of ensuring that Heimberg was punished now that Borysław had again come under Soviet control.

Indeed, survivors in Poland did not seem to struggle with self-imposed censorship and taboos about involving non-Jewish authorities in pursuing and punishing breaches of Jewish communal solidarity. The wounds were still raw, as was the need to establish a renewed sense of dignity by reclaiming the authority over their own community. Michal Leonowicz-Gerszowski from Kopiczyńce (today Kopychyntsi, Ukraine) recalled Jewish collaboration with the Germans and ended his testimony with a laconic personal comment which pointed to deep conflicts that tormented survivors and tore apart survivor families and communities: "My brother married a sister of a Jewish militiaman who had turned my sister in. I am no longer on speaking terms with him."[42] Thus, it seems that no sense of taboo stopped Jewish survivors from speaking about the collaboration of their non-Jewish neighbors or the dishonorable behavior of their own, both in Jewish and general forums. Yet, if survivors did not whitewash local collaboration or the role of the Jewish functionaries, were there other issues they did choose not to talk about?

OTHER COMMUNAL TABOOS

While many communal norms no longer applied in narrating the Holocaust, some taboos were broken, and others were reinforced. Survivors did not hesitate to assert that the cruelty inflicted on individual Jews broke them psychologically. The testimonies are replete with accounts of Jewish humiliation, suffering, and powerlessness. Pesach Herzog reported that during the pogrom on July 4, 1941 in Tarnopol, Jewish men who were tortured in the town square went mad.[43] Still, graphic descriptions of sexual violence against Jewish women remained taboo. Giving an account of a pogrom that began in Lwów on July 25 and in which 15,000 people were killed, Ryszard Ryndner explained that "women were robbed, and men were stripped naked and taken to Piaskowa Góra where they were all shot."[44] Tellingly, he made no mention of the fact that Jewish women were raped and sexually assaulted in the course of these events. It may still have been easier to elaborate on the degradation of Jewish men than on that of Jewish women. However, even this taboo did not completely silence stories of sexual violence, although these tend to be limited to short statements about instances of rape or mere allusions to sexual violence. Moreover, some male survivors did draw attention to instances of rape which they considered an important part of their account. Dawid Berber of Stanisławów (today Ivano-Frankivsk, Ukraine) mentioned the names of two women who had been raped during the final liquidation of the ghetto in February 1943.[45] Ignacy Feiner and Isser Reinharz reported an instance of attempted rape in the ghetto in Przemyśl on May 10, 1943, although their focus was on the brave response of a male Jew whom the Germans then publicly executed.[46]

The testimony of the young secondary school graduate Sonia Katzman offers us an insight into the limits of narrating such events. In her handwritten notes, Katzman mentioned an incident that occurred in January 1942 at the Ukrainian police station in Brody where she had performed forced labor cleaning and translating. The deputy commander of the police, a man named Pawluk, approached her and began to "flirt with me, came too close to me." When she fought him off, he threatened her, telling the young woman she would not be so lucky the next time they met.[47] However, in the taped version of the testimony, she only stated that she had "an unpleasant incident with one of the Ukrainians–Pawluk."[48] The testimony given by women generally tends to focus on instances of sexual abuse and rape that were witnessed rather than those personally experienced.[49]

In the aftermath of the Second World War, survivors began testifying about the destruction of their communities and the loss of their families. Shaped by the agendas behind the documentation projects, these testimonies were intended to safeguard the memory of the crimes committed and lives lost, help prosecute the perpetrators, and create a historical record for future generations that was constructed by the Jews themselves rather than relying on the records of the perpetrators. Political circumstances, individual trajectories, and communal norms made a decisive mark on these early–not yet settled–accounts. It made a difference if the discussion was confined to survivors, or if it involved the Jewish community more broadly or a state institution; and whether the principal purpose was one of straightforward documentation, of "setting the record straight," or of seeking legal retribution. In particular, the Central Jewish Historical Commission worked to document crimes primarily within the Jewish community and had only a marginal, if any, impact on the non-Jewish Polish memory of German occupation.[50] Nevertheless, in the moment of reckoning, survivors testified about local collaboration and the role of some Jewish functionaries who abetted the Final Solution, broaching topics that could prove both painful and precarious. Likewise, survivors' testimonies detailed pogroms and cases of murder, looting, and betrayal committed under German occupation by non-Jewish local populations, including ethnic Poles. Indeed, in contrast to later accounts and popular memorialization, there seems to have been little self- or institutionally imposed political censorship.

In Friedman's case, omissions and misrepresentations in his account high-light the fact that experiences of violence are narrated differently in different political contexts and for varying audiences. Striving for recognition and agency, survivors testified at the Jewish Historical Commission and for Polish courts. How can we account for this apparent lack of constraint in discussing politically volatile issues? The members of the Commission counted on the backing of the new Polish government. Survivors also testified about instances of fellow Jews breaking the bonds of communal solidarity. However, there were still elements, notably sexualized violence against Jewish women, that remained largely off-limits.

How, then, should one relate to the body of testimonies left behind by Holocaust survivors? Political, communal, and personal constraints on articu-lating the fates of Jewish communities and families raise questions about this systematically collected historical documentation. During the brief immediate postwar period, in the midst of political chaos and mass migration, survivors understood that different narratives could be delivered in the Soviet Union and in Poland, or if one intended to leave Eastern Europe altogether. Reading early testimonies in comparison with accounts recorded later reveals inconsistencies that are not only a function of trauma and faulty memory but also of survivors' cleareyed understanding of what could be said where. Indeed, communal and personal constraints shaped early testimonies. Survivors' postwar interpretations were sensitive to the specific political climate and intended audiences, and their emerging project of documenting the Holocaust was shaped by the goals they set for their testimonies. In other words, like historical texts, these testimonies were carefully thought out and strategized. Survivors knew that they could not simply count on the power—and horror—of their stories to gain a hearing or legitimacy. Right from the start, in telling the story of the Holocaust, survivors exercised agency and shaped their accounts according to various political contexts and circumstances.

---

[1] Pylyp Lazarovych Fri[e]dman, "Stenohrama zapysu spohadiv," January 22, 1946, TsDAHOU, f. 166, op. 3, spr. 246, ark. 78–89, EHRI Online Course in Holocaust Studies, English ver-sion, accessed July 12, 2019, https://training.ehri-project.eu/sites/training.ehri-project.eu/files/Ukraine%20A10%20translation_0.pdf.

[2] Fri[e]dman, "Stenohrama zapysu spohadiv," 80.

[3] Kai Struve, *Deutsche Herrschaft, Ukrainischer Nationalismus, Antijüdische Gewalt. Der Som-mer 1941 in der Westukraine* (Berlin: De Gruyter Oldenbourg, 2015), 247–253, also 14–221.

[4] Fri[e]dman, "Stenohrama zapysu spohadiv," 81.

[5] Fri[e]dman, "Stenohrama zapysu spohadiv," 84.

[6] Friedman only alluded to the murder of Symon Petliura (1879–1926), the president of the short-lived Ukrainian National Republic, who was blamed for the bloody pogroms in the Ukraine in the aftermath of the First World War. For this reason, the Ukrainian-born Jewish journalist Samuel (Sholem) Schwarzbard shot and killed Petliura in Paris in 1926. A French court acquitted Schwarzbard the following year. See David Engel, "Introduction," in *The*

Assassination of Symon Petliura and the Trial of Scholem Schwarzbard 1926–1927. A Selection of Documents, ed. David Engel (Göttingen: Vandenhoeck & Ruprecht, 2016), 7–95. In his testimony, Friedman may also have been alluding to a more politically volatile question of the bodies left behind by the Soviets in the prisons in Lviv. See Paul Hanebrink, *A Specter Haunting Europe. The Myth of Judeo-Bolshevism* (Cambridge, MA: The Belknap Press of Harvard University Press, 2018), 133–136, 142–143.

7   Fri[e]dman, "Stenohrama zapysu spohadiv," 84.

8   See Roni Stauber, *Laying the Foundation for Holocaust Research. The Impact of the Historian Philip Friedman* (Jerusalem: Yad Vashem, 2009); unsigned letter, Warsaw, August 14, 1981, Yad Vashem Archives, O.6 (Poland Collection), folder 419.

9   On the activities of the Central Jewish Historical Commission see Laura Jockusch, *Collect and Record! Jewish Holocaust Documentation in Early Postwar Europe* (New York: Oxford University Press, 2012), 84–120.

10   Philip Friedman, *Roads to Extinction: Essays on the Holocaust* (New York, Philadelphia: Conference on Jewish Social Studies, JPS, 1980), 245.

11   Friedman, *Roads to Extinction*, 246.

12   Friedman, *Roads to Extinction*, 247.

13   Friedman, *Roads to Extinction*, 249.

14   Jockusch, *Collect and Record!*, 87.

15   *Instrukcje dla zbierania materiałów historycznych z okresu okupacji niemieckiej* (Łódź: CKŻP, Komisja Historyczna, 1945), 11.

16   *Instrukcje dla zbierania materiałów historycznych*, 11.

17   *Instrukcje dla zbierania materiałów historycznych*, 12.

18   Ryszard Ryndner, testimony written down by M. Lewenkopf [?] in September 1944, Archiwum Żydowskiego Instytutu Historycznego (Archives of the Jewish Historical Institute, AŻIH), 301/18, 1 (author's translation).

19   AŻIH, 301/18, 5

20   Pesach Herzog, testimony written down on September 6, 1942[?] by M. Lewenkopf, AŻIH, 301/20 (author's translation).

21   AŻIH, 301/87, 2.

22   AŻIH, 301/87, 3.

23   See "I/4 1945 grudzień–Zeznanie Rudolfa Redera złożone przed sędzią Janem Sehnem z Komisji Zbrodni Niemieckich" in *Obóz zagłady w Bełżcu w relacjach ocalonych i zeznaniach polskich świadków*, ed. Dariusz Libionka (Lublin: Państwowe Muzeum na Majdanku, 2014), 36.

24   For example, in his account from Złoczów, Mendel Ruder stated that his wife and son had briefly been hidden by a Polish woman in the city (AŻIH, 301/87, 2).

25   In Stanisławów, they allegedly purchased tickets from the Germans in August 1942 to come and watch Jews being hanged from the lamp posts along one of the main streets. Dawid Berber, born August 18, 1910 in Stanisławów, merchant, testimony written down by Ida Gliksztejn in Bytom, December 15, 1946, AŻIH, 301/91, 2.

26   AŻIH, 301/1, 3(12). Assisted by the Polish conductor whom he paid for his help, he made it to Lublin and then to Łączna.

27   See AŻIH, 301/1, 3 and 14(5). The testimony was recorded in Lublin on September 2, 1944.

28   See Jan T. Gross, *Neighbors. The Destruction of the Jewish Community in Jedwabne, Poland* (Princeton: Princeton University Press, 2001). See the critical edition of his testimonies in *Wokół Jedwabnego*, vol. 2: *Dokumenty*, ed. Paweł Machcewicz and Krzysztof Persak (Warsaw: IPN, 2002).

29   See Gabriel N. Finder and Alexander V. Prusin, "Jewish Collaborators on Trial in Poland, 1944–1956," in *Polin* 20 (2008), 126–127.

30   Fri[e]dman, "Stenohrama zapysu spohadiv," 82.

31   Fri[e]dman, "Stenohrama zapysu spohadiv," 82.

32   *Instrukcje dla zbierania materiałów historycznych*, 11–12

[33] AŻIH, 301/20, 2.

[34] AŻIH, 301/1, 3.

[35] AŻIH, 301/18, 3.

[36] AŻIH, 301/18, 4.

[37] Protocol of the court hearing, June 5, 1946 r., Instytut Pamięci Narodowej (Institute of National Remembrance, IPN) Lu, 315/226, 127. See also the sentence in the name of the Republic of Poland, June 5, 1946, IPN Lu, 315/226, 139–140.

[38] Two of them had close ties to the communist authorities: Kestenbaum worked for the official newspaper, *Sztandar Młodych (The Banner of Youth)*, and Doner was listed as a government official but had earlier been employed by the Security Services. IPN Lu, 315/226, 134.

[39] Protocol of the notification of crime committed, Lublin, April 11, 1945, IPN Lu, 315/226, 7.

[40] IPN Lu, 315/226, 7.

[41] Protokół zeznania, May 11, 1945, IPN Lu, 315/226, 10.

[42] AŻIH, 301/70, 6.

[43] AŻIH, 301/20.

[44] AŻIH, 301/18, 1.

[45] AŻIH, 301/91, 3.

[46] AŻIH, 301/73, 1, recorded by Taffet.

[47] Testimony of Sonia Katzman, born in Brody in 1922, taken on January 17, 1945, AŻIH, 301/39, 2.

[48] Testimony of Sonia Katzman, 2.

[49] Atina Grossmann notes a similar pattern in German women's accounts of rapes by Soviet soldiers. Atina Grossmann, "A Question of Silence. The Rape of German Women by Occupation Soldiers," *October* 72 (1995), 42–63.

[50] As Jockusch notes: "From the postwar perspective of most ethnic Poles, the wartime experiences of Poles and Jews remained two separate stories, and hence a fundamental 'division of memory' separated both groups." Jockusch, *Collect and Record!*, 88. See also Monika Rice, *"What! Still Alive?!" Jewish Survivors in Poland and Israel Remember Homecoming* (Syracuse: Syracuse University Press, 2017), 65–85.

BIBLIOGRAPHY

"I/4 1945 grudzień–Zeznanie Rudolfa Redera," in *Obóz zagłady w Bełżcu w relacjach ocalonych i zeznaniach polskich świadków*, edited by Dariusz Libionka, 36–42. Lublin: Państwowe Muzeum na Majdanku, 2014. / **Engel, David.** "Introduction." In *The Assassination of Symon Petliura and the Trial of Scholem Schwarzbard, 1926–1927. A Selection of Documents*, edited by David Engel, 7–95. Göttingen: Vandenhoeck & Ruprecht, 2016. / **Finder, Gabriel N.,** and **Alexander V. Prusin**, "Jewish Collaborators on Trial in Poland, 1944–1956." *Polin* 20 (2008), 122–148. / **Friedman, Philip.** *Roads to Extinction: Essays on the Holocaust.* New York, Philadelphia: Conference on Jewish Social Studies, JPS, 1980. / **Gross, Jan T**. *Neighbors. The Destruction of the Jewish Community in Jedwabne, Poland.* Princeton: Princeton University Press, 2001. / **Grossmann, Atina**. "A Question of Silence. The Rape of German Women by Occupation Soldiers." *October* 72 (1995), 43–63. / **Hanebrink, Paul**. *A Specter Haunting Europe. The Myth of Judeo-Bolshevism.* Cambridge, MA: The Belknap Press of Harvard University Press, 2018. / *Instrukcje dla zbierania materiałów historycznych z okresu okupacji niemieckiej.* Łódź: CKŻP, Komisja Historyczna, 1945. / **Jockusch, Laura**. *Collect and Record! Jewish Holocaust Documentation in Early Postwar Europe.* New York: Oxford University Press, 2012. / **Machcewicz, Pawet, and Krzysztof Persak,** eds. *Wokót Jedwabnego, vol 2: Dokumenty.* Warsaw: IPN, 2002. / **Rice, Monika**. *"What! Still Alive?!" Jewish Survivors in Poland and Israel Remember Homecoming.* Syracuse: Syracuse University Press, 2017. / **Stauber, Roni**. *Laying the Foundation for Holocaust Research. The Impact of the Historian Philip Friedman.* Jerusalem: Yad Vashem, 2009. / **Struve, Kai**. *Deutsche Herrschaft, Ukrainischer Nationalismus, Antijüdische Gewalt. Der Sommer 1941 in der Westukraine.* Berlin: De Gruyter Oldenbourg, 2015.

BIAŁYSTOK
THE DEAD CITY

KATA BOHUS

> My survival seemed meaningless as I spotted a portion of the barbed
> wire fence, a remnant of the destroyed Bialystok ghetto. I felt guilty that
> I survived and my loved ones did not. What meaning could my life have
> when all the love that I had known from childhood had been wrenched
> away by the Nazis? I was torn between wanting to enter the broken
> frame of my house in which, to my horror, I might find the skeletons
> of my lost relatives, and leaving—which I could not physically bring
> myself to do.
>
> Srolke Kot, 1947[1]

Before the Second World War, the city of Białystok was one of the main Jewish
centers in Eastern Poland. At the end of the 19th century, Jews constituted more
than two thirds of the city's population and on the eve of the Second World War,
still almost half of Białystok's inhabitants were Jews.[2] In September 1939, the city
came under Soviet rule under the provisions of the Molotov-Ribbentrop Pact,
then was occupied by Nazi Germany in the summer of 1941, during the offensive
against the Soviet Union. Shortly afterwards, the entire Jewish population of
Białystok, about 50,000 people, was forced into a ghetto. Mass deportations
began in the spring of 1943, mostly towards the Treblinka and Majdanek camps.
Faced with the final liquidation of the ghetto, an armed Jewish insurrection
broke out on August 16. The uprising lasted a month and by the time it ended,
only a minority of the Jews who had taken part had managed to escape and
join the partisans in the nearby forests. A handful of Jews stayed alive by living
under assumed identities in the city.[3] Otherwise, the entire Jewish community of
Białystok was destroyed. The commemoration and retelling of this dramatic
story of desperate heroism in the face of Nazi brutality became a defining
element of the identity of the small postwar Jewish community.

Białystok was one of the first Polish cities liberated by the Red Army in
July 1944. About 1,085 Jews returned to the city, some local residents, some
from neighboring villages.[4] What they found was ruins, desolation, and despair.
A young survivor described this experience as follows.

The Great Synagogue of Białystok in the 1920s.
At this time, about 50,000 Jews lived in the city.
The Joseph and Margit Hoffmann Judaica Postcard
Collection at the Folklore Research Center of the
Mandel Institute of Jewish Studies, The Hebrew
University of Jerusalem

The ruins of the Great Synagogue, 1948. The Ghetto
Fighters' House Museum / The Photo Archive, Western
Galilee, Israel

I was told that several [Jews] were staying at a building on 24 Kupiecka Street, which I found in a state of total disrepair, making it difficult to enter. Climbing the stairs, I went into a dark room and found an emaciated old woman sitting on a broken chair near a table listing to one side because it lacked one leg. I asked her whether Jews lived here and she replied, in a barely audible voice, yes.[5]

Despite the devastation, the Jewish community began to revive. A Jewish Reconstruction Committee was established and took on the task of organizing housing and social assistance for Jewish returnees. It operated a kosher soup kitchen which served several hundred portions of lunch each day, a kosher butcher shop, and even a small *yeshiva*.[6] The Committee also acquired a building at the main intersection of the city which served as the first temporary home for Jewish returnees and those in transit.[7] In October 1944, this temporary body became the Jewish Communal Council. It resided in a former synagogue building, the Piaskower Beit-Midrash,[8] along with other Jewish communal organizations. The Council was headed by long-term resident and survivor of the Białystok ghetto Szymon Datner.[9] A trained historian, Datner also wrote the first account of the destruction of the city's ghetto.[10] Later, he became the head of the Białystok Jewish Regional Committee, a branch of the Central Committee of Jews in Poland, which took on the task of Jewish political representation. The Cytron Synagogue, which had escaped destruction, became the community's main synagogue. A library, housing some 2000 books and named after Pejsach Kaplan, the renowned Jewish writer and editor of the former Białystok daily newspaper *Undzer Leben*, opened in August 1944.[11]

Communal institutions helped not only local survivors, but also Jews arriving in the city from the liberated concentration camps and from their harsh exile in the Soviet Union, en route to other destinations. Assistance provided to returnees was financed mainly from funds transferred by the JDC and the substantial aid from Jewish *landsmanshaftn*, Jewish immigrant hometown associations across the United States and South America. For example, the Białystoker community in Buenos Aires organized eight tons of food to be sent to their city of origin in May 1946.[12]

Remembrance of the city's ghetto, the ghetto uprising, and the resistance movement was central to the memorial celebrations that thematized recent history for the survivors in Białystok. On August 16, 1945, on the second anniversary of the ghetto's dissolution, a stone obelisk was erected at the cemetery at Żabia Street, bearing the inscription: "In memory of 60,000 Jewish Brothers from the Białystok ghetto murdered by the Germans–who will live in the hearts of the few Jews who survived. The nation of Israel lives on." In 1946, another monument was erected in memory of the combatants in the ghetto, and two

Survivors in Białystok celebrate Passover, 1946.
Emanuel Ringelblum Jewish Historical Institute, Warsaw

The Cytron Synagogue in Białystok after the war,
1945–1946. Emanuel Ringelblum Jewish Historical
Institute, Warsaw

years later, a mausoleum was constructed at the Jewish cemetery in memory of the Jewish insurgents. In these early years, the main emphasis of the commemorations was on Jewish heroism and the will to survive. "A tragic funeral celebration is both our victory and revenge,"[13] Szymon Datner claimed in 1945, emphasizing that the survival of even a handful of Jews in Białystok was a victory over Hitler. Even so, no further monuments were erected in the immediate postwar period. In 1947, Datner argued in an article that no further funds for such endeavors were necessary; money should rather be spent on helping Jews to obtain exit visas.[14]

The reasons behind Datner's change of mind are manifold and reflect the factors which contributed to the failure of a postwar Jewish revival in Białystok. The hostile attitude of the local Polish population and the resurgence of popular antisemitism was a major driving force of Jewish flight from the city. For example, Ewa Kracowski returned to Białystok after the war, only to find her family's old home occupied by Poles who did not let her in, forcing her to sleep in the courtyard. This prompted Kracowski to leave the city within days.[15] Several antisemitic incidents in the vicinity of Białystok—including the murder of several members of a *kibbutz* (which had been established by the Gordonia Zionist youth movement) on a train between Białystok and Warsaw in 1946—and the bloody pogrom in Kielce led to a mass exodus. Right before the pogrom, in June 1946, a record number of 1,567 Jews were registered with the Regional Committee in Białystok. Within a month, this number shrank to 1,269, and by the end of the year, there were only 883 Jews left in the city.[16] The founding of the State of Israel and the consolidation of communist rule in Poland also contributed to the emigration of many survivors. Finally, the state-sponsored antisemitic campaign in Poland in 1968 delivered the final blow to the postwar experiment, and the Jewish community ceased to exist. By 1997, only five Jews officially lived in Białystok, and Szymon Bartnowski, who called himself "the last Jew of Białystok," died in 2000.[17] The fragile attempt to re-establish Jewish life in the city ended in failure. Jewish Białystok became a city of ghosts, an imagined homeland in the hearts and souls of the dispersed diaspora of Jews around the world who originated from there.[18]

[1] English text from: "Jews in Bialystok after the War," The Bialystoker Center, accessed August 19, 2019, http://www.zchor.org/bialystok/yizkor9.htm#jews.

[2] "Bialystok (Rus. Belostok)," Encyclopedia Judaica, accessed July 4, 2019, https://www.jewish-virtuallibrary.org/bialystok; Sara Bender, *The Jews of Białystok during World War II and the Holocaust* (Waltham, MA: Brandeis University Press, 2008), 19.

[3] Bender, *The Jews of Białystok*, 296.

[4] "A History of Bialystok, Poland," The Bialystoker Synagogue, accessed July 4, 2019, http://www.bialystoker.org/bialystok.htm.

[5] Srolke Kot, "Bialystok in August 1944," in *The Bialystoker Memorial Book*, ed. Bialystoker Center (New York: Bialystoker Center, 1982), 121–122.

Commemoration of the Białystok ghetto uprising at the memorial obelisk erected in 1945 at the cemetery on Żabia street, 1947. Emanuel Ringelblum Jewish Historical Institute, Warsaw

Funeral of three members of the Gordonia kibbutz
movement who were murdered on a train near
Białystok, 1946. Emanuel Ringelblum Jewish Historical
Institute, Warsaw

6 Awrom Krawets, "The First Passover after the War," in *The Bialystoker Memorial Book*, ed. Bialystoker Center (New York: Bialystoker Center, 1982), 122–123.

7 Rebecca Kobrin, *Jewish Bialystok and Its Diaspora* (Bloomington: Indiana University Press, 2010), 218.

8 Arnon Rubin, *The Rise and Fall of Jewish Communities in Poland and their Relics Today*, vol. 1: *District Białystok* (Tel Aviv: A. Rubin, 2006), part II/33.

9 See the biographical section for more information on Datner.

10 Datner's book, *Walka i zagłada białostockiego ghetta* (*The Fight and Destruction of the Białystok Ghetto*) was published in 1946 by the Provincial Jewish Historical Commission in Białystok.

11 Izchok Bornsztejn, "Memorial in Tribute to the Victims," in *The Bialystoker Memorial Book*, ed. Bialystoker Center (New York: Bialystoker Center, 1982), 120.

12 Joanna Sadowska, "Epilog Historii Białostockich Żydów–Okres Powojenny," in *Kres Świata Białostockich Żydów*, ed. Daniel Boćkowski, Ewa Rogalewska, and Joanna Sadowska (Białystok: Muzeum Wojska w Białymstoku, Galeria Ślendzińskich w Białystoku, 2013), 65.

13 Sadowska, "Epilog Historii Białostockich Żydów," 79.

14 Kobrin, *Jewish Bialystok*, 221.

15 Kobrin, *Jewish Bialystok*, 218–219.

16 Sadowska, "Epilog Historii Białostockich Żydów," 58.

17 Rebecca Kobrin, "Bialystok," The YIVO Encyclopedia of Jews in Eastern Europe, accessed June 13, 2019, http://www.yivoencyclopedia.org/article.aspx/Bia%C5%82ystok; Sadowska, "Epilog Historii Białostockich Żydów," 55.

18 For a particular Białystoker identity and its many forms, see Kobrin, *Jewish Bialystok and Its Diaspora*.

CHAIKA (CHAYA) GROSSMAN (1919–1996)

Chaika (Chaya) Grossman was a Zionist activist and Jewish underground leader during the Second World War. Born into a Zionist family in Białystok, Grossman was involved in the Hashomer Hatzair Zionist youth movement from a young age. She helped organize the Białystok ghetto revolt that took place on August 16, 1943 during the liquidation of the ghetto. Afterwards, she arranged hiding places for those who were able to escape. For the next year, Grossman cultivated her ties to the Soviet partisans in the Białystok region and, for a time, lived among them in the forests. During the war, Grossman's father was shot by the Germans and her mother was killed in the Majdanek concentration and extermination camp. Her two sisters survived, but her brother disappeared after being conscripted into the Red Army.

After the war, Grossman became a member of the Central Committee of Jews in Poland and was sent as a delegate to the World Zionist Conference in London (1945) and the World Zionist Congress in Basel (1946). She was also actively involved in the *Bricha* and *Aliyah Bet* movements in Poland, devoting herself to the assistance of Jews seeking to reach Palestine. In May 1948, Grossman immigrated to the newly established State of Israel on board the SS Providence. She settled in Kibbutz Evron and soon married her former Hashomer youth movement leader, Meir Orkin, who had immigrated from Białystok in 1936. In 1949, Chaika Grossman wrote her book, *The Underground Army*, about Jewish resistance in Białystok. The day she finished it, she gave birth to her first daughter Leah. Chaika and Meir later had another daughter, Yosefa. In 1950, Grossman was elected head of the Ga'aton Regional Council. From 1969 to 1981, she also served in the Israeli Knesset.

Chaika Grossman in Great Britain during the World Zionist Conference in London, 1945. National Science and Media Museum, Bradford, United Kingdom

Chaika Grossman (second from left) on the fourth anniversary of the uprising in the Białystok ghetto, during the solemn march to the mass grave, 1947. Emanuel Ringelblum Jewish Historical Institute, Warsaw

Chaika Grossman with her husband Meir Orkin and daughter Leah after their immigration to Israel, 1950. United States Holocaust Memorial Museum, Washington, D.C., courtesy of Meir Orkin

SZYMON DATNER
(1902–1989)

Szymon Datner was born in Kraków. He received a traditional religious education and later studied philosophy, earning a doctorate in anthropology in 1927. From 1929, he worked in a Hebrew high school in Białystok and started a family. During the Second World War, he participated in the resistance movement in the Białystok ghetto. He managed to escape from there in the summer of 1943 and joined the Soviet resistance. His older daughter, who also belonged to the underground organization in the ghetto, was killed during the ghetto uprising. His wife and younger daughter were probably murdered in the Treblinka extermination camp.

Shortly after the war, Datner returned to Białystok. He was the head of the Jewish Regional Committee there until 1946. He married Edwarda Orłowska, the provincial head of the Polish Communist Party, in 1946. In 1949, they had a daughter, Helena.

Datner took part in the early efforts to record accounts of the war. He collected information and reports about the Holocaust in the Białystok area. The Jewish Historical Commission published his book, *Walka i zagłada Białostockiego Ghetta* (*The Fight and the Destruction of the Białystok Ghetto*) in 1946.

In 1947, he attempted to travel to Palestine to visit his father. He encountered many obstacles on the way and ended up in a detention camp in Cyprus. After escaping from there, he managed to enter Palestine illegally where he stayed for a few months. After his return to Poland in May 1948, he started working for the Jewish Historical Institute. He was dismissed in 1953, after protesting against the publication of an article in the institute's bulletin which condemned the JDC as a Zionist organization. After his dismissal, he had to work as a bricklayer for years. From 1958 onwards, he worked in the Central Commission for the Investigation of Nazi Crimes. In 1969, his postdoctoral thesis (*Habilitation*) was accepted by the Historical Institute of the Polish Academy of Sciences. In the years 1969 and 1970, he served as the director of the Jewish Historical Institute.

Szymon Datner standing beside the well which hid the entrance to the Jewish underground's bunker at 7 Chmielna Street in the Białystok ghetto, 1945–1947. In all likelihood his older daughter, who was a member of the Jewish underground, was killed there. Ghetto Fighters' House Museum / The Photo Archive, Western Galilee, Israel

Members of the presidium of the Jewish Regional Committee in Białystok. Szymon Datner is second from the right, 1945–1948. Emanuel Ringelblum Jewish Historical Institute, Warsaw

ART PRINTS
AS A MEDIUM FOR THE DOCUMENTATION AND MEMORIALIZATION OF THE GENOCIDE

ERIK RIEDEL

The "camp art" produced by prisoners in the various concentration, forced labor, and death camps all over Nazi-occupied Europe was not directed at any specific audience. Whenever these images were produced, their future fate was as uncertain as that of their creators. Even so, most of these artists wanted to document what went on in the camps as precisely as possible, in the hope that their artworks might serve as a form of testimony for posterity, for the world outside the camps, the world as it would be after liberation.[1] When the war ended, this situation changed fundamentally. Now, the images, which had often been created in secret and preserved in various hiding places, could be recovered and displayed to the public. This is exactly what happened in the immediate postwar years. All over Europe, images created in the camps and ghettos depicting the persecution and annihilation of European Jewry were exhibited and published.

Esther Lurie (1913–1998) was born in Latvia and studied stage design and painting. In the summer of 1941, while visiting her sister in Lithuania, she was arrested and interned in the Kovno (Kaunas) ghetto. She was subsequently deported and imprisoned in the Stutthof concentration camp and the forced labor camp in Leibitsch (Lubicz) in Pomerania. Following her liberation by the Red Army, Lurie made her way to a refugee camp in Italy, where she arrived in March 1945. There, with the help of British Jewish soldiers from Palestine, she was able to exhibit her drawings from the camps and publish them in a small volume.[2]

Leo Haas (1901–1987) had worked as a painter, graphic artist, and carica-turist in Vienna and Czechoslovakia from 1926 on. Following the annexation of the Czech part of Czechoslovakia by the German Reich in 1939, Haas was arrested and imprisoned in a number of forced labor and concentration camps. Among other tasks, he was forced to work as a draftsman in Theresienstadt and for the counterfeiting operation in Sachsenhausen. Following his liberation,

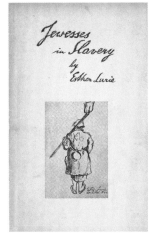

Leo Haas, *Hunger*, from: *12 původních litografií z německých koncentračních táborů* (*12 Original Lithographs from German Concentration Camps*), Prague, 1947, lithograph, 28,3 x 45 cm. Akademie der Künste, Berlin, Kunstsammlung, Inv.-No.: Leo Haas I 479, © David Haas, Daniel Haas, Ronny Haas, Michal Haas Foell

Esther Lurie, *Jewesses in Slavery*, Rome, 1945 (book cover). Jewish Museum Frankfurt, © Descendants of the Artist

Lea Grundig, *Refugees*, 1944, from: *Im Tal des Todes*
(*In the Valley of Death*), 1947, ink, brush, 44,8 x 59,2 cm.
Akademie der Künste, Berlin, Kunstsammlung, Inv.-No.:
Lea Grundig 2411, © VG Bild-Kunst, Bonn 2019

Zinovii Tolkatchev, *Flowers of Oświęcim*, Kraków, 1947
(dust jacket). Private collection, Frankfurt am Main.
In this edition, the image titles are printed in Polish, Russian, English, French and German.

Haas was able to recover his hidden images, and they served as the basis for the collection of prints he published in Prague in 1947, *From German Concentration Camps*.[3]

However, during the immediate postwar years not only artists who had survived the ghettos and camps responded to the genocide perpetrated against European Jewry that would later become known as the Holocaust or the Shoah with artistic means. Rather, exiled artists, who had observed events from afar, also exhibited and published artistic responses to the persecution and annihilation of European Jewry.[4] One of them was Lea Grundig (1906–1977). Her approach was largely shaped by the attempt to imagine the unimaginable and visualize the increasingly detailed reports and eyewitness testimonies about the genocide. Following her graduation from the Academy of Fine Arts in Dresden, Grundig had joined the Communist Party of Germany (Kommunistische Partei Deutschlands, KPD) in 1926; there, she helped found the local chapter of the Association of Revolutionary Artists (Asso). Threatened both as a Jew and a communist, she fled to Slovakia in 1939 and from there to Palestine, where she arrived in 1940. Here, she created her print collections *In the Valley of Death*, *Ghetto*, and *Ghetto Uprising*. The first of these was published in Dresden in 1947, even before Grundig returned to the Soviet occupation zone for good some two years later.[5]

Those artists who arrived with the Allied troops in the areas formerly occupied by Germany approached the Shoah from yet another vantage point. Initially, they too had only indirect knowledge of the atrocities and were now abruptly confronted with the emaciated survivors and huge numbers of corpses. Their shock and trauma are clearly discernible in their works of art.[6] Zinovii Tolkatchev (1903–1977), a native of Belarus, studied art in Moscow and later held a chair at the Institute of Fine Arts in Kiev. Working as an official artist for the Red Army, he arrived in the Majdanek death camp soon after its liberation in 1944 and was among those who liberated Auschwitz in 1945. The collections of drawings he made there, *Majdanek* and *The Flowers of Auschwitz*, were exhibited in numerous Polish towns and then published in 1945. The Polish government presented the published collections to Allied politicians and military figures as a gift. Tolkatchev fell from grace in the Soviet Union in the 1950s because of his "Zionist" works, having illustrated books by Sholem Aleichem and others.[7]

These few examples may suffice to illustrate the various perspectives of Jewish artists responding to the Shoah in the immediate postwar period. What their works have in common, though, is the fact that they were published in the immediate postwar years; they are thus exemplary of the prolific production that commenced in 1945 of prints, portfolios of prints, and art books responding to the Shoah. Other examples include: the wood engravings of Miklós Adler (1909–1965) published in Debrecen (Hungary) in 1947, some of which had also been included in the *Survivors' Haggadah* that appeared in Munich the year before;[8] the linocuts of Endre Bálint (1914–1986); or the *24 Drawings* published by Jerzy Zielezinski (1914–1982) in Munich in 1946.[9]

What makes this publication of substantial numbers of prints and art books responding to the genocide so remarkable is the fact that these are not private renderings relying on more introspective artistic techniques. Prints, print collections, and art books are, after all, artistic media inherently addressed to a wider public. That Jewish artists opted for these modes of reproduction and publication indicates that many of them regarded their artistic work not primarily as means for coping with their experiences. Rather, they were intent on communicating them and bearing witness in public. Like the innumerable testimonials and various contemporaneous projects undertaken by Jewish historians to document the crimes perpetrated by the Nazis, these works of art actively contributed to the discourse on the genocide perpetrated against European Jewry.[10] How lively this discourse initially had been before it came to a standstill during the Cold War soon thereafter, is demonstrated not least by this extensive production of art prints in the immediate postwar years.

[1] It is telling that Ziva Amishai Maisels gave the first chapter of her groundbreaking study on camp art and testimony the title, "I am a camera." See Ziva Amishai-Maisels, *Depiction and Interpretation. The Influence of the Holocaust on the Visual Arts* (Oxford: Pergamon, 1993), 3–18.

[2] Esther Lurie, *Jewesses in Slavery* (Rome: Jewish Soldiers' Club, 1945). See also Esther Lurie, *A Living Witness. Kovno Ghetto, Scenes and Types. 30 Drawings and Water-Colours with Accompanying Text* (Tel Aviv: Dvir, 1958); Pnina Rosenberg, "Esther Lurie, 1913–1998," accessed August 20, 2019, http://art.holocaust-education.net/explore.asp?langid=1&submenu=200&id=6#1f.

[3] On Haas, see Wolf H. Wagner, *Der Hölle entronnen. Stationen eines Lebens. Eine Biografie des Malers und Graphikers Leo Haas* (Berlin: Henschel, 1987).

[4] Ludwig Meidner (1884–1966) is a case in point. In exile in Britain, he created a collection with the title *Massacres in Poland* (alternatively, *The Suffering of the Jews in Poland*). See Shulamith Behr, "Ludwig Meidner's Cycle *Leiden der Juden in Polen* (1942–1945) and Holocaust Knowledge: Toward a Methodology," in *Ludwig Meidner. Expressionismus, Ekstase, Exil/Expressionism, Ecstasy, Exile*, ed. Erik Riedel and Mirjam Wenzel (Berlin: Gebr. Mann, 2018), 279–297.

[5] On Grundig, see her autobiography: *Gesichte und Geschichte* (Berlin: Dietz, 1958); Oliver Sukrow, *Lea Grundig, sozialistische Künstlerin und Präsidentin des Verbandes Bildender Künstler in der DDR (1964–1970)* (Frankfurt a. M.: Peter Lang, 2011).

[6] The works of the war artists Edgar Ainsworth (1905–1975) and Feliks Topolski (1909–1987) are cases in point. See Edgar Ainsworth, "Victim and Prisoner," *Picture Post*, September 22, 1945, accessed August 20, 2019, https://www.iwm.org.uk/collections/item/object/95; Feliks Topolski, *Three Continents, 1944–45: England, Mediterranean convoy, Egypt, East Africa, Palestine, Lebanon, Syria, Iraq, India, Burma front, China, Italian campaign, Germany defeated* (London: Methuen, 1946).

[7] Zinovii Tolkatchev, *Flowers of Oświęcim* (Cracow: M. H. Rubin, 1947). This volume and a second book with the title *Majdanek* were first published in Cracow in 1945. On Tolkatchev, see *Private Tolkatchev at the Gates of Hell. Majdanek and Auschwitz Liberated. Testimony of an*

Artist, ed. Yehudit Shendar (Jerusalem: Yad Vashem, 2005); https://www.yadvashem.org/yv/de/exhibitions/tolkatchev/about_tolkatchev.asp, accessed August 20, 2019.

8   See *A Survivors' Haggadah. Written, designed, and illustrated by Yosef Dov Sheinson with woodcuts by Miklós Adler*, ed. Saul Touster (Philadelphia: JPS, 2000) and the contribution on Pesach 1946 in this volume.

9   On Bálint, see Dániel Véri, "A holokauszt és a zsidó identitás szimbolikus ábrázolásai (1939–1960) (Bálint Endre, Martyn Ferenc, Major János és Maurer Dóra grafikái)," in *Szigorúan ellenőrzött nyomatok. A magyar sokszorosított grafika 1945–1961 között*, ed. Gábor Pataki (Miskolc: Herman Ottó Múzeum – Miskolci Galéria, 2018), 40–71. Although Zielezinski was not himself Jewish, he and his Jewish fiancée were interned in the Warsaw Ghetto and subsequently deported to Auschwitz. After the war, he moved to the United States where he worked as a book illustrator under the name George Ziel. See Kathrin Hoffmann-Curtius, *Judenmord. Art and the Holocaust in Post-war Germany* (London: Reaktion, 2018), 100–114; Lynn Munroe, "George Ziel," accessed August 20, 2019, http://lynn-munroe-books.com/list62/GEORGE_ZIEL2.htm; Lynn Munroe Books, "George Ziel 2014 Update," accessed August 20, 2019, http://lynn-munroe-books.com/list62/Zielupdate.htm.

10   See also the contribution by Natalia Aleksiun in this volume.

Miklós Adler, *The Wagon*, from: *16 fametszete* (*16 Woodcuts*), Debrecen, 1947. YIVO Institute for Jewish Research, New York. In the introduction, the artist writes, "This book has no title, because you cannot find a word to describe what happened to European Jews in recent years."

POSTWAR VIOLENCE
AGAINST JEWS IN CENTRAL AND EASTERN EUROPE

JOANNA TOKARSKA-BAKIR

One of the more shocking aspects of immediate postwar history is the wave of anti-Jewish pogroms that swept Central and Eastern Europe, as well as cities that had never been occupied by the Nazis, in the first years after the Second World War.[1] In fact, this chapter in the long history of anti-Jewish violence began even before the end of the war, in Soviet occupied Kirghizia. During Passover in 1943 a group of Jews, including the director of the local preschool Rokhl Tversky, was accused of kidnapping a Russian boy whose father was an important figure in the local army.[2] The child was soon found, but Tversky, who attempted in vain to draw the attention of the authorities to the political character of the rumors, was silenced by dismissal from his job.

The second attempt at a pogrom, this time accompanied by the slogan, "Death to Jews!", was recorded in the summer of 1944 in Dnepropetrovsk (now Dnipro) in eastern Ukraine, shortly after the Red Army had set off from the city to march on Berlin.[3] The reactions of the authorities (including the Central Committee of the Ukrainian Soviet Socialist Republic) to these excesses were muted in the extreme. While the incidents were not denied, the authorities showed no interest in treating them as a systematic phenomenon connected with postwar restitution. They increased in intensity, however, with the return of those Jews who had survived the war deep in the heart of the USSR and were now trying to recover their homes which, in the interim, had been occupied by their Ukrainian neighbors, many of whom were collaborators implicated in the extermination of the survivors' family members.

Caskets of pogrom victims in Kielce, Poland, 1946.
Photo: Julia Pirotte, Emanuel Ringelblum Jewish
Historical Institute, Warsaw

Defendants at the trial after the pogrom in
Kunmadaras held in the Great Hall of Szolnok
County, 1946. Hungarian Telegraphic Agency,
Budapest

POGROMS IN 1945

Ironically, anti-Jewish violence continued to occur in Soviet and Soviet-dominated territories shortly after liberation. Between May and July 1945, the unrest spread to Rubtsovsk in Altai Krai (West Siberia), a city that the war had never reached.[4] An incident which began as a dispute over a chicken at the local bazaar ended as an anti-Jewish pogrom at the city's stadium.[5] On May 2, 1945, anti-Jewish incidents were also reported in Košice, Czechoslovakia (now Slovakia).[6] Jewish attempts to recover property lost during the war provided the pretext for these attacks.[7] The situation was further inflamed by groundless accusations of Jews trying to evade military service behind the frontlines in the Soviet Union and, in Czechoslovakia, of collaboration with the Nazis. Jewish soldiers were in fact active combatants in many armies and resistance groups fighting against the Nazis. The accusation of "Jewish cowardice," as well as that of collaboration, served to cover the actual intentions of the accusers who were eager to pre-empt the recovery of Jewish property and divert attention from their own past deeds.

Several pogroms in early to mid-1945 in Poland point to a political factor which motivated them. The killing of fourteen Jews in Leżajsk in southeastern Poland has only recently been reconstructed in detail. During the night of February 18–19, 1945, a group of Holocaust survivors living together (for safety reasons) in premises including Puderbeutel's restaurant and Chaskiel Potascher's house at 19 Mickiewicza Street, were murdered. A number of Polish and Soviet soldiers temporarily staying in Leżajsk had been billeted with them. In the attack, mounted by a unit under Józef Zadzierski comprising members of the National Armed Forces (*Narodowe Siły Zbrojne*, NSZ) and the National Military Organization (*Narodowa Organizacja Wojskowa*, NOW), the houses came under artillery and grenade fire. The inhabitants only surrendered when the assailants blasted a hole in the wall from the courtyard. After gaining entrance to the house, the guerillas shot all those inside, including women, children, and the elderly. The opinion of the doyen of nationalist Polish historiography, Marek Jan Chodakiewicz, that the Jews died "on NKVD premises" has no basis in reality.[8]

On March 1, 1945, the same underground unit carried out a similar attack in Kisielów (killing seven, including three children) and another on March 31, 1945 in Kańczuga (killing thirteen, including one pregnant woman, Chana Krieger, and three children). Another six Jews perished at the hands of assailants in Polish uniforms in the night of April 18-19 in Klimontów Sandomierski; another twelve, including eight women, on May 24, 1945 in Czyżew-Osada; and a further eight on May 27, 1945 in Przedbórz.[9] This list could be continued. In virtually every case, the murders were motivated by the victims' alleged collaboration with the NKVD, the hated representative organization of Soviet occupation, which the perpetrators considered sufficient grounds for murdering even unborn children.

The toxic blood libel legend as a motif in anti-Jewish violence surfaced in pogroms in the Polish-Ukrainian borderlands, where it was enhanced by its historical precedents, still present in local memory.[10] In late March and early April 1945, a rumor suggesting that Jews were abducting children started circulating in the Polish town of Chełm. The local militia charged a small group of Jews with bleeding a Christian boy and tortured one of the accused.[11] The first real pogrom took place on June 11-12, 1945 in Rzeszów (Poland), following the murder of Bronia Mendoń, a teenage girl whose body, disfigured by rats, was found on Tannenbauma Street in the cellars of a house in which some of the tenants were Jews. The Jewish residents were framed as the immediate suspects, partly due to the unprofessional investigation conducted by officers of the Citizens' Militia (*Milicja Obywatelska*, MO, the communist police) who were convinced that the Jews were guilty. Only the forensic analysis of the blood found in the Jews' apartments proved that it had come from the slaughter of chickens (one of the tenants was a *shokhet*, a ritual butcher).

Another source which forejudged the Jews' guilt was a widely disseminated report by an anti-communist underground organization. In this case, Jews were accused not only of needing children's blood for their Passover *matzah* (the alleged justification of the blood libel since the Middle Ages), but also of using it for regenerative "transfusions." Rzeszów's Jews were saved by the efficient intervention of the local communist Office of Security (*Urząd Bezpieczeństwa*, UB), which had been alerted by a Jewish Pole, Roman Orłowski, a deputy commander of the Voivodeship Headquarters of the local Civil Militia. The UB had all those in danger quickly evacuated from the city.[12]

Two days later, on June 14, 1945, a similar pogrom broke out on Krakovsky Square in Lvov (now Lviv), Ukraine.[13] It was triggered by rumors about Jews abducting Polish and Ukrainian children and hiding their corpses in the cellar of the synagogue. Even though the synagogue was thoroughly searched, no traces were found that would have indicated the murder of children.[14] Ivan Fedak, a metalsmith who had incited the crowd and called on them to burn down the synagogue, turned out to have been a serial collaborator: a confidant of the wartime German police force, a guard in the camp for Jews in Lvov and, after the war, also an informer for the NKVD.[15] These examples point to a particularly toxic mix of traditional antisemitic beliefs (i.e., blood libel accusations), racial ideas propagated by Nazi ideology, and the policies instituted by the liberating Soviets. All these factors, put together, led to anti-Jewish violence perpetrated by local populations in the postwar period.

The blood libel accusation also played a role during the pogrom in Kraków, Poland, which began on July 27, 1945, with rumors that a child had been abducted by a Jewish woman on Kleparski Market Place.[16] This was followed on August 11–12, 1945, by a full-scale pogrom in the Kraków quarter of Kazimierz.[17] It began with provocations by young boys who threw stones at the Kupa Synagogue at 27 Miodowa Street while a Saturday service was in progress. The provocateurs were caught by the *shammes*, the synagogue janitor (or, according to another source, by a Jewish soldier of the Polish Army) who attempted to hand them over to the Citizens' Militia (MO). He was prevented from doing so by twelve-year-old Antoni Nijaki who later testified that a man wearing the uniform of the MO had ordered him to run out of the synagogue shouting that the Jews had tried to murder him.[18] The boy's cries sparked an attack by the crowd gathered there. They forced their way into the synagogue, began vandalizing it, and sought to set fire to the interior. The religious scrolls and books were destroyed, and the few remaining Jews who had recently returned to their town after the Shoah and were praying there were dragged out into the street and beaten. Aside from civilians, the attackers included railroad workers, MO officers, and Polish soldiers. However, Soviet soldiers came to the aid of the victims. The perpetrators also forced their way into the Jewish hostel at 26 Miodowa Street and the Jewish Students' House at 3 Przemyska Street. In other parts of the city, including on Szczepański Square, the women in the market stalls announced their intentions to "shut up shop and go beat Jews," while at the Tandeta bazaar in Kazimierz they cried: "The Jews have crawled out of the holes, the Jews have multiplied like bugs, and we need to finish off the Jews."[19] The crowd forced its way into homes, ransacking them and beating up Jews.[20] Two persons were killed in the pogrom and many were injured.

Several pogroms also occurred in the Slovakian parts of Czechoslovakia: in Prešov,[21] Humenne, and Michalovice in July 1945, and in the towns of Vel'ké Topol'čany,[22] Chynorany, and Žabokreky[23] in September of that year. Vel'ké Topol'čany had a strong tradition of extreme right-wing sympathies and had seen three-quarters of its Jewish community perish during the war. The return of Jewish property, confiscated during the war as part of the "Aryanization process," caused ongoing tensions, though this was not merely a localized problem. The immediate pretext for the September pogrom was supplied by rumors that a local school run by nuns was to be closed down or nationalized. The numbers of protestors outside the school mushroomed, soon reaching several thousand (in a town of 9,000). Wild rumors circulated about Jews tearing the crosses off the walls and attacking the nuns, and about Jewish plans to pave the streets with Christian skulls. There were calls for Jewish children to be expelled from the school and Jewish doctors, accused of murderous intentions in connection with the compulsory vaccination of young people, to be barred from practicing their profession. One of the doctors, K. Berger, was dragged out of the besieged school by the crowd but miraculously escaped almost certain death by hiding in the building of the communist Office of National Security (*Národna bezpecnost*, NB). The authorities' response to the pogrom was sluggish: few officers were sent to quell the unrest. Meanwhile, anti-Jewish unrest also swept the Polish towns of Przemyśl,[24] Radomsk, Łódź, Zwoleń, Chełm again (August 14, 1945),[25] and Bydgoszcz.[26]

On September 4, 1945, a pogrom erupted in the Ukrainian capital, Kiev (now Kyiv), where on Bazarnaya Street an NKVD officer, Josif Rozenshtein, got into a fight with two drunken Red Army soldiers on leave, Ivan Grabar and Nikolai Mielnik. They had insulted Rozenshtein with the derogatory epithet "Tashkent partisan," which was commonly used to refer to Jews evading military service behind the front.[27] Rozenshtein, who sustained injuries in the brawl, found out where his attackers were staying, donned his NKVD officer's uniform and, accompanied by two armed friends, set out to arrest them. When they put up resistance, he shot and killed them with his service pistol. The shots alarmed a Ukrainian militiaman patrolling Kitaevskaya Street who, on arriving at the scene, overpowered Rozenshtein. Rozenshtein was later sentenced to death and executed by a firing squad.

The files from the investigation analyzed by Ilya Luvish reveal a background to the dispute typical for the postwar period. The family of one of the soldiers who insulted Rozenshtein was staying in an apartment which used to belong to Jews. They fled to Uzbekistan during the war, survived, and returned to Kiev in February 1945. The Jewish owners' attempt to reclaim the apartment angered one of the soldiers involved in the incident who took out his anger on Rozensthein. Although the authorities attempted to pacify the situation by arresting Rozenshtein, the crowd wanted to see the Jews subjected to some form of collective punishment. The funeral of Grabar and Melnik on September 7, 1945, escalated into a demonstration, and subsequently into a pogrom at Galitsky Market which lasted several hours and left five people dead (some of them Jews) and more than one hundred wounded.[28]

POGROMS IN 1946

In May and July 1946, anti-Jewish incidents were reported in Hungary, in the cities of Kunmadaras and Miskolc.[29] Shortages on the market provided the background to the events in Kunmadaras. The communist government reacted to the problem with a campaign against "speculators" whom it systematically portrayed with "Semitic" features. As in the case of pogroms in Poland and the Soviet Union described above, a combination of traditional antisemitic beliefs, circulating rumors and communist policies provided the spark that led to anti-Jewish violence. In this case, surreal rumors about Jews producing sausages from the corpses of children who had disappeared in the town of Karcag were circulating among the population.[30] The pogrom against the tiny group of Jews in Kunmadaras–of the 250 who had lived there before the war, only 75 survived– mushroomed out of a banal dispute over the price of eggs at the market. The altercation pitted a Jewish merchant called Klein against his customers who accused him of inflating his prices in order to "destroy the Hungarian nation." One of them was Eszter Kabai Tóth, the wife of Zsigmond Tóth who liked to put it about town that "it was the Jews who kidnapped the children who disap- peared, and so they should all hang."[31] At the trial of the perpetrators it came to light that some of those who took part in the pogrom had previously served in a Hungarian SS regiment. This was nothing new in a country where, as Peter Kenez writes, the communist party had around 500 000 members in 1945, of whom half were Jewish Holocaust survivors from Budapest and the other half fascists, former members of the Arrow Cross Party who had still been killing the Jews only months before.[32] Communist authorities made no attempt to address the causes of Hungarian popular antisemitism.

On July 4, 1946, the bloodiest of all the postwar pogroms took place in Kielce, Poland. It left more than forty people dead and more than one hundred injured.[33] Here again, the spark was the blood libel myth, a neat fit with the story of eight-year-old Henio Błaszczyk who claimed to have been abducted by Jews. The incident was reported to a civilian employee of the MO, Stefan Sędek, who before the war had founded the Kielce branch of the quasi-fascist party, the National Radical Camp (*Obóz Narodowo-Radykalny*, ONR). The MO patrol that he dispatched to search the Jewish Committee premises spread the rumor as it went that the Jews were holding children prisoner there. A crowd gathered rapidly and surrounded the building in the belief that there were corpses of murdered children in its cellars. Many members of the MO in Kielce joined the angry crowds in the assault. The forces of the communist secret police (UB) as well as the Soviet troops present in Kielce were hesitant to intervene, and the bloodshed was only halted by the arrival of military reinforcements stationed near Warsaw.

Murders were also committed on trains passing through Kielce and the city of Częstochowa (located roughly one hundred miles to the west of Kielce). In the fast-tracked trial, nine of the participants in the pogrom were sentenced to death, which quelled the inflamed mood for a time. The most recent archival research into the biographies of the Kielce MO officers who were dispatched to the pogrom has revealed that many of them had served in anti-communist underground organizations during the war and were implicated in wartime murders of Jews. As in other countries in the Soviet bloc, the Soviet-installed authorities of the Office of National Security in Kielce lacked legitimacy and, in an attempt to curry favor, sought the sympathy of the "masses" by turning a blind eye to antisemitism.[34]

Mourners bearing wreaths and banners grieve at
the funeral of the Kielce pogrom victims, July 8,
1946. United States Holocaust Memorial Museum,
Washington D.C., courtesy of Leah Lahav

Funeral procession for the pogrom victims in Kielce, July 8, 1946. Photo: Julia Pirotte, Emanuel Ringelblum Jewish Historical Institute, Warsaw

After reaching an apogee in the summer of 1946, the wave of rumors with the potential to spark pogroms spread to further Polish towns, including Tarnów, Kraków again, Częstochowa, Radom, Ostrowiec Świętokrzyski, Białobrzegi, Dęblin, Łódź, Skarżysko-Kamienna, Starachowice, Pionki, and Kalisz. In this latter city, the rumor spread that the Jews had abducted 24 boys, drunk their blood, and sold their corpses to the Ukrainians (or "Soviets"), who processed them as sausage meat.[35]

In August 1946, the spark that ignited the pogroms reached Slovakia again, where a wave of violence engulfed towns including Veľka Bytča, Bratislava,[36] Nové Zámky, Žilina, Komàrne, Čadca, Dunajská Streda, and Ispoľske Šahy. It was not extinguished until 1948, after the attempted pogrom in Bratislava, and was briefly reignited in the 1950s. In Poland, the last cases of social unrest incited by the blood libel were reported at Easter and in May 1947, in places including Bytom, Białystok, and the Brzesko district, and in 1949 in Częstochowa, Włocławek, and Kraków. These rumors ultimately only caused a gathering of crowds rather than actual pogroms.

The discussion surrounding postwar pogroms has produced many controversial issues such as the question of provocation by the NKVD or the Zionists (who allegedly attempted to force the emigration of the Jews to Palestine in this way), the role of the blood libel as a trigger for pogroms, and the role of women in initiating pogroms. The "provocation by women" hypothesis has been particularly widely touted, especially in relation to the Kielce pogrom. Both an investigation conducted by the Polish Institute of National Remembrance (*Instytut Pamięci Narodowej*, IPN) around the year 2000 and the most recent research have shown that there is no evidence to support this thesis.[37] The suggestion that women played a particularly prominent role in the pogroms is founded on a misunderstanding indicative of long-standing assumptions regarding gender roles. Because women have conventionally been associated with protective roles in the family, forms of assertive behavior considered perfectly ordinary when displayed by men are assumed to reflect "abnormally high" levels of aggression when displayed by women.

INDIVIDUAL VIOLENCE

We define pogroms as a form of social control in which a depraved majority uses violence to show a minority its place,[38] and in which the principle of collective responsibility is employed uncritically in respect to the latter group. Using this definition, there were around fifty pogroms against Jews in Central and Eastern Europe in the years between 1945 and 1948. If, however, we broaden our definition to encompass not only acts of collective violence but also individual attacks on Jews, that figure becomes hard to estimate.[39]

Like many other crimes, postwar attacks on Jews were rarely motivated unequivocally by one single factor. Assaults on the pretext of "the Jews' collaboration with the communists" which, in the eyes of some Polish historians, still provides a blanket justification for these murders, almost always comprised an element of looting. For Holocaust survivors who were confronted with the enmity of the society which had seized their property, such "collaboration" was the only means of physical survival aside from emigration. Even though the economic policies of the communist party constituted a threat to the economic interests and even the very livelihood of the Jews, to many, the communists nonetheless seemed the only force capable of protecting them from popular antisemitism.[40]

Owing to lack of space we cannot discuss in full the heated ongoing discussions about the causes of postwar violence against Jews in each of the European countries mentioned in this paper. Of the many theories in currency, we will look at two which are relevant to address the specific Polish postwar situation: the general semiotic theory and the historically specific theory.

Yuri Lotman analyzed mass behaviors of people in times of crisis in a high-profile study of early modern witch trials. He called into question common-sense theories of violence as a reaction to increased strain, concluding instead that it is often not the case that panic erupts in response to a threat, but that anxiety is in fact the cause of the violence.[41] A society overcome by anxiety whose source it cannot establish projects that fear onto a semiotically constructed hostile object. The latter is identified on the basis of the codes of the frightened society itself, not on the basis of objective reality, and is usually the weakest and least threatening element of the group overcome by fear.[42] The choice of this group, Lotman writes, is based on a paradoxical minority/majority dialectic. While the initial assumption is that "we" are the majority, the rising tide of fear causes the conviction to spread that "there are people among us who represent hidden alien forces that must be identified and neutralized. Before long, the phobia moves to the next level, where the masses themselves begin to feel like a minority: we are surrounded by enemies."[43] This is how witch hunts started in the middle ages. In the postwar context, Polish society was overcome by anxiety from multiple inchoate sources that was then projected onto the Jewish minority perceived as a threatening majority.

As for the historically specific theory, the Polish scholar Andrzej Żbikowski has noted that the "desire for an 'ethnic purge'–to make permanent the ethnic landscape produced by the Holocaust"[44] had been an important element of the political plans of some Polish conspiratorial circles even before the end of the war. This aim was a reflection of attitudes widespread in the Polish provinces from the moment when the vast cultural capital of Polish Jewry was plundered by the occupiers and subsequently, as "abandoned property" was taken over by Poles.

The postwar persecution of Jews in the Kielce region, for instance, bears clear hallmarks of economically motivated ethnic cleansing. It has been calculated that among the approximately 2,000 Jewish Poles who survived the war in the region (around one to two percent of their prewar number), between March 1945 and July 4, 1946, roughly one hundred were murdered. If we include the victims of the Kielce pogrom, this means that within a year and a half of the end of the war, on average, one in fourteen Jews was killed (i.e., approximately seven percent of the survivors).[45] The culmination of this violence, which has been referred to by some as the fourth phase of the Holocaust, was the aforementioned pogrom in Kielce on July 4, 1946. The very next day, the greatest wave of emigration in Poland's history began, which ended in more than 100,000 Jewish Poles leaving the country.

[1] For the definition of a pogrom, as used in this paper, please see footnote 38.
[2] Nisn Rozental, *Yidish lebn in ratnfarband* (Tel Aviv: I. L. Peretz, 1971), 164, cited in Elissa Bemporad, "Empowerment, Defiance, and Demise: Jews and the Blood Libel Specter under Stalinism," *Jewish History* 26 (2012), 355.
[3] Amir Weiner, *Making Sense of War: The Second World War and the Fate of the Bolshevik Revolution* (Princeton: Princeton University Press, 2001), 192.
[4] A group of workers from the Altai agricultural machinery factory in Rubtsovsk, letter to Solomon Mikhoels of the Jewish Anti-Fascist Comittee, July 12, 1945 (document no. 39), in *War, Holocaust and Stalinism: A Documented Study of the Jewish Anti-Fascist Committee in the USRR*, ed. Shimon Redlich et al., (Luxemburg: Harwood Academic, 1995), 228–230. Ilya Luvish, "From the Lonely Cellar to the Crowded Street: The Progression of Anti-Semitic Manifestations in Postwar Poland and the Soviet Union, 1944–1947" (Senior Honors Thesis, Northeastern University, 2005).
[5] Weiner, *Making Sense of War*, 191–235.
[6] Anna Cichopek, *Beyond Violence: Jewish Survivors in Poland and Slovakia, 1944–1948* (Cambridge: Cambridge University Press, 2014), 217–218.
[7] Mordechai Tsanin, *Iber shteyn un shtok. A rayze iber hundert horev-gevorene kehiles in Poyln* (Tel Aviv: Letste nayes, 1952), 178–180.
[8] Mirosław Surdej, *Okręg Rzeszowski Narodowej Organizacji Wojskowej–Narodowego Zjednoczenia Wojskowego w latach 1944–1947* (Rzeszów: IPN, 2018), 337.
[9] See Joanna Tokarska-Bakir, "Terror in Przedbórz. The Night of 27/28 May 1945," *East European Politics, Societies* and Cultures (forthcoming).
[10] See Joanna Tokarska-Bakir, *Légendes du sang. Pour une anthropologie de l'antisémitisme chrétien* (Paris: Albin Michel, 2015).
[11] S. Herszenhorn, IX Sprawozdanie z działalności Referatu d.s. Pomocy Ludności Żydowskiej za m-c marzec 1945, 4 kwietnia 1945, ka. 5, MiP, 753, Central Archives of Modern Records (Archiwum Akt Nowych, AAN), Warsaw.
[12] Krzysztof Kaczmarski, *Pogrom którego nie było. Rzeszów 11–12 czerwca 1945. Fakty, hipotezy, dokumenty* (Rzeszów: Instytut Pamięci Narodowej, 2008), 34.
[13] Luvish, "From the Lonely Cellar to the Crowded Street," 9–19.
[14] Operational report of the search signed by the public prosecutor of the Lvov *oblast* ("region"), Lavreniuk, and the head of the Lvov special group of the NKVD, Malar, dated June 14, 1945,

Courtyard of the emergency center in Bratislava, with Polish Jewish refugees who fled after the Kielce pogrom, summer 1946. JDC Archives, New York

Akta sprawy Fedaka, Derzavnyi Arkhiv Lvivskoi Oblasti (DALO). Derżavny Archiv Lvivskoj Obłasti fond P-3258, vol. 2, case 4757 II-1567.

[15] Joanna Tokarska-Bakir, *Pod klątwą. Społeczny portret pogromu kieleckiego* (Warsaw: Czarna Owca, 2018), vol. 1, 14, 175–177 and chapter 12.

[16] Wolność i Niezawisłość (Freedom and Independence, WiN) archive collection, State Archive in Kraków, Poland, under reference no. ANKr 1214, 923, UW II.

[17] Cichopek, *Beyond Violence*, 123–127.

[18] According to NKVD sources, the perpetrators were people in uniform who stormed into the synagogue and arrested four Jews on a charge of ritual murder. The Jews were taken to a nearby police station. Thereafter, "many militiamen started to arrest and beat Jews." See Siergiej Krivienko, "Raporty z Polski," *Karta* 5.15 (1995), 32.

[19] Report on the anti-Jewish events in Kraków on Saturday, August 11, 1945, fo. 14, 295/VI/28, KC PPR, AAN.

[20] Julian Kwiek, Żydzi, *Łemkowie, Słowacy w województwie krakowskim w latach 1945–1949/50* (Kraków: Księgarnia Akademicka, 2002), 61–68.

[21] Chronicle of the Town of Prešov 1945–1948, 110–112, Okresný národný výbor v Prešove, I. manipulačné obdobie (1930) 1945–1948, State Regional Archive in Prešov.

[22] Ivan Kamenec, "Protižidovský Pogrom v Topoľčanach v Septembri 1945," *Studia Historica Nitriensia* 8 (2000), 85–97.

[23] In nearby Zabokreky, people started congregating in the evening of September 24, talking of children who had died after being inoculated by a Jewish doctor in Topol'čany. Some members of local Jewish families were assaulted. Two families left the village for the night out of fear, and their homes were looted; others were robbed while they were on their way. Hana Kubátová, "A zsidókról kialakult kép a háború utáni Szlovákiában," *Regio*, 24.2 (2016), 63–80, 68.

[24] Four men, who apparently believed the blood libel myth, attacked a Jewish family living in Przemyśl, killing the man and his son-in-law and injuring his daughter on June 21, 1945. A dispatch, 24, 303/I, CKŻP, Prezydium, Archive of the Jewish Historical Institute (AŻIH).

[25] A dispatch, 178–180, 303/24, 1945, CKŻP, Prezydium, AŻIH.

[26] Alina Cała, *Żyd–wróg odwieczny: Antysemityzm w Polsce i jego źródła* (Warsaw: Nisza, 2012), 470.

[27] The antisemitic term *zhid* is used, rather than the correct form *evrey*, for "Jew." See John D. Klier, "'*Zhid*': Biography of a Russian Epithet," *Slavonic and East European Review* 60.1 (1982), 1–15. See also: Sheila Fitzpatrick, "Annexation, Evacuation, and Antisemitism in the Soviet Union, 1939–1946," in *Shelter from the Holocaust. Rethinking Jewish Survival in the Soviet Union*, ed. Mark Edele, Sheila Fitzpatrick, and Atina Grossmann (Detroit: Wayne State University Press, 2017), 144.

[28] Luvish, "From the Lonely Cellar to the Crowded Street"; Weiner, *Making Sense of War*, 192, 375–377. Archival documentation: d. 1394, op. 23, fo. 1, Tsentralnyi Dzerzhavnyi Arkhiv Hromadskykh Organizatsii Ukrainuu (TsDAHOu, formerly the Central Party Archives of Ukraine).

[29] See János Pelle, *Az utolsó vérvádak. Az etnikai gyűlölet és a politikai manipuláció kelet-európai történetéből* (Budapest: Pelikán Kiadó, 1995), 149–246; Peter Kenez, *Hungary: From the Nazis to the Soviets. The Establishment of the Communist Regime in Hungary, 1944–1948* (Cambridge: Cambridge University Press, 2006), 160–161.

[30] Péter Apor, "The Lost Deportations and the Lost People of Kunmadaras: A Pogrom in Hungary, 1946," *Hungarian Historical Review* 2.3 (2013): 584, *n*43.

[31] Apor, "The Lost Deportations," 584, *n*43.

[32] According to estimates by Peter Kenez, the Hungarian Communist Party comprised, *inter alia*, two radically different groups of members: Budapest Jews who had survived the Holocaust and for whom the Soviet invasion was undeniably a liberation, and terrified low-ranking members of the fascist Arrow Cross Party. For the latter, joining the Communist Party was an attempt to conceal the fact of their collaboration. They were assisted in this by their Jewish comrades who found themselves, for the first time, in a privileged position (Kenez: *Hungary:*

From the Nazis to the Soviets, 46). This form of compromise between former enemies, when neither side can win, may be referred to, following Richard White, as "the middle ground." Richard White, *The Middle Ground. Indians, Empires, and Republicans in the Great Lakes Region, 1650–1815* (Cambridge: Cambridge University Press, 2011). Symptoms of this are visible in the structure of authority in Kielce, Poland, where the biggest of the postwar pogroms played out.

33 Bożena Szaynok, *Pogrom Żydów w Kielcach, 4. VII 1946 r.* (Warsaw: Bellona, 1992); Jan Tomasz Gross, *Fear: Anti-Semitism in Poland After Auschwitz* (New York: Random House, 2006).

34 Tokarska-Bakir, *Pod klątwą*. Prior to this, similar aspects of communist authority in Poland immediately after the war were examined by Anita J. Prażmowska, "The Kielce Pogrom 1946 and the Emergence of Communist Power in Poland," *Cold War History* 2.2 (2002), 101–124. She noticed a rapid increase in the number of members of the communist party (PPR) who had previously been members of the AK. This may be interpreted as a form of ideological conformism similar to that seen in Hungary and described by Kenez.

35 See Andrzej Paczkowski, "Raporty o pogromie," *Puls* 50.3 (1991), 107–120.

36 Report by the regional commander of the State Police about anti-Jewish disturbances in Slovakia, August 1–4, 1946, and security measures adopted, August 1946, (document 6) in *Československo a Izrael v letech 1945–1956: Dokumenty*, ed. Marie Bulínová (Prague: Ustav pro soudobe dejiny AV ČR, 1993), 35–38; Ivica Bumová, "Protižidovské výtržnosti v Bratislave v historickom kontexte," *Pamäť národa* 3 (2007), 14–29.

37 *Reflections on the Kielce Pogrom*, ed. Łukasz Kamiński and Jan Żaryn (Warsaw: IPN, 2006); Tokarska-Bakir, *Pod klątwą*.

38 I use the definition of pogroms coined by Werner Bergmann on the basis of the conception of Roberta Senechal de la Roche. See Roberta Senechal de la Roche, "Collective violence as social control," *Sociological Forum* 11.1 (1996), 1. Pogroms are defined here "as a one-sided and non-governmental form of social control, as 'self-help by a group' that occurs when no remedy from the state against the [perceived, often illusory] threat which another ethnic group poses can be expected." Werner Bergmann, "Ethnic Riots in Situations of Loss of Control: Revolution, Civil War, and Regime Change as Opportunity Structures for Anti-Jewish Violence in Nineteenth- and Twentieth-Century Europe," in *Control of Violence*, ed. Wilhelm Heitmeyer et al. (New York: Springer, 2011), 487.

39 David Engel, "Patterns of Anti-Jewish Violence in Poland, 1944–1946," *Yad Vashem Studies* 26 (1998), 43–85. Andrzej Żbikowski estimates the number of victims to be at least 650–750. Andrzej Żbikowski, "The Post-War Wave of Pogroms and Killings," in *Jewish Presence in Absence: The Aftermath of the Holocaust in Poland, 1944–2010*, ed. Feliks Tych and Monika Adamczyk-Garbowska (Jerusalem: Yad Vashem, 2014), 69.

40 Kenez, *Hungary: From the Nazis to the Soviets*, 155.

41 This corresponds to the contention of Roy F. Baumeister that "it is wrong to say that emotions are for initiating behavior, and it is even mostly wrong to say that emotions cause behavior. Instead, behavior pursues emotions. Emotions are an important consequence of behavior rather than a cause." Roy F. Baumeister, *The Cultural Animal: Human Nature, Meaning, and Social Life* (Oxford: Oxford University Press, 2005), 267.

42 Yuri Lotman, "Okhota za ved'mami. Semiotika strakha/Witchhunts: semiotics of fear," in *Trudy po znakovym sistemam/Sign Systems Studies* 26 (1998), 61–82.

43 Lotman, *Okhota za ved'mami*, 63–64, 80.

44 Andrzej Żbikowski, "The Post-War Wave of Pogroms," 69.

45 Tokarska-Bakir, *Pod klątwą*, vol. 1, 145.

BIBLIOGRAPHY

Apor, Péter. "The Lost Deportations and the Lost People of Kunmadaras: A Pogrom in Hungary, 1946." *Hungarian Historical Review* 2.3 (2013), 566–604. / **Baumeister, Roy F.** *The Cultural Animal: Human Nature, Meaning, and Social Life*. Oxford: Oxford University Press, 2005. / **Bemporad, Elissa.** "Empowerment, Defiance, and Demise: Jews and the Blood Libel Specter under Stalinism." *Jewish History* 26.3–4 (2012), 343–361. /**Bergmann, Werner.** "Ethnic Riots in Situations of Loss of Control: Revolution, Civil War, and Regime Change as Opportunity Structures for Anti-Jewish Violence in Nineteenth- and Twentieth-Century Europe." In *Control of Violence*, edited by Wilhelm Heitmeyer et al., 487–516. New York: Springer, 2011. / **Bulínová, Marie, ed.** *Československo a Izrael v letech 1945–1956: Dokumenty*. Prague: Ustav pro soudobe dejiny AV ČR, 1993. / **Bumová, Ivica.** "Protižidovské výtržnosti v Bratislave v historickom kontexte." *Pamäť národa* 3 (2007), 14–29. / **Cała, Alina.** *Żyd–wróg odwieczny: Antysemityzm w Polsce i jego źródła*. Warsaw: Nisza, 2012. / **Cichopek, Anna.** *Beyond Violence: Jewish Survivors in Poland and Slovakia, 1944–1948*. Cambridge: Cambridge University Press, 2014. / **Engel, David.** "Patterns of Anti-Jewish Violence in Poland, 1944–1946." *Yad Vashem Studies* 26 (1998), 43–85. / **Fitzpatrick, Sheila.** "Annexation, Evacuation, and Antisemitism in the Soviet Union, 1939–1946." In *Shelter from the Holocaust. Rethinking Jewish Survival in the Soviet Union*, edited by Mark Edele, Sheila Fitzpatrick, and Atina Grossmann. Detroit: Wayne State University Press, 2017, 133–160. / **Gross, Jan T.** *Fear: Anti-Semitism in Poland After Auschwitz*. New York: Random House, 2006. / **Kaczmarski, Krzysztof.** *Pogrom którego nie było. Rzeszów 11–12 czerca 1945. Fakty, hipotezy, dokumenty*. Rzeszów: Instytut Pamięci Narodowej, 2008. / **Kamenec, Ivan.** "Protižidovský Pogrom v Topoľčanoch v Septembri 1945." *Studia Historica Nitriensia* 8 (2000), 85–97. / **Kamiński, Łukasz** and **Jan Żaryn, ed.** *Reflections on the Kielce Pogrom*. Warsaw: IPN, 2006. / **Kenez, Peter.** *Hungary: From the Nazis to the Soviets. The Establishment of the Communist Regime in Hungary, 1944–1948*. Cambridge: Cambridge University Press, 2006. / **Klier, John D.** "'Zhid': Biography of a Russian Epithet." *Slavonic and East European Review* 60.1 (1982), 1–15. / **Krivienko, Siergiej.** "Raporty z Polski." *Karta* 5.15 (1995), 28–52. / **Kubátová, Hana.** "A zsidókról kialakult kép a háború utáni Szlovákiában," *Regio* 24.2 (2016), 63–80. / **Kwiek, Julian.** *Żydzi, Łemkowie, Słowacy w województwie krakowskim wlatach 1945–1949/50*. Kraków: Księgarnia Akademicka, 2002. / **Lotman, Yuri.** "Okhota za ved'mami. Semiotika strakha/Witchhunts: semiotics of fear." *Trudy po znakovym sistemam/Sign Systems Studies* 26 (1998), 61–82. / **Luvish, Ilya.** "From the Lonely Cellar to the Crowded Street: The Progression of Anti-Semitic Manifestations in Postwar Poland and the Soviet Union, 1944–1947." Senior Honors Thesis, Northeastern University, 2005. / **Paczkowski, Andrzej.** "Raporty o pogromie." *Puls* 50.3 (1991), 107–120. / **Pelle, János.** *Az utolsó vérvádak. Az etnikai gyűlölet és a politikai manipuláció kelet-európai történetéből*. Budapest: Pelikán Kiadó, 1995. / **Prażmowska, Anita J.** "The Kielce Pogrom 1946 and the Emergence of Communist Power in Poland." *Cold War History* 2.2 (2002), 101–124. / **Redlich, Shimon et al., ed.** *War, Holocaust and Stalinism: A Documented Study of the Jewish Anti-Fascist Committee in the USRR*. Luxemburg: Harwood Academic, 1995. / **Rozental, Nisn.** *Yidish lebn in ratnfarband*. Tel Aviv: I. L. Peretz, 1971. / **Senechal de la Roche, Roberta.** "Collective violence as social control." *Sociological Forum* 11.1 (1996), 97–128. / **Surdej, Mirosław.** *Okręg Rzeszowski Narodowej Organizacji Wojskowej–Narodowego Zjednoczenia Wojskowego w latach 1944–1947*. Rzeszów: IPN, 2018. / **Szaynok, Bożena.** *Pogrom Żydów w Kielcach, 4. VII 1946 r.* Warsaw: Bellona, 1992. / **Tokarska-Bakir, Joanna.** *Légendes du sang. Pour une anthropologie de l'antisémitisme chrétien*. Paris: Albin Michel, 2015. / **Tokarska-Bakir, Joanna.** *Pod klątwą. Społeczny portret pogromu kieleckiego*. Warsaw: Czarna Owca, 2018. / **Tokarska-Bakir, Joanna.** "Terror in Przedbórz. The Night of 27/28 May 1945." *East European Politics, Societies* and Cultures (forthcoming). / **Tsanin, Mordechai.** *Iber shteyn un shtok. A rayze iber hundert horev-gevorene kehiles in Poyln*. Tel Aviv: Letste nayes, 1952. / **Weiner, Amir.** *Making Sense of War: The Second World War and the Fate of the Bolshevik Revolution*. Princeton: Princeton University Press, 2001. / **White, Richard.** *The Middle Ground. Indians, Empires, and Republicans in the Great Lakes Region, 1650–1815*. Cambridge: Cambridge University Press, 2011. / **Żbikowski, Andrzej.** "The Post-War Wave of Pogroms and Killings." In

Jewish Presence in Absence: The Aftermath of the Holocaust in Poland, 1944–2010, edited by Feliks Tych and Monika Adamczyk-Garbowska, 67–94. Jerusalem: Yad Vashem, 2014.

JULIA PIROTTE
AND THE DOCUMENTATION
OF THE KIELCE POGROM

KATA BOHUS

Julia Pirotte was born into a poor Jewish family in Konskowola, a small town in Poland, in 1908 as Julia Diament. She was active in leftist political movements from a young age. In 1934, following threats of imprisonment for her political activities, she fled Poland. While seeking refuge in Brussels, she met activist Jean Pirotte and the couple were married in 1935. During the 1930s, Julia Pirotte worked as a journalist and enrolled in a photography course. She moved to France in 1940 and joined her sister Mindla as a member of the Résistance. Mindla was caught, tortured, and then executed by the Vichy regime in 1944. To this day, Julia Pirotte's photographs of the 1944 uprising in Marseille, of members of the Résistance in the city, and of the arrival of the Allies are recognized as important documents pertaining to the Second World War.

In 1946, Pirotte returned to Poland and continued working as a photo-journalist. She was employed by the periodicals *Trybuna Wolności* and *Żołnierz Polski*. On the night of July 4, 1946, she traveled by train from Warsaw to the town of Kielce. She had been commissioned by the editor-in-chief of *Żołnierz Polski* to report on the pogrom there. The task was dangerous: she had to be accompanied by a Polish officer because, even after the pogrom, trains passing through Kielce were scrutinized for Jews by civilians and railway guards who beat and, in some cases, murdered Jewish passengers.

In Kielce, Julia Pirotte took photographs of the massacred and desecrated corpses of pogrom victims, visited the survivors in the hospital, and documented the funeral procession as well. She was the only photojournalist present in the town at the time. Most of the photographs she took—and there were more than one hundred—were confiscated by the communist secret police organ, the Office of Security (*Urząd Bezpieczeństwa*). Consequently, she had to redo the negatives from proofs, but, as a result of her efforts, some of the photos did get published in the Polish press in 1946.

Julia Pirotte's self-portrait, 1942–1943. Emanuel
Ringelblum Jewish Historical Institute, Warsaw

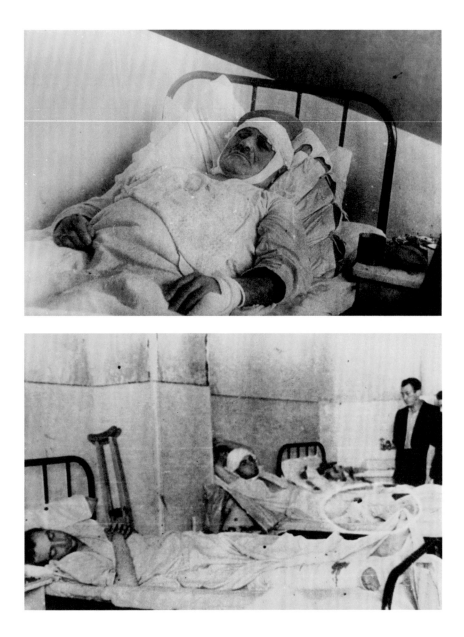

Jewish men wounded during the Kielce pogrom
in hospital, 1946. Photo: Julia Pirotte, Emanuel
Ringelblum Jewish Historical Institute, Warsaw

Coffins of the pogrom victims in Kielce, 1946.
Photo: Julia Pirotte, Emanuel Ringelblum Jewish
Historical Institute, Warsaw

Jewish soldiers of the Polish Army in the funeral
procession of the pogrom victims in Kielce, 1946.
Photo: Julia Pirotte, Emanuel Ringelblum Jewish
Historical Institute, Warsaw

STORIES OF MIGRATION AND REPATRIATION FROM THE SOVIET UNION

SHIFTING BORDERS AND POPULATION GROUPS

KATHARINA FRIEDLA

Judith Karliner-Gerczuk was born in Berlin in 1927. Her parents, Elias and Klara, were Polish nationals who had moved to Germany soon after the First World War. In October 1938, the family was arrested in Berlin and deported to Poland. At first, the Karliners were forced to stay in the refugee camp in Zbąszyń. Not until the summer of 1939 were they allowed to leave the camp and join their relatives in the town of Stanisławów in Eastern Poland (which is today the Ukrainian city of Ivano-Frankivsk). When the Second World War began, the town was occupied by the Soviets. As the situation there became increasingly precarious, Judith's father volunteered to go to the Soviet Union as a laborer. In January 1940, the Karliners, along with thousands of other Polish nationals, were brought to the Caucasus in cattle cars. From there, the family was subsequently transferred to Saratov (in the eponymous oblast on the Volga). In an interview, Judith Karliner-Gerczuk recalled these events as follows:

> Hitler had a very good teacher in Stalin. Because in Russia was exactly the same thing what we went through in Germany. [...] I want to let known the future generations what was going on. Because some people say, 'Oh, you were not in a camp, so you didn't go through so much.' But for me it was a trauma practically from childhood on.[1]

In April 1946, as the postwar repatriation of the Polish nationals who had come to the Soviet Union began, Judith and her family were able to leave the USSR.

Their transport took them to the Lower Silesian town of Kłodzko (which the Germans had called Glatz). The Karliners' trajectory reflects the history of the Holocaust in a transnational and multidimensional way. As Polish citizens and Jews, they were subjected to the horrors of the Second World War, first by the National Socialist regime and subsequently, under difficult conditions, in the Soviet Union. In 1938, the Germans deported them to Poland, where the family had to make sense of their new circumstances. A few months later, the Soviet occupation began, and eventually they had to flee again, this time to the Soviet Union. The biography of the Karliners thus bears witness to various forms of exile and the complexities of survival.

Like Judith Karliner-Gerczuk, Cyla Berman-Zylbertal, who was born in Zamość in 1931, also ended up in the Soviet Union with her family. Following the German occupation of Poland, they were able to flee, in January 1940, to the part of the country under Soviet control. In June of that year, during the next wave of deportations of Polish citizens to the Soviet Union, they were transferred to the Siberian city of Krasnoyarsk, which is located on the Trans-Siberian Railway line and the Yenisei River. Only Cyla Berman-Zylbertal, her two younger sisters, and her younger brother survived. In March 1946, the siblings arrived in Lower Silesia on one of the repatriation transports. In an interview, Cyla Berman-Zylbertal recalled her experience as follows:

> Well, it was heaven on earth... In Siberia, we left the graves
> of four of our relatives behind, each in a different location. [...]
> Our grandmother, Sara Zylber, died in the Soviet Union.
> We also lost my older sister Rozalia there. She was thirteen
> at the time. My father died in the winter of 1942–43.
> And my mother died just before we left for Ukraine in 1944.[2]

Judith Karliner-Gerczuk and Cyla Berman-Zylbertal were among the roughly 230,000 Polish Jews who survived the Shoah in the Soviet Union.[3] Most of them had either fled from the part of Poland occupied by Germany at the beginning of the Second World War or, having been denounced as "class enemies and political undesirables," were arrested in the part of Poland occupied by the Soviets between 1939 and 1941 and deported to the USSR. In addition, some Polish Jewish refugees moved further into Soviet territory as they fled from the advancing Wehrmacht following the German invasion, and some came to the Soviet Union individually, mostly in search of work. Whether they fled, were deported, or evacuated, most of the (relatively speaking: very few) Polish Jews who survived the Shoah and the horrors that followed the German invasion of their country did so in the Soviet Union.

Refugees in the Soviet Union baking *matzot* for Passover, ca. 1945. United States Holocaust Memorial Museum, Washington D.C., courtesy of Hynda Szczukowski Halpren

A group photograph of Polish Jewish refugees in Bukhara (Uzbek Soviet Republic), 1941–1945. United States Holocaust Memorial Museum Washington D.C., courtesy of Pessia Polak

Polish Jews who had spent the war years in the Soviet Union looking out of the train that returned them to Poland, ca. 1946. Photo: John Vachon, JDC Archives, New York

Although many of the survivors described the deportation of their families to the Soviet Union as a stroke of good fortune, the experience of their exile there was painful and distressing. Most of the deportees and refugees lost their relatives and homes, and many of them ended up stateless. In the forced labor camps, prisons, detention centers, and other places of banishment in the Soviet Union, in *kolkhozes* (collective farms) in Kazakhstan and Uzbekistan, and in urban centers such as Archangelsk, Krasnoyarsk, or Irkutsk, they endured poverty, hunger, and epidemics. Many caught malaria and typhus. Older Jews frequently died of exhaustion. Even so, most of them survived thanks to their harsh involuntary exile under Stalin.

After the Second World War, most of the Polish Jewish survivors were repatriated under an agreement signed by the Soviet Union and the Provisional Polish Government of National Unity on July 6, 1945. The hundreds of transports bringing repatriates back from the Soviet Union began to arrive as early as the spring of 1946. Most of the trains went to the former German territories that had been ceded to Poland. Judith Karliner-Gerczuk, Cyla Berman-Zylbertal, and their surviving relatives too were among the repatriates who now arrived in the so-called "Recovered Territories."[4]

"NAYE GRENETSEN–NAYE HOFENUNGEN" ("NEW BORDERS–NEW HOPES")[5]

The Potsdam Conference in August 1945 once again redrew the borders in Europe. The four victorious powers determined that large parts of eastern Germany should henceforth fall under Polish administration. The Neumark in eastern Brandenburg, two-thirds of Pomerania, the southern part of East Prussia, and the bulk of Silesia were allotted to Poland. It, in turn, was forced to cede its Eastern region, the so-called "Kresy," to the Soviet Union. Even though millions lost their homes in the process, the Big Four at the table in Potsdam considered population transfers, forced migration, resettlement, and expulsion legitimate means of realpolitik.

The massive transfers began as soon as the fighting in Lower Silesia had ended with the German capitulation in Breslau on May 6, 1945. The German population was removed, and Poles were settled in its place. Silesia became Śląsk. Gradually, the territory was purged of the remnants of German settlement, systematically Polonized, and celebrated as one of the "Recovered Territories."[6]

The Jewish activist Jakub Egit, who had survived the war in the Soviet Union and went on to chair the Jewish Regional Committee in Lower Silesia (*Wojewódzki Komitet Żydów na Dolny Śląsk*), offered an account of how the idea emerged to create a center of Jewish life in Lower Silesia when he visited there with his friend, the Zionist activist Yitzhak (Antek) Zuckerman, a survivor of the Warsaw Ghetto:

> In early July 1945, my friend Yitzhak Zuckerman and I arrived in Lower Silesia. It was my goal to revive Jewish life on this soil where Hitler had annihilated Polish Jewry. Since their former houses and towns had been destroyed, the Jewish survivors were able to begin their new lives in Lower Silesia. There was no way back for them.[7]

Initially, it was mostly Polish Jews, survivors of the Gross-Rosen concentration camp and its numerous subsidiaries, who settled in the area. When the main camp in Gross-Rosen was liberated by the Red Army on February 8–9, 1945, some 10,000 Polish Jews were still alive in the various camps.[8]

Historians estimate that somewhere between 60,000 and 80,000 Polish Jews survived the Shoah in occupied Poland.[9] On June 15, 1945, the Central Committee of Jews in Poland had 73,965 Jews on its books who had registered with the regional Jewish Committees throughout the country.[10] Like most Polish survivors of the Shoah, some of the former Jewish prisoners from the camps in Lower Silesia who had previously lived in central Poland returned to their home towns. After the time they had spent in the concentration and forced labor camps, or in hiding, whether in the towns and villages, in the bunkers in the woods, or with the partisans, their former homes seemed the obvious next stop. Yet for most of them, this attempt to return to their former lives failed dramatically. Having returned home, they were generally confronted with the hostility of their Polish neighbors. The experience of the war had done nothing to ameliorate the stereotypes and prejudices that had long been widespread in Polish society.[11] Many of the Jewish survivors' former neighbors showed neither empathy for, nor solidarity with them. On occasion, the utter indifference displayed by most non-Jews towards the Jews turned into hatred.[12] Upon their deportation, Jews were forced to leave behind houses, apartments, businesses, workshops, and other assets all over Poland; most of these were then appropriated by the Polish neighbors while the country was under German occupation. Few were willing to hand back these assets to their surviving Jewish owners. Frequently, disputes about the restitution of the expropriated assets led to violent abuse and, in some cases, murder. In the summer of 1945, anti-Jewish unrest and pogroms erupted in some Polish cities, such as Rzeszów, Lublin, Radom, Częstochowa, and Kraków.[13] This atmosphere culminated in the pogrom in Kielce in July 1946 in which 42 Polish Jews were killed.[14] In addition, returning to their former homes, the survivors found that all their relatives, friends, and acquaintances had disappeared. Having to face up to this permanent loss where they had once lived swayed most of the survivors to move on and build their

new lives elsewhere. Psychologically, their determination to live amongst people who had been shaped by similar experiences also played an important role.
The survivors formed a quite distinct group, given the fears and trauma with
which they had to contend. Those who had survived in Poland either emerged
from hiding places and were able to move freely for the first time in years, or
had been shaped by the terrible and tormenting experiences of the ghettos and
concentration camps. The majority of survivors, those who were repatriated
from the Soviet Union, had also been affected by the turmoil of the war. Their
exile in Siberia and Central Asia had been characterized by hunger, illness, and
poverty. Returning from the Soviet Union, they were exhausted and in poor
health.

Against the backdrop of the survivors' futile attempts to return to their
former homes, Lower Silesian cities such as Wrocław, Dzierżoniów, Wałbrzych,
Legnica, and Bielawa seemed well-suited to allow them to establish their new
lives. The newly acquired territories in the West, which included the large cities
of Wrocław und Szczecin, also offered the Jews much greater security than
Poland's central regions. Here, the Jews and the Poles were both new settlers.
They had to build new lives for themselves and were able to take over the houses,
factories, and infrastructure left behind by the Germans. Moreover, Jews and
Poles alike still had very fresh memories of the Germans as their common
enemy. Unlike elsewhere, the issue of the earlier appropriation of Jewish assets by
Poles did not arise here. Finally, illegal anti-communist organizations such as the
antisemitic National Armed Forces (*Narodowe Siły Zbrojne*, NSZ) were not as
strong here as they were in central Poland.[15]

The fact that houses, apartments, and estates that had previously belonged to Germans were waiting for new owners clearly favored the settlement
of Jews in Lower Silesia. With the exception of the "Fortress Breslau," the
war had caused little destruction in the region, which offered the new settlers
a well-developed agricultural and industrial infrastructure. Moreover, the factories and farms left behind by the Germans provided numerous employment
opportunities.

The government in Warsaw responded positively to the suggestions of the
surviving Polish Jews regarding their settlement in Lower Silesia because they
matched its own concept for the resettlement of the "Recovered Territories,"
which envisaged that the area should be populated, and its economy developed,
in short order.[16] As early as June 1945, the Council of Ministers passed a resolution "On the Intensification of the Resettlement Program" that integrated
the repatriation program in a comprehensive national population policy.[17] It
was designed to ensure that the "recovered" Polish territories were populated as
promptly as possible and integrated into the new, "socialist" and "democratic"
Poland. The roughly 230,000 repatriated Jews who had survived the war in the

Soviet Union and, in so doing, escaped the Shoah, were allotted a distinct role in this plan. Consequently, approximately half of the surviving Polish Jews settled in the former German territories of Lower Silesia and Western Pomerania.

On July 1, 1945, 7,860 Jews were registered with the Jewish Committees in Lower Silesia. By January 1, 1946, this number had risen to 18,210.[18] The bulk of the Jews settling in the area subsequently arrived in the course of their systematic repatriation from the Soviet Union. Between January 1 and July 31, 1946, more than 120 transports brought a total of 86,563 Jewish repatriates to Lower Silesia.[19]

REPATRIATION—THE DIFFICULT RETURN HOME

Along with her mother and brother, Marie Brandstetter (*née* Mania Zelwer), born in Błaszki near Kalisz in 1933, fled to the part of Poland occupied by the Soviets and was deported from there to Siberia. In December 1945, the three returned to Poland and initially moved to the Lower Silesian city of Legnica (which the Germans had called Liegnitz). In her memoirs, she recalled her feelings on the eve of her return to Poland:

> It came time for us to leave Russia. [...] We all were excited to be going home. I wondered if there was a home left for us or if we would find any of the family there, or, for that matter, anyone alive. We had such a big family before the war, so many aunts, uncles and cousins; who had survived, I wondered?[20]

Marie Brandstetter's sentiments were shared by many returnees from the Soviet Union. They returned home with great curiosity but also with uncertainty and fear over the relatives and friends they had left behind when they left for the USSR. As soon as they arrived, they found out that their relatives who had stayed in Poland had been murdered and their former homeland had become a Jewish cemetery. Given the unimaginable scale of the tragedy, they could barely grasp the reality of the Shoah. The world they had left behind in 1939 no longer existed. There was nowhere for them to return. They were not welcome in their former homes. The situation in war-ravaged Poland alarmed many. When the returnees reached the Polish border, they were often confronted with virulent antisemitism. Morris Gruda, born in Różań in 1919, spent the war in the Soviet Union and returned to Poland in the spring of 1946, where he settled in Dzierżoniów.[21] When the train crossed the border and made a short stop, he got off the train and met a non-Jewish Polish returnee with whom he struck up a conversation. "Oh, have a lot of Jews survived?" he was asked. "You don't even speak a good Polish but with a Russian accent. You don't belong here."[22] Other Polish Jewish returnees were confronted with similar questions and statements: "'What are you coming back for? Couldn't you stay in Russia?'; 'The Russians take our coal and give us Jews.'; 'A pity that Hitler didn't finish you all off to the last one.'"[23]

Cyla Berman-Zylbertal and her siblings were also among the Jews now arriving in Lower Silesia. She described her journey to, and arrival in, the region as follows:

> We travelled by train to the western territories, we already knew this. We did not care. There was no point in returning to our town, we knew, there was nothing there for us anymore—neither our house nor our family, nothing. [...] We arrived in Wrocław [...] The PUR[24] staff took us to Viktoriastraße 7, it was still called that at this time, all the streets still had German signs. We were allotted a ground-floor apartment in the rear building [...] My brother and I stood by as the Germans were evicted. [...] Once we got to Wrocław, we thought we were in heaven. Here, Jewish life was well organized and none of us needed to live in fear.[25]

As Cyla explained in the interview, she and her siblings initially received food and clothing packages from UNRRA, the Jewish Committee, and the official Jewish community. The responsibility for the reception and support of the Jewish returnees lay with the Jewish Regional Committee and its repatriation department. Funding was provided by a number of institutions, foremost the JDC, the Central Committee of Jews in Poland, and the Polish government.

The roughly 90,000 Jews in Lower Silesia formed a significant proportion of the Jewish population in Poland at this time. In July 1946, some 250,000 Jews were registered with the statistical department of the Central Committee of Jews in Poland, most of whom lived in Lower Silesia, Szczecin, Łódź, and Upper Silesia.[26]

"A NAYE LEBN GEYT OYF" (A NEW LIFE BEGINS)[27]

Shortly after the war, Jacob Pat, who had fled to New York in 1938, was commissioned by the New York-based Jewish Labor Committee to travel to Poland and survey the situation of the surviving Jews. His travel reports were published in Yiddish as *Ash un fayer. Iber di khurves fun Poyln* (*Ash and Fire: Through the Ruins of Poland*) in New York in 1946. Following particularly traumatic stops such as in the ruins of the Warsaw Ghetto, Rychbach/Dzierżoniów was his first destination in

Jewish DPs in Lower Silesia wait to be resettled into
apartments near Reichenbach (later Dzierżoniów)
or Waldenburg (later Wałbrzych), 1945. United States
Holocaust Memorial Museum, Washington D.C.,
courtesy of Mahli Lieblich

Lower Silesia. In his travelogue, he related his initial impression of the Jewish life recently established in the region:

> I arrived in Rychbach on the evening of *shabbos*. [...] I was extremely surprised, it was like landing on a different planet. It is a beautiful city, which had not been damaged [...] It has a large market square [...] Jews are walking about, standing around in small groups, busily strutting to and fro [...] One had soon expelled the Germans, and Jews have settled there. Thousands more from the Soviet Union are expected. [...] As I look into the side street, I notice a large illuminated sign–to my great surprise. I had not previously seen anything like it in Poland. A Yiddish sign in Yiddish letters, lit up electrically, reading: Cultural Center. You will not see this in Warsaw, Łódź, Białystok, Kraków, Częstochowa, or Katowice–only in Rychbach is this possible. [...] "A Jewish city is being created here," the Jewish actor [...] Symche Natan, who recently arrived here from the Soviet Union, tells me. [...] Today, after Oświęcim–a Jewish dance in the Cultural Center of Rychbach. Have these Jews dancing in the hall risen from the ashes? ... –No, they are no specters, no ghosts, they are real, living Jews. They are simply miracle Jews. They are Jews from the concentration camps and forests or returnees from the Soviet Union.[28]

This account of a flourishing Jewish life in Poland seems extremely counterintuitive, especially when one takes into account that the Second World War had only been over for the better part of a year. Pat's travelogue conveys a sense of the extent and dimension of Jewish settlement in Lower Silesia. As his account indicates, new Jewish institutions and organizations were established in Lower Silesia to cater to the massively growing number of Jewish repatriates from the Soviet Union. Among their urgent tasks was the provision of healthcare, the so-called "productivization,"[29] and the securing of housing and work. The Jewish Regional Committee and its various branches in smaller localities in the area took on these extremely important functions. They provided accommodation for the Jews and helped them with their search for work, housing, and, quite often, for surviving family members as well.

The political leeway granted Jews in Poland in the immediate postwar years favored a broad spectrum of political parties that replicated the Jewish politics of interwar Poland.[30] While some had survived in Poland in hiding, the majority of politically active Jews were repatriates from the Soviet Union. For the various political parties, Lower Silesia was particularly fertile territory. The Zionist parties were able to establish numerous *kibbutzim* in various parts of Lower Silesia. In Wrocław alone, there were thirteen of them, mostly run by the extremely popular Ihud (Unity) Party.[31] It was especially the young Jewish survivors who arrived as aliens in the region and were often the only members of their family to survive who tended to begin their new lives in the *kibbutzim*.[32]

The Jewish newcomers to Lower Silesia also revived the religious structures that had been wiped out during the Second World War. Moreover, numerous Jewish schools (where Hebrew and Yiddish were the languages of instruction), clinics, and orphanages were launched. One of the most important cultural activities involved the creation of a Yiddish press and publishing sector. Given this diverse range of independent Jewish activities, the prerequisites for the consolidation of a "Yiddish *Yishuv*" in Lower Silesia initially seemed to be in place. Yet this soon turned out to be an illusion.

This measure of independence and pronounced desire for Jewish self-determination in Poland immediately after the war resulted principally from the experience of the war, which had set the Jews apart from the Polish majority population. It also resulted from postwar antisemitism, a source of fear but also of solidarity among the Jews. The activists among the Jewish communists and the representatives of the Bund in particular pushed ahead with the revival of Jewish life in Poland. In addition, Jews in Poland, like their peers in other European countries at the time, received funding from foreign organizations. Yet their efforts gradually came to an end. On an individual level, the majority of Polish Jews already saw no future for themselves in the country. Most of the repatriates from the USSR decided to flee to the DP camps in western Europe.

The creation of the State of Israel in the spring of 1948 transformed the relationship between the Polish People's Republic and the Jews. As a result of the power dynamics at play, Polish government policy was aligned with Moscow's stance towards the newly established state. The situation in Poland became extremely tense, and the anti-Jewish signals emanating from the Soviet Union contributed substantially to its further deterioration. The emerging rivalry between the superpowers in the Middle East had grave consequences for the Jews in Poland and the other Eastern European states. As the evolving Cold War intensified, a new political alliance formed, which saw Israel increasingly draw closer to the U.S. and distance itself from the policies of the communist states (and the Soviet Union in particular). This created a new political constellation that not only robbed the Jews in the Eastern European states of their newly won independence but also precipitated a renewed rise of discriminatory practices towards them. The postwar fate of the Jews in Poland was determined by these emerging fault lines. The extremely unstable domestic situation in Poland also militated against the consolidation of Jewish life in the country after the Shoah.

Hence, the new *Yishuv* in Lower Silesia did not flourish for long. As the Stalinization of the party and country gained momentum from 1949 onwards, pluralism became a thing of the past. Jewish schools were nationalized and the

Shmuel Willenberg shooting footage of members
of the Ihud Zionist group in Lower Silesia, 1947.
United States Holocaust Memorial Museum, Washington
D.C., courtesy of Shmuel and Ada Willenberg

Former German shops turned into Jewish food stores
in Reichenbach (later Dzierżoniów), 1945–1950.
Photo: Brauislau Aidler, Yad Vashem, Jerusalem

independent Jewish cooperatives and healthcare system disbanded. The Central Committee of Jews in Poland and its local branches, including the Jewish Regional Committees, were also dissolved.[33]

Given the centralization and Stalinization of the Polish People's Republic in the early 1950s, most Jews saw emigration as their only option. For many of the Jewish returnees, Poland was merely an intermediate stop on their way, first, to the DP camps in Germany and, from there, to other countries, especially Israel and the U.S. Their flight and emigration were motivated not least by their experience of the communist regime in the Soviet Union during the years of their exile there. According to the statistics of the Central Committee of Jews in Poland, roughly 200,000 Polish Jews between 1944 and 1949 had been repatriated from the Soviet Union.[34] Between 1945 and 1947, some 130,000 Jews left the country.[35] In 1948, the repatriation from the Soviet Union was officially terminated, and the authorities in Poland prohibited any further emigration.

The experience of Judith Karliner and her family reflects the odyssey of Polish Jews in a multidimensional perspective. Their painful experiences did not end with their return to Poland. They too saw no future for themselves in there. In April 1946, Judith and her family crossed the Soviet-Polish border. They initially moved to the Lower Silesian town of Kłodzko and later from there to Wrocław. As soon as they arrived in Poland, they tried to find a way of moving on to the American occupation zone in Germany. Judith joined a *kibbutz* for a short while, hoping this might give her the opportunity to get to Germany illegally via Czechoslovakia, but to no avail. For the time being, the Karliners were stuck in Poland, their consistent efforts to emigrate notwithstanding. They were not able to leave the People's Republic until the next large wave of Jewish emigration from Poland in September 1957. Judith Karliner then moved to Berlin and, from there, to Australia, where she settled in Melbourne.[36] That brought an end to the protracted, painful, and distressing trajectory of exile, flight, deportation, repatriation, and renewed exile, which had led her across several constantly shifting borders.

---

[1] Judith Karliner-Gerczuk, Interview 26867, March 3, 1997, Melbourne, Australia, Tape 2 (22:00 Min.) and Tape 4 (00:50 Min.), USC Shoah Foundation Visual History Archive (USC VHA).

[2] Interview with Cyla Berman-Zylbertal, held in Polish on September 15, 2006 and September 9, 2007 in Wrocław (author's archive).

[3] Recent research assumes that somewhere between 200,000 and 230,000 Polish Jews escaped the Shoah by going to the Soviet Union. Mark Edele and Wanda Warlik, "Saved by Stalin? Trajectories and Numbers of Polish Jews in the Soviet Second World War," in *Shelter from the Holocaust. Rethinking Jewish Survival in the Soviet Union*, ed. Mark Edele, Sheila Fitzpatrick, and Atina Grossman (Detroit: Wayne State University Press, 2017), 95–131.

[4] Formerly German areas such as Lower Silesia and Western Pomerania were referred to by the Polish propaganda as "*Ziemie Odzyskane*" ("Recovered Territories").

[5] "New Borders—New Hopes". Shmuel Leyb Shnayderman, *Tsvishn shrek un hofenung* (Buenos Aires: Tsentral-farband fun Poylishe Yidn in Argentine, 1947), 285.

[6] See Gregor Thum, *Die fremde Stadt. Breslau 1945* (Berlin: Siedler, 2003).

[7] Jakub Egit, *Tsu a nay lebn (tsvay yor yidisher yishev in Nidershlesye)* (Wrocław: Farlag Nidershlesye, 1947), 21; Jakub Egit, *Grand Illusion* (Toronto: Lugus, 1991), 44. In contrast to Egit, Cukierman assumed that the Polish survivors of the Shoah had only one option, namely, to move to Palestine and contribute to the creation of a Jewish state. Zuckierman left Poland in 1947 and moved to Palestine.

[8] Wojewódzki Komitet Żydowski, Sig. 5, Bl. 37, Archiwum Państwowe Wrocław (APWr).

[9] Given the enormous fluctuation, it is difficult to determine the exact number of surviving Jews. On this, see, *inter alia*, Albert Stankowski and Piotr Weiser, "Demograficzne skutki Holokaustu," in *Następstwa zagłady Żydów. Polska 1944–2010*, ed. Feliks Tych and Monika Adamczyk-Garbowska (Lublin: UMSC, 2011), 15–38. Somewhere between 60,000 and 80,000 Polish Jews likely survived the German occupation. See, Natalia Aleksiun and Dariusz Stola, "'Wszyscy krawcy wyjechali'. O Żydach w PRL," *Biuletyn Instytutu Pamięci Narodowej* 2 (2008), 391–409.

[10] Natalia Aleksiun, *Dokąd dalej? Ruch syjonistyczny w Polsce (1944–1950)* (Warsaw: TRIO, 2002), 63.

[11] The complex and dramatic Polish–Jewish "coexistence" in Poland immediately after the war has been studied extensively. See, *inter alia*, Jan T. Gross, *Fear: Anti-Semitism in Poland After Auschwitz* (Princeton: Princeton University Press, 2006); *Golden Harvest: Events at the Periphery of the Holocaust*, ed. Jan T. Gross and Irena Grudzińska-Gross (Oxford: Oxford University Press, 2011); Marcin Zaremba, *Wielka Trwoga. Polska 1944–1947. Ludowa reakcja na kryzys* (Kraków: Znak, 2012); *Następstwa zagłady Żydów*, ed. Feliks Tych and Monika Adamczyk-Garbowska; Łukasz Krzyżanowski, *Dom którego nie było. Powroty ocalałych do powojennego miasta* (Wołowiec: Czarne, 2016); *Dalej jest noc. Losy Żydów w wybranych powiatach okupowanej Polski*, ed. Barbara Engelking and Jan T. Grabowski (Warsaw: Centrum Badań nad Zagładą Żydów, 2018); Joanna Tokarska-Bakir, *Pod klątwą. Społeczny portret pogromu kieleckiego* (Kraków: Znak, 2018).

[12] See Alina Skibińska, "Powroty ocalałych i stosunek do nich społeczeństwa polskiego," in *Następstwa zagłady Żydów*, ed. Feliks Tych and Monika Adamczyk-Garbowska (Lublin: UMSC, 2011), 39–70; Andrzej Żbikowski, "Morderstwa popełniane na Żydach w pierwszych latach po wojnie," in *Następstwa zagłady Żydów*, ed. Feliks Tych and Monika Adamczyk-Garbowska (Lublin: UMSC, 2011), 71–93.

[13] On this, see Joanna Tokarska-Bakir's contribution to this volume.

[14] Joanna Tokarska-Bakir's two-volume monograph, *Pod klątwą*, is the most recent study on the pogrom in Kielce.

[15] CKŻP, Sig. 303/I/1, Bl. 104f, Archive of the Jewish Historical Institute in Warsaw (AŻIH).

[16] On the Polonization of the "Recovered Territories" and Jewish efforts in this context, see Kamil Kijek, "Aliens in the Lands of the Piasts: The Polonization of Lower Silesia and Its Jewish Community in the Years 1945–1950," in *Jews and Germans in Eastern Europe. Shared and Comparative Histories*, ed. Tobias Grill (Berlin: De Gruyter, 2018), 234–255.

[17] See Jan Czerniakiewicz, *Repatriacja ludności polskiej z ZSRR. 1944–1948* (Warsaw: PWN, 1987), 37.

[18] WKŻ, Sig. 5, Bl. 35, APWr.

[19] CKŻP, Sig. 303/V/401 (no pagination) and Sig. 303/V/3, AŻIH.

[20] Marie Brandstetter, *Mania's Angel. My Life Story* (n.p.: Author's edition, 1995), 69. See also the interview with Marie Brandstetter, February 7, 2001, San Francisco, U.S.A., Bay Area Holocaust Oral History Project, No. 1999.A.0122.397, RG-50.477.0397, United States Holocaust Memorial Museum Archive.

[21] The city the Germans had called Reichenbach until 1945 was briefly renamed Rychbach (Yiddish) after the war. The name was then Polonized to Dzierżoniów in 1946. On this, see Kamil Kijek's contribution to this volume.

[22] Morris Gruda, *Tricks of Fate. Escape, Survival, and Rescue, 1939–1945* (Toronto: Mosaic

Press, 2006), 236. See also Morris Gruda, Interview 14395, April 22, 1996, Thornhill/Ontario, Canada, USC VHA.

[23] Rachela Tytelman-Wygodzki, *The End and the Beginning. August 1939–July 1948* (n.p.d: Author's edition, 1998), 36.

[24] *Państwowy Urząd Repatriacji*, the national repatriation authority.

[25] Interview with Cyla Berman-Zylbertal.

[26] Elżbieta Hornowa, "Powrót Żydów polskich z ZSRR oraz działalność opiekuńcza Centralnego Komitetu Żydów w Polsce," *Biuletyn Żydowskiego Instytutu Historycznego* no. 133/134 (1985), 105–122.

[27] Egit: *Tsu a nay lebn*, 21.

[28] Jacob Pat, *Ash un fayer. Iber di khurbes fun Poyln* (New York: „CYCO" Bicher-Farlag, 1946), 211, 212, 213.

[29] This term emerged in the 1880s to denote attempts to integrate the destitute and homeless Jews whom the tsarist administration had banished from the countryside into the capitalist production process in the Polish towns and cities. Although the term always had antisemitic overtones, it was still used after the war.

[30] They included the Bund, Poale Zion, Hitahdut, and Ihud.

[31] CKŻP, Sig. 324/1169, Bl. 12, AŻIH.

[32] See Avinoam Patt, *Finding Home and Homeland: Jewish Youth and Zionism in the Aftermath of the Holocaust* (Detroit: Wayne State University Press, 2009).

[33] See Hersz Smolar, *Oyf der letster positsye mit der letster hofenung* (Tel Aviv: I. L. Peretz, 1982), 192–193.

[34] Anna M. Rosner, *Obraz społeczności ocalałych w Centralnej Kartotece Wydziału Ewidencji i Statystyki CKŻP* (Warsaw: Żydowski Instytut Historyczny, 2018).

[35] Albert Stankowski, "How many Polish Jews survived the Holocaust?" in *Jewish Presence in Absence: The Aftermath of the Holocaust in Poland, 1944–2010*, ed. Feliks Tych and Monika Adamczyk-Garbowska (Jerusalem: Yad Vashem, 2014), 205–217.

[36] Karliner-Gerczuk, USC VHA interview, Tapes 3 und 4.

BIBLIOGRAPHY

Aleksiun, Natalia. *Dokąd dalej? Ruch syjonistyczny w Polsce (1944–1950).* Warsaw: TRIO, 2002. / **Aleksiun, Natalia,** and **Dariusz Stola.** "'Wszyscy krawcy wyjechali'. O Żydach w PRL." *Biuletyn Instytutu Pamięci Narodowej* 2 (2008), 391–409. / **Brandstetter, Marie.** *Mania's Angel. My Life Story.* N.p.: Author's edition, 1995. / **Czerniakiewicz, Jan.** *Repatriacja ludności polskiej z ZSRR. 1944–1948.* Warsaw: PWN, 1987. / **Edele, Mark,** and **Wanda Warlik.** "Saved by Stalin? Trajectories and Numbers of Polish Jews in the Soviet Second World War." In *Shelter from the Holocaust. Rethinking Jewish Survival in the Soviet Union,* edited by Mark Edele, Sheila Fitzpatrick, and Atina Grossman, 95–131. Detroit: Wayne State University Press, 2017. / **Egit, Jakub.** *Tsu a nay lebn (tsvay yor yidisher yishev in Nidershlesye).* Wrocław: Farlag Nidershlesye, 1947. / **Egit, Jakub.** *Grand Illusion.* Toronto: Lugus, 1991. / **Engelking, Barbara,** and **Jan Grabowski,** eds. *Dalej jest noc. Losy Żydów w wybranych powiatach okupowanej Polski. Warsaw:* Centrum Badań nad Zagładą Żydów, 2018. / **Gross, Jan T.** *Fear: Anti-Semitism in Poland After Auschwitz.* Princeton: Princeton University Press, 2006. / **Gross, Jan T.,** and **Irena Grudzińska-Gross.** *Golden Harvest: Events at the Periphery of the Holocaust.* Oxford: Oxford University Press, 2011. / **Gruda, Morris.** *Tricks of Fate. Escape, Survival, and Rescue, 1939–1945.* Toronto: Mosaic Press, 2006. / **Hornowa, Elżbieta.** "Powrót Żydów polskich z ZSRR oraz działalność opiekuńcza Centralnego Komitetu Żydów w Polsce." *Biuletyn Żydowskiego Instytutu Historycznego* no. 133/134 (1985), 105–122. / **Kijek, Kamil.** "Aliens in the Lands of the Piasts: The Polonization of Lower Silesia and Its Jewish Community in the Years 1945–1950." In *Jews and Germans in Eastern Europe. Shared and Comparative Histories,* edited by Tobias Grill, 234–255. Berlin: De Gruyter, 2018. / **Krzyżanowski, Łukasz.** *Dom którego nie było. Powroty ocalałych do powojennego* *miasta*. Wołowiec: Czarne, 2016. **/ Pat, Jacob.** *Ash un fayer. Iber di khurbes fun Poyln*. New York: "CYCO" Bicher-Farlag, 1946. **/ Patt, Avinoam.** *Finding Home and Homeland: Jewish Youth and Zionism in the Aftermath of the Holocaust*. Detroit: Wayne State University Press, 2009. **/ Rosner, Anna M.** *Obraz społeczności ocalałych w Centralnej Kartotece Wydziału Ewidencji i Statystyki CKŻP*. Warsaw: Żydowski Instytut Historyczny, 2018. **/ Shnayderman, Shmuel Leyb.** *Tsvishn shrek un hofenung*. Buenos Aires: Tsentral-farband fun Poylishe Yidn in Argentine, 1947. **/ Skibińska, Alina**. "Powroty ocalałych i stosunek do nich społeczeństwa polskiego." In *Następstwa zagłady Żydów. Polska 1944–2010*, edited by Feliks Tych and Monika Adamczyk-Garbowska, 39–70. Lublin: UMSC, 2011. **/ Smolar, Hersz.** *Oyf der letster posit-sye mit der letster hofenung*. Tel Aviv: I. L. Peretz, 1982. **/ Stankowski, Albert.** "How many Polish Jews survived the Holocaust?" In *Jewish Presence in Absence: The Aftermath of the Holocaust in Poland, 1944–2010*, edited by Feliks Tych and Monika Adamczyk-Garbowska, 205–217. Jerusalem: Yad Vashem, 2014. **/ Stankowski, Albert,** and **Piotr Weiser.** "Demograficzne skutki Holokaustu." In *Następstwa zagłady Żydów. Polska 1944–2010*, edited by Feliks Tych and Monika Adamczyk-Garbowska, 15–38. Lublin: UMSC, 2011. **/ Thum, Gregor.** *Die fremde Stadt. Breslau 1945*. Berlin: Siedler, 2003. **/ Tokarska-Bakir, Joanna.** *Pod klątwą. Społeczny portret pogromu kieleckiego*. Kraków: Znak, 2018. **/ Tych, Feliks,** and **Monika Adamczyk-Garbowska,** eds. *Następstwa zagłady Żydów. Polska 1944–2010*. Lublin: UMSC, 2011. **/ Tytelman-Wygodz-ki, Rachela.** *The End and the Beginning. August 1939–July 1948*. N.p.: Author's edition, 1998. **/ Zaremba, Marcin.** *Wielka Trwoga. Polska 1944–1947. Ludowa reakcja na kryzys*. Kraków: Znak, 2012. **/ Żbikowski, Andrzej.** "Morderstwa popełniane na Żydach w pierwszych latach po wojnie." In *Następstwa zagłady Żydów. Polska 1944–2010*, edited by Feliks Tych and Monika Adamczyk-Garbowska, 71–93. Lublin: UMSC, 2011.

REICHENBACH/ RYCHBACH/ DZIERŻONIÓW
A CENTER FOR JEWISH LIFE IN POLAND IN A PERIOD OF TRANSITION, 1945–1950[1]

KAMIL KIJEK

> Today, after Oświęcim–a Jewish dance in the Cultural Center of Rychbach. Have these Jews dancing in the hall risen from the ashes? … –No, they are no specters, no ghosts, they are real, living Jews. They are simply miracle Jews. They are Jews from the concentration camps and forests or returnees from the Soviet Union.
>
> Jacob Pat, 1946

For a short time after the war, the small Lower Silesian town of Reichenbach im Eulengebirge, which briefly became known as Rychbach before being renamed Dzierżoniów in 1946, unexpectedly became home to a lively Jewish community with autonomous political, cultural, and religious institutions, something unique in postwar Eastern Europe where most of Jewish life had been extinguished. By the summer of 1946, Jews made up almost half of its population and until 1950, their proportion never dropped below 20 percent. In this brief and intense period, Dzierżoniów was a significant center of Jewish settlement in Poland, albeit one largely forgotten today.

POSTWAR JEWISH SETTLEMENT IN AND AROUND DZIERŻONIÓW

Lower Silesia was the site of a major German concentration camp, Gross-Rosen. When it was liberated by Soviet troops, there were some 10,000 Polish Jews among its prisoners.[2] On May 13, 1945, a few days after their liberation, former camp

Street scene in Rychbach/Dzierżoniów, 1945–1947.
Emanuel Ringelblum Jewish Historical Institute, Warsaw

Building of the Jewish Regional Committee in Rychbach,
later Dzierżoniów, 1945–1948. Emanuel Ringelblum
Jewish Historical Institute, Warsaw

A group of *kibbutz* members of the Dror Zionist youth
movement in Rychbach/ Dzierżoniów, standing in a
roll call assembly, 1946. The Ghetto Fighters' House
Museum / The Photo Archive, Western Galilee, Israel,
courtesy of Baruch Altschuler and Benjamin Anolik

Wolf Arbesman, the first Jewish farmer to settle in postwar Rychbach/Dzierżoniów, 1945. Taube Department of
Jewish Studies, University of Wrocław

inmates formed the Committee for the Aid of Former Jewish Camp Prisoners (*Komitet Pomocy Żydom z Obozów Koncentracyjnych*). Following a favorable assessment of the suitability of Lower Silesia (part of the so-called "Recovered Territories" taken over by Poland from Germany) for Jewish settlement by the Warsaw-based Central Committee of Jews in Poland and the Ministry of Internal Affairs, the Reichenbach Jewish Committee was created to oversee further developments.[3]

Around 7,000 of these Polish Jews newly present in Lower Silesia were ready to stay.[4] Many of them had nowhere to go; their families had been killed and their communities destroyed by the Nazis. In many cases, their assets had been taken by their neighbors. In Lower Silesia, by contrast, they were able to take over flats, businesses, factories, and farms previously owned by expelled Germans. This process was also supported by the Polish state. In places like Rychbach, the presence of Polish Jews, recognized as ultimate victims of Nazi Germany, served as legitimization for Polish claims to the territory and the expulsion of German inhabitants.

In the summer of 1945, the Rychbach Jewish Committee started to develop local institutions for providing housing, work, welfare, and health care. Meanwhile, the number of Jews living in the town continued to grow. On July 6, 1945, the new Polish government reached an agreement with the victorious Soviets regarding the repatriation of Polish citizens from the Soviet Union.[5] Polish authorities and Jewish leaders in Poland agreed that Lower Silesia would be the best place for settling the majority of more than 100,000 Jews arriving from the Soviet Union in the first half of 1946.[6] This decision resulted in the quick growth of the Rychbach Jewish community. In January 1946, 3,873 Jews were registered in the town with another 3,000 in the surrounding area.[7] With the arrival of the Jews from the Soviet Union, by July 1946, Dzierżoniów had become the town with the highest Jewish share of the population in postwar Poland (around 50 percent). After the Kielce pogrom in July 1946, tens of thousands of Jews fled Poland, most of them to DP camps in the American occupation zone of Germany. Nevertheless, Jewish flight from Dzierżoniów was much less intense than from other parts of the country, as Jews lived in a large, protected, closely-knit community there.

Those who had settled in the town drew in more Jews who had not initially intended to stay. Frieda Pertman, for example, recalled that she and her family were on their way from the Soviet Union to another Lower Silesian town. Their train stopped for a couple of hours in Dzierżoniów and her husband, Chaim, went for a walk. On the street, he met his former neighbor Yaacov Ponczak, who told him that a cousin of Chaim's was also living in town. As a result, the Pertmans spontaneously decided to get off the train and settle in Dzierżoniów.[8]

In June 1947, Dzierżoniów still had 6,250 Jewish inhabitants and another 6,000 Jews lived in the surrounding area.[9] Many of them continued to believe that there was a future for Jews in Poland. Even after the mass flight in the summer of 1946, Jews still made up a quarter of the local population in Dzierżoniów. They had their own representatives on the town council and even a vice-president in the municipal administration. The town's Jewish Committee, assisted by the JDC, helped local Jews find housing and work while it also provided healthcare, schooling, professional training, and distributed clothing, food, and financial aid. It played a crucial role in arranging employment for thousands of Jews in two branches of local industry: textile production and radio-construction. With the help of the committee, Jews opened arts and crafts cooperatives, and until 1949 they played a leading role in this sector of the economy in Dzierżoniów. The Jewish Committee had already acquired five agricultural farms and established the first Jewish agricultural school in Dzierżoniów by November 1945.[10] In September 1947, there were 135 Jewish farms in the area, making it the center of Jewish agriculture in Poland.[11]

The Jewish community of Dzierżoniów created an impressive network of welfare institutions. They had their own children's home and health clinic, both a Yiddish and a Hebrew primary school, several after-school daycare centers, a library, and, for some time, even a Yiddish theater. Various Zionist organizations established their party headquarters, youth centers, cooperatives, and *kibbutzim* in and around the town.[12]

Even though after 1945, Poland was ruled by a regime opposed to religion, in the second half of the 1940s, Judaism could still be practiced in the country. Dzierżoniów had its own Jewish congregation which used the town's large synagogue. There was also a second *shul*, a cemetery, a *cheder*, and a *mikveh*. Despite all this, Jews in Lower Silesia were constantly confronted with various forms of antisemitism. Some Poles, including people critical of the new communist regime and even some members of the new local elite, dreamt of Dzierżoniów as an exclusively Polish town, cleansed of both Germans and Jews.[13] When Jews were murdered and Jewish homes and institutions attacked in and around Dzierżoniów in 1946,[14] the local Jewish community organized its own self-defense units, in close cooperation with the state's security forces who also armed them.

TRANSNATIONAL CONNECTIONS, ATTITUDES TOWARDS COMMUNISM, AND THE DEMISE OF THE JEWISH COMMUNITY IN DZIERŻONIÓW

For the Jews of Dzierżoniów, the heavy burdens of antisemitism, postwar poverty, and the hardships of a socialist economy were alleviated by the enormous help they received from the American Jewish community, an expression of modern

Armed members of the Jewish militia guarding the House
of Culture in Rychbach/Dzierżoniów, 1946.
Emanuel Ringelblum Jewish Historical Institute, Warsaw

A mass assembly of Dzierżoniów Jews listening to the
radio broadcast and awaiting the UN decision on the
partition of Palestine, 1947. The Ghetto Fighters' House
Museum / The Photo Archive, Western Galilee, Israel

Jewish transnationalism, a multidimensional connection between various centers of the Jewish world. For the Jews in and around Dzierżoniów, these transnational connections were helpful not only economically and culturally but also politically, because they protected them against full dependence on the authoritarian communist state.

Not all of the Jews gathered in Lower Silesia wanted to stay in Poland and many of their leaders also advocated emigration. This was the course of action promoted by the Zionists, the most popular Jewish political movement in postwar Poland. Swelled by the arrival of repatriates from the Soviet Union, they unofficially organized illegal emigration of Jews to Palestine (*Bricha*) while formally supporting the reconstruction of the Jewish community in Poland. In Lower Silesia, their goal was to enroll arriving Jews in Zionist cooperatives (*kibbutzim*) and prepare them for *aliyah* as soon as the time was right.[15] The first such *kibbutzim* were opened in the Rychbach area at the end of July and beginning of August 1945.[16] Many Jews from the town participated in military training for the *Haganah* and, later on, the Israel Defense Forces.[17] Local Zionist culture was also transnational because Jews were highly engaged in everything that concerned the *Yishuv* in Palestine. They celebrated the United Nations' decision regarding the partition of Palestine and Israel's Declaration of Independence.

The attitudes of Dzierżoniów's Jews towards the communist system varied, ranging from full-fledged admiration and support to rejection and even illegal political activity. Jewish survivors undoubtedly had good reasons to be attracted to Communism. Many of them acknowledged that they owed their lives to the Red Army. Moreover, the communist-dominated government had afforded the Jews full legal, social, and economic equality. Finally, the communist government guaranteed a Polish and Jewish presence in newly acquired Lower Silesia, and indeed provided protection against antisemitic violence. However, most Jews were ambivalent, critical, or even hostile towards the Soviet presence and communist authoritarianism. After all, most Jews in Lower Silesia had been repatriates from the Soviet Union and, while being grateful for its harsh shelter, they had no illusions about Communism.

Zionism was the most popular political current among the Jews of Dzierżoniów, as among the entire Polish Jewish community. Its interaction with communism was complex and tense. In August 1945, the Jewish Committee in Dzierżoniów evicted a group trying to establish a *kibbutz* in a communal facility because the committee believed that they harbored anti-Soviet views.[18] Besides legal Zionist activities, from 1946 until 1950, both Brit ha-Hayal and Betar (two right-wing Zionist revisionist organizations considered illegal by the communist authorities) operated in Dzierżoniów.[19]

Some elements of the new political reality were problematic for all Jews. Communists, unpopular among the country's population, sought to legitimize their power by promoting Polish ethnic nationalism, especially in the territories recently acquired from Germany. The Jews of Dzierżoniów and Lower Silesia had to take part in this nationalist legitimization. Thus, they engaged with the creation of nationalist discourse and popular consciousness, which would later undermine their own place in the social, cultural, and political landscape of the region.[20]

The same dynamic operated in general politics. All legal Jewish parties in and around Dzierżoniów supported the communists in the referendum of June 1946 and the elections of January 1947 (both falsified by the authorities), thereby sealing the communist takeover of power in Poland. As the regime became increasingly authoritarian, it began to attack Jewish socio-political pluralism, autonomy, and ties to the western Jewish world. The "war on commerce" announced by the government in 1947 hit many of Dzierżoniów's Jews engaged in commerce particularly hard. The "Exhibition of Recovered Territories" held in Wrocław in the summer of 1948 was meant to feature the local Jewish community. But just before the opening, the authorities decided to remove the Jewish pavilion because they felt there should be no place for a public display of Jewish ethnic identity in Poland.[21]

The situation took a decisive turn for the worse in the second half of 1948, when Stalin signaled a change in the Communist Bloc's policy towards Zionism. Poland's Jews were ordered to break relations with the World Jewish Congress. The following year, all legal Jewish political parties were disbanded. Zionist Jews were urged to leave for Israel, risking imprisonment if they stayed. In 1950, the Jewish Committees were dissolved and connections with transnational Jewish welfare organizations like the JDC were broken. All official Jewish life came under communist control. Dzierżoniów's Jewish community, while still present (with 2000 to 3000 members until the years 1956–1957), had lost the richness and uniqueness so vividly manifested in the first postwar years.

[1] The research for this article was funded in part by the Polish National Science Center grant no. 2014/15/G/HS6/04836 ("Jews and Germans in Polish Collective Memory: Two Case Studies of Memory Formation in Local Communities after the Second World War").

[2] Archiwum Żydowskiego Instytutu Historycznego (AŻIH), Wojewódzki Komitet Żydowski na Dolnym Śląsku 145 (WKŻ 145), 5, k. 37–38.
[3] AŻIH, WKŻ 145, 1, k. 1; Jonas Turkow, *Nokh der bafrayung. Zikhroynesk* (Buenos Aires: Tsentral-farband fun Poylishe Yidn in Argentine, 1959), 230–231.
[4] YIVO Archives, RG 116, Poland 3, Folder 6.
[5] Józef Adelson, "WW Polsce zwanej ludowąą," in *Najnowsze dzieje Żydów w Polsce w zarysie (do 1950 roku)*, ed. Jerzy Tomaszewski (Warsaw: Wydawnictwo Naukowe PWN, 1993), 390–391.
[6] Hana Shlomi, "Reshit ha-hitargenut shel yehude Polin be-shilhe milhemet ha-olam ha-sheniya," in *Asupat mehkarim le-toldot she'erit ha-peletah ha-Yehudit be-Polin, 1944–1950* (Tel Aviv: Tel Aviv University, 2001),) 78–79.
[7] AŻIH, WKŻ 145, 5, k. 20.

8 Kamil Kijek, Interview with Frieda Pertman, Baltimore, February 2009.

9 AŻIH, WKŻ 145, 9, k. 118.

10 AŻIH, 145 WKŻ DS, 1, k. 33.

11 AŻIH, WKŻ 145, 5, k. 139; YIVO Archives, RG 116, Poland, Folder 20.

12 YYRDC, 55 (1), 55 (3); Natalia Aleksiun, *Dokąd dalej? Ruch syjonistyczny w Polsce (1944–1950)* (Warsaw: Centrum Badania i Nauczania Dziejów Żydów w Polsce im. Mordechaja Anielewicza, Wydawnictwo Trio, 2002), 178, 181, 194–195.

13 Turkow, *Nokh der bafrayung*, 236; AŻIH, WKŻ 145, 1, k. 6; AŻIH, WKŻ 145, 5, k. 91; Archiwum Państwowe we Wrocławiu (APWr), 331/VI Urząd Wojewódzki we Wrocławiu, Wydział Społeczno-Polityczny (UWW), 697, k. 6–14, 37–38, 40, 74–77, 97; APWr, 331/VI UWW, 698, k. 141, 149.

14 Alina Cała, *Ochrona bezpieczeństwa fizycznego Żydów w Polsce powojennej. Komisje Specjalne przy Centralnym Komitecie Żydów w Polsce* (Warsaw: Żydowski Instytut Historyczny im. Emanuela Ringelbluma, 2014), 195, 281, 287.

15 Yaad Yari Research & Documentation Center (YYRDC), 1–2, 48 (1); 48 (3).

16 YYRDC, 1–2, 48 (1); 48 (3).

17 Helga Hirsch, *Gehen oder bleiben? Juden in Schlesien und Pommern, 1945–1957* (Göttingen: Wallstein, 2011), 173–175.

18 David Engel, *Bein shihrurs li-verihah: nitsoleivehns ha-sho'ah be'polin veha-ma'avaks"p-m' al hanhagatamha, 1944–1946* (Tel Aviv: Am Oved, 1996), 115–116.

19 Archiwum Instytutu Pamięci Narodowej, BU 0259/447, 4, 27, 30–31.

20 Kamil Kijek, ""Aliens in the Lands of the Piasts: The Polonization of Lower Silesia and Its Jewish Community in the Years 1945–1950,"" in *Jews and Germans in Eastern Europe. Shared and Comparative Histories*, ed. Tobias Grill (Berlin: De Gruyter Oldenbourg, 2018), 234–255.

21 Hersh Smolar, *Oyf der letster pozitsye mit der letster hofenung* (Tel Aviv: I. L. Peretz, 1982), 152.

FELIKS NIEZNANOWSKI (1926–2017)

Feliks Nieznanowski was born into a poor Jewish family in the Old Town of Warsaw. After the German invasion of the city in 1939, he escaped to the Soviet-occupied side of Poland. He survived the war in the Soviet Union, working in the steel industry.

Nieznanowski returned to Poland with the repatriation wave of 1946, settling in Dzierżoniów. He found his brother there as well, who had also survived in the Soviet Union. All other members of his immediate family were murdered during the war. In Dzierżoniów, Feliks Nieznanowski joined the Fighting Youth Union (*Związek Walki Młodych*, ZWM), a communist youth organization established during the war to fight the Germans. He was responsible for the distribution of JDC-funded goods arriving in the town, a role that embroiled him in many conflicts. In a later interview, Nieznanowski gave a detailed description of the political and practical battles between the various Jewish groups in the town.

In 1947, he was drafted into the Polish army and left Dzierżoniów. He became a professional soldier, graduated from the military academy in Łódź, and moved up the ranks. He settled in Warsaw and married in 1952. He and his wife Henryka had two children; their daughter, Ewa, was born in 1953, and their son, Witold, a year later. All the while, he kept in touch with his Jewish acquaintances in Dzierżoniów. His brother moved to Israel in the 1950s, but Feliks Nieznanowski stayed in Warsaw until the end of his life.

Feliks Nieznanowski (left) with a friend in Dzierżoniów, 1945–1947. Private collection, Ewa Buszko (*née* Nieznanowski), Warsaw

Feliks Nieznanowski (third from left) with a group of young Jews in Dzierżoniów, 1945–1947. Private collection, Ewa Buszko (*née* Nieznanowski), Warsaw

Registration certificate issued by the Jewish Regional Committee for Feliks Nieznanowski, 1946. Private collection, Ewa Buszko (*née* Nieznanowski), Warsaw

JAKUB EGIT
(1908–1996)

Jakub Egit was born in a Jewish shtetl called Borysław. He was active in leftist Jewish political movements from a young age. Together with his wife and son, he managed to flee to the Soviet Union during the war, surviving under harsh circumstances in Kazakhstan. He separated from his wife there and returned to Poland with the Red Army in 1944, only to learn that his parents and siblings had perished in the Shoah.

Egit was active in the Jewish Faction of the Polish Workers' Party after the war. He strongly believed in the necessity to create a strong, culturally autonomous Jewish settlement in postwar Poland. He worked towards this goal as chairman of the Jewish Regional Committee in Lower Silesia (*Wojewódzki Komitet Żydów na Dolny Śląsk*) between 1945 and 1949.

However, by the end of the 1940s, the Polish communist leadership withdrew its support for Jewish autonomy, which it now viewed as an expression of Jewish nationalism. Egit was dismissed from his post at the Jewish Regional Committee. "[M]y dream of a new life for a resurrected, flourishing Jewish community upon the soil of a democratic Poland was dead," he wrote about his bitter feelings at the time.[1]

After his dismissal, he found employment as a journalist for Yiddish newspapers in Warsaw. In February 1953, he was arrested on fabricated charges about activities to separate Lower Silesia from the Polish People's Republic. As a result, he spent eight months in prison. In 1957, he emigrated to Canada with his family.

[1]   Jakub Egit, *Grand Illusion* (Toronto: Lugus, 1991), 100.

Jakub Egit's portrait from a photo album about Jewish life in postwar Lower Silesia, 1945–1946. Emanuel Ringelblum Jewish Historical Institute, Warsaw

American actress Molly Picon during a visit to Dzierżoniów, 1946. Picon, sitting in the bottom row with flowers, was one of the biggest stars of Yiddish film at the time. Egit is first from the right in the bottom row. Emanuel Ringelblum Jewish Historical Institute, Warsaw

PROTECTING THE EUROPEAN BRANCH OF THE JEWISH DIASPORA
THE AMERICAN JEWISH JOINT DISTRIBUTION COMMITTEE IN EUROPE AFTER THE HOLOCAUST

LAURA HOBSON FAURE

The slow liberation of Europe marked the beginning of a difficult period for its surviving Jews. While the immediate threat of murder ceased in most places, families and support networks had been separated and destroyed, leading Jewish individuals to seek outside help for their most basic resources. The American Jewish Joint Distribution Committee (JDC, or Joint), established in New York in 1914 to distribute American Jewish assistance to the victims of the First World War was, by far, the largest aid provider to European Jews in the post-Holocaust period. As Europe was being liberated, the JDC was able to send American staff to formerly occupied areas, first to Italy, then, in late 1944, to France, and only much later, in late summer 1945, to Austria and Germany.

This overview of the JDC's efforts to provide emergency aid and reconstruct European Jewish life in the aftermath of the Holocaust will explore how it confronted the major issues of postwar reconstruction. By providing extensive aid to Jewish populations in flux, usually supplementing and at times replacing state aid, the JDC protected what remained of the European branch of the Jewish diaspora at a critical juncture. At the same time, the fact that European Jewish reconstruction was financed in large part by American Jews was a source of tension with local Jews: on what model should European Jewish life be rebuilt? The JDC, Jewish survivors, and communal leaders responded to this question differently.

Warehouse and trucks of the JDC in Germany, 1946. Jewish Americans sent over 194 million dollars to Europe from 1945 to 1948 through the JDC. JDC Archives, New York

A survivor irons clothes in a JDC-supported workshop in Budapest, 1945-1948. The number from the concentration camp tatooed on her arm is still visible. Magyar Zsidó Múzeum és Levéltár, Budapest.

Postwar France provides a key example of the tensions inherent in the reconstruction process. With 180,000 to 200,000 Jewish survivors, and more arriving daily (primarily from Eastern Europe), France inspired hope for the continuity of European Jewish life. Under the JDC's auspices, French Jewish welfare was centralized and professionalized. The JDC helped import new structures, such as centralized fundraising and Jewish community centers. One leading scholar has suggested that this represented a form of cultural imperialism.[1] My own research has pointed to the ambiguities of American Jewish philanthropy in the reconstruction of French Jewish life by showing how American Jewish aid led to a negotiated reconstruction process: French Jews also shaped how this aid was implemented, at times *even agreeing* with theirAmerican funders. French Jewish reconstruction, then, involved not only the French Republic and its Jewish inhabitants. It was also a transnational process, shaped in large part by American Jewish organizations and individuals.[2]

Hungary serves as an interesting comparison to France. If the postwar Jewish populations of these two countries were similar in size (roughly 180,000 to 200,000 at the end of 1945), the magnitude of their losses was radically different. France had roughly 330,000 Jews in 1940, 80,000 of whom were deported or executed during the war, whereas in Hungary, more than 500,000 of some 800,000 Jews were murdered in the final phases of the war, and an additional 12,000 died from starvation after liberation.[3]

Food remained scarce for months to come, and the economy proved unstable. If all Hungarians faced these difficulties, the Jews' situation was more acute since months of underground survival during the genocide left many weakened. Unlike others, they could no longer rely upon extended family and support networks. Nonetheless, American Jewish aid directed exclusively to Jews was prone to criticism and exploitation, even before the 1949 communist takeover. The JDC was able to operate in Hungary on the condition that it would also provide "non-sectarian" aid and use Hungarian banks to exchange its dollars. Moreover, it was not able to send an American representative until 1947. In the meantime, by 1947, almost 2,800 Hungarians were working for the JDC to provide emergency relief to thousands. Tensions inevitably arose when the American JDC representative arrived with the goal of streamlining what was the JDC's most expensive program.[4]

These issues were also relevant in other parts of Europe with smaller survivor communities. A recent shift in the historiography has focused attention on the *She'erit Hapletah*—the Surviving Remnant—as agents in the rebuilding of Jewish life and seeks to understand American Jewish aid as an integral part of European postwar reconstruction.[5] Recent scholarship on the JDC suggests that in the post-Holocaust period, there were three candidates for 'lead role' in the reconstruction of Jewish life in post-war Europe: (1). local Jewish survivors and/or newcomers [...] (2) overseas Jewish welfare organizations, and (3) national or local governments. [...]. Divergent ideas on how to organize Jewish life abounded, not only between 'local' Jews and overseas Jewish welfare organizations but also within the local Jewish populations themselves.[6]

These tensions, coupled with a rapidly changing geopolitical situation, led to local differences in the implementation of JDC aid programs. When the JDC and European Jews set out to reconstruct Jewish life together, the JDC worked with a basic set of guidelines throughout Europe but, as the following table underscores, place mattered, as the engagement of the JDC varied considerably from country to country.

ANNUAL JDC AID TO EUROPE 1945–1948[7]

	JEWISH POPULATION	JDC AID (IN US DOLLARS)			
Year	1945	1945	1946	1947	1948
Austria and Germany	50,000–65,000	317,000	3,979,500	9,012,000	7,320,000
Belgium	12,000	1,917,000	1,801,000	1,354,000	1,024,000
France	80,000–200,000	1,998,000	2,831,000	5,906,000	3,583,000
Hungary	180,000	3,837,000	9,499,000	10,898,000	8,463,000
Poland	60,000–80,000	1,684,000	7,666,000	5,603,000	2,955,000
Total		17,698,000	33,473,500	46,054,000	30,945,000

JDC FUNDING IN A MOMENT OF FLUX

Between 1945 and 1948, Jewish Americans sent more than $194 million to Europe through the JDC.[8] However, as we just saw, JDC funding was not distributed equally throughout Europe or evenly according to the number of surviving Jews in a given country. For example, even though France had the largest Jewish population in formerly occupied Western Europe, in 1945, it received the same amount as Belgium whose Jewish population was less than a tenth of that of France.[9] Poland and the American occupation-zone of Germany and Austria received considerably more funding than other countries with more Jewish survivors, although this too was still deemed "wildly insufficient."[10] In the years from 1945 to 1948, Hungary, whose surviving Jewish population was about the same size as that of France, received between 23 and 27 percent of the JDC's funding, while only eight to ten percent of the organization's funds went to France.[11]

The uneven distribution of JDC funding was in part linked to the geopolitical situation. The emergence of Cold War tensions, as well as Zionism,
complicated the administration of JDC aid. In the interwar period, the JDC's
American leadership was primarily opposed to the Zionist movement but by the
late 1940s, the JDC had accepted the creation of a Jewish state. Yet the very act
of reconstructing European Jewish life was inherently political since it provided
European Jews with the option of staying put. On the ground, the JDC sought
to maintain a neutral stance but it was confronted with illegal immigration to
Palestine and varying state attitudes toward these efforts.

Indeed, Europe's surviving Jews, a small and vulnerable population,
were on the move in the years following the war, searching for family members
and stability. Poland provides the most acute example of this phenomenon. In
the aftermath of the war, tens of thousands of Jews who had sought refuge in
the Soviet Union were repatriated, quickly increasing the Jewish population to
as many as 280,000 individuals. However, the 1946 Kielce pogrom and other
incidents of antisemitic violence, along with growing Cold War tensions, led
most of these Jews to flee Poland.

Even before the 1948 creation of the State of Israel, Palestine drew
Europe's surviving Jews away from their native countries. These migrations
affected Jewish communities across Europe very differently. For example, in the
period between 1948 and 1951, more than 100,000 Jews left for Israel from
Poland and a similar number from Romania. In the same period, only 3,000 left
France and 1,000 the Netherlands.[12] As these numbers show, Jews in the Soviet
Bloc were more likely to leave for Israel than those in Western Europe, suggesting
that it was conditions in Eastern Europe during the early Cold War, and not
necessarily Zionist ideology, that fueled this migration. The communist show
trials of the 1950s, which targeted individuals of Jewish origin, accusing them
of cosmopolitanism and treason, demonstrate the vulnerability of Jewish populations in the Soviet Bloc.[13]

In the decades after the Second World War, Jews remained a visible minority and as such were especially affected by Cold War tensions, the creation of
Israel, and the decolonization of the British and French empires. This resulted in
new migratory patterns, causing some Jews to leave Europe, while others sought
refuge there. Caught between opposing nationalist and communist factions,
Jews were disproportionally present among the individuals fleeing Hungary
in the midst of the 1956 Hungarian Revolution. Many of these Jews settled
in Western Europe where they encountered refugees from Muslim countries,
such as Egyptian Jews, who were expelled from their country in the years 1956
and 1957. Such displacements, along with the unraveling of the French empire,
allowed France to recover (and eventually surpass) its prewar demographics,
albeit with an entirely different Jewish population. In the unstable decade that

followed the Second World War, JDC funding provided European Jews with emergency funds to manage these migrations and, along with the Hebrew Sheltering and Immigrant Aid Society (HIAS), the JDC often took a more direct role by processing visas, renting hotel rooms, and arranging transportation.

The influx of JDC aid to postwar Europe can be divided into three distinct periods, corresponding to the phases of emergency relief and long-term reconstruction. If in the first period, from liberation until the creation of the State of Israel, emergency relief to children and refugees was of major importance, in the years between 1948 and 1954, the JDC slowly shifted its focus to prioritize training and the importation of new structures to centralize Jewish welfare in each European country. A final chapter of postwar reconstruction began in 1954, when funding became available from the Conference on Material Claims against Germany.

THE CASE OF CHILDREN AND OTHER YOUNG SURVIVORS

Scholars working on the JDC agree that in the period immediately following liberation, the organization focused principally on meeting the basic needs of the surviving Jewish populations. Concern for the children and other young survivors represents a central theme in Jewish reconstruction, yet also one that shows the complexities of American Jewish aid, since local aspirations for the young survivors at times conflicted with those of the JDC.

The JDC funded local Jewish aid initiatives and organizations to help individuals of all backgrounds regardless of their circumstances–citizens, refugees, the elderly, and the young–by providing food, shelter, legal aid, and loans. In France, for example, the JDC funded 35 organizations, which in turn ran 115 aid institutions.[14] This allowed the JDC to assist 50,000 individuals–some 25 to 28 percent of the Jewish population–indirectly in 1945 alone.[15] A key priority in this period was finding a solution for surviving Jewish children. As Daniella Doron and Tara Zahra have recently pointed out, Jewish children, like the other "lost children" of Europe who came of age amidst the upheaval of war, provoked passionate debates on collective identity and nation-building.[16]

A comparison of the ways in which Jewish child survivors were cared for in France and Hungary–similar only in the size of their Jewish populations–is instructive. Funded by the JDC, local Jewish organizations in both places established a network of Jewish children's homes reflecting the full spectrum of religious orientations and political ideologies, from Orthodox to Zionist to communist. A 1948 JDC report indicated that the JDC was funding 54 children's homes in France, 36 in Romania, 31 in Hungary, fifteen in Poland, ten in Germany, eight each in Belgium and Italy, four in Czechoslovakia, and one each in Austria, Greece, Holland, and Yugoslavia.[17]

In keeping with interwar Jewish childcare practices, children's homes were still widespread in Europe. Built on the model of prewar collective pedagogy,[18] children's homes were a familiar and efficient model of care that accommodated large groups of children while providing a Jewish setting for their upbringing. While foster care did exist, many Jewish children, even those with living parents, were placed in Jewish children's homes. According to historian Viktória Bányai, Hungarian Jewish parents preferred children's homes for a critical practical reason: the children in these homes received more food. Furthermore, the homes proved to be an efficient training ground for Hungarian Zionist organizations.[19]

Daniella Doron notes that in France, the unprecedented crisis cast doubt within French Jewish welfare organizations on the ability of Jewish families to protect their community's most precious resource—its youth. Hence, they favored children's homes.[20] In both Hungary and France, however, local Jews quickly expressed dissatisfaction with this system. For Hungarian child protection expert and JDC employee Géza Varsányi, the children's homes created an unhealthy dependence on charity. In July 1945, he argued for reintegrating children back into their families, while supporting these families with an extensive network of services.[21] In France, where a perceived failure of the family initially caused social workers to encourage group homes, these pedagogical methods also gave way to doubt. Would youth raised in these homes be able to function as normal adults? Educators feared a "silver-spoon syndrome"[22] with deeper, gendered implications for future Jewish families: would girls learn to care for their own children?

The children's home model points to a certain tolerance of European ways among JDC representatives. Indeed, it is somewhat paradoxical that the American organization willingly funded collective homes; in the same period in the United States, American social workers, following Freudian theory, endorsed foster care in the nuclear families, which served "the children's 'best interests'" and reflected "American values of individualism, self-reliance and family solidarity."[23]

While JDC social workers were clearly aware of these debates, they still funded children's homes. Furthermore, even more significant, especially in light of the emerging Cold War tensions, the American organization supported homes of all ideological orientations, including communist ones.[24] The JDC's funding of Zionist homes is also somewhat curious, suggesting that the JDC delegated childcare to local Jews, putting pragmatism over politics.

Nonetheless, in both Hungary and France, the JDC did shape children's lives. In 1947, a drastic new JDC policy led to a major reduction in the number

Compelling photos were needed to keep the donations coming. The young refugee Reva Ehrlich, who fled from Poland, is being fitted for a new pair of shoes at the UNRRA Düppel Center for displaced persons. She is showing off her new shoes to Eli Rock, Chief of JDC Operations in Berlin, as well as to an anonymous UNRRA camp police officer in the Berlin-Schlachtensee DP camp, ca. 1946–1948. Photos: Al Taylor, JDC Archives, New York of children cared for in children's homes. Predictions of an economic recession and a slow-going fundraising campaign in the United States forced the JDC to start radically cutting back its programs in 1947. This reduction reflected a larger shift in JDC policy: country directors, who until then had sought to distribute JDC funds as widely as possible, felt the time had now come to cultivate self-sufficiency. In France, under the direction of veteran American relief official Laura Margolis, JDC workers wrote that they "cut budgets with a conscious purpose of 'shocking' agencies into facing reality."[25] Hungary experienced a similar situation under the direction of JDC director Israel Jacobson. Budget cuts were accompanied by new policies for childcare. In France, starting from September 1947, the JDC no longer systematically supported summer camps or the placement costs in children's homes for those children who had two living parents and—most controversially—it no longer provided funds for youth over the age of eighteen who were living in children's homes.[26] In Hungary, the "unmaking of the children's home network"[27] began at exactly the same moment. This new policy was confirmed at the Paris Country Directors Conference in April 1948, mobilizing the American family placement model to justify the budget cuts. The new JDC care guidelines stated: "Our general policy is to strengthen family life and therefore to minimize the use of institutions as the solution for child care problems."[28]

In both France and Hungary, similar JDC policies led to children being sent home to their parents or relatives. In France, orphans over the age of eighteen were emancipated, forcing them to leave the places that had become their home and the people that made up their surrogate families. Some of them reported feeling completely abandoned, some grouped together to rent hotel rooms, others slept in parks. To this day, this change in policy is a source of considerable anger and confusion. Some have suggested that it was due to a shift in priorities after the creation of the State of Israel, which did divert some JDC funding from European reconstruction in order to help refugees in the new state.[29] One must also take into account the American nature of the aid. American social work was driven by a strong belief in cultivating self-sufficiency. Furthermore, American Jewish donors were showing signs of fatigue. Funds were simply less abundant and budgets needed to be cut.

LONG-TERM RECONSTRUCTION: IMPORTING AMERICAN STRUCTURES?

The issue of children and other young survivors points to a strong similarity between two extremely different European countries. However, long-term reconstruction policies led to divergent outcomes in similar countries and converging outcomes in very different societies. Questioning the JDC's capacity to import (and thus impose) American models provides a means to assess its power. Did the JDC use its funding "like the promoters of the Marshall Plan, who flexed their financial muscle in France [...] to impose their own objectives,"[30] as one scholar has claimed? Were this true, one would expect all of the JDC's beneficiaries to have followed its policy of establishing a central welfare organization to coordinate fundraising and planning on a nation-wide level. In the aftermath of the Holocaust, JDC representatives were adamant about centralizing fundraising and domestic welfare under a national umbrella, as American Jews had done with the United Jewish Appeal in 1939.[31] While the JDC's efforts proved successful in the Netherlands, France, and Yugoslavia (to cite only a few examples), the JDC did not, however, achieve the same results in Belgium.

The reasons for this divergent outcome reflect the fact that American aid, while influential, was not as powerful as the structural factors shaping life in Jewish communities throughout Europe. In France, for example, a politically diverse group of Jewish leaders who had organized Jewish self-help and resistance under German occupation grew increasingly concerned that the JDC was making decisions on their behalf. In late 1946, they decided to form an advisory committee, designed to counterbalance the weight of the JDC. By the fall of 1947, the American director of the JDC in France, Laura Margolis, managed to convince this group to establish a new organization, based on the United Jewish Appeal, which could then serve as a French-led successor organization to the JDC. The fact that Margolis was a woman most likely played a role in her French partners' willingness to endorse this structure. Margolis had initially brought in an American (male) expert to work with the French Jewish leaders but they refused to cooperate with him. In contrast, Margolis' accommodating and humble attitude, along with her mastery of French, helped her garner more support among local Jews.[32] As one of the only female leaders in the organization and a veteran of wartime JDC relief efforts in Cuba and Shanghai, it is quite possible that Margolis learned to walk softly, honing her ability to negotiate with powerful men. This skill paid off in France, yet structural and historical factors, inherent to French Jewish life, also encouraged centralization. Since the end of the nineteenth century, French Jewish life had been fairly centralized in Paris. Even though a distinct Jewish community reestablished itself in Alsace-Lorraine after the war, the Paris-centric bias among the French population in general contributed to the acceptance of a Paris-based central structure. Furthermore, for all its political and ethnic diversity, the postwar Jewish community in France was, in comparison to others in Europe, relatively homogeneous in religious terms. These structural factors can help explain why, with Margolis's guidance,

Almond blossoms in Apulia, Italy. The JDC assisted
refugees who were on their way to Palestine and
provided them with agricultural training in camps near
Bari, where many were waiting to sail to Palestine, ca.
1945–1948. JDC Archives, New York

French Jews created the *Fonds Social Juif Unifié* in October 1949, which gradually replaced the JDC.

In the years from 1945 to 1950, the surviving Jewish population in Yugoslavia, which numbered about 12,000 individuals in 1946, also channeled JDC funding through a central structure, the Autonomous Relief Committee (ARC), and thereafter, under the auspices of the Federation of Jewish communities. As Emil Kerenji has recently shown, the JDC and the Yugoslavian Jewish leadership initially created the ARC in 1945, yet the JDC was not in fact able to send a representative to Yugoslavia until the fall of 1946. Even in the absence of American JDC leadership, Yugoslavian Jews embraced a centralized structure, in continuity with the prewar period. The Federation of Jewish Religious Communities of Yugoslavia was re-established by its former president in October 1944, a decision shaped by postwar structural constraints. As Kerenji observes: "This centralization of leadership was a result of the new constellation of power in Yugoslavia in the first years after the war. The regime itself was highly centralized and based in Belgrade, and if the Jewish leaders were to organize a humanitarian effort–especially one funded by a western organization–they needed to be close to the center of power and speak in one voice."[33]

While France and Yugoslavia demonstrate two contrasting examples of welfare centralization, the case of Belgium presents an altogether different scenario. As Veerle Vanden Daelen's research has shown, this country had two very different Jewish communities: a small, primarily Orthodox one in Antwerp and a much larger one in Brussels, which was mostly communist and secular. Importantly, Antwerp's community had strong ties to the diamond industry, which exceptionally allowed for some Antwerp Jews to find refuge in New York during the Second World War. This created an informal New York-based lobby for the postwar Antwerp community, lending support to its Orthodox initiatives. The JDC struggled to reconcile the two very different communities in Brussels and Antwerp in order to unite their welfare organizations as they had done elsewhere. Eventually, under pressure from the Antwerp Jews in New York, the JDC gave up and decided to let the highly organized Jews in Antwerp manage their funding separately from those in Brussels.[34]

This transnational and comparative perspective on the JDC's aid programs shows that despite the significance of its funding and personnel, structural and historical factors proved perhaps more determinant than the power of the JDC in shaping postwar Jewish life. European Jewish reconstruction was the outcome of a complex negotiation among local Jewish communities, European states, and the American Jewish aid organization. JDC funding played a crucial role in providing relief to vulnerable populations in the emergency period following the war, as seen here in the case of children, and in establishing long-term structures to administer Jewish communal life. Nonetheless, local desires and structural, historical, and geopolitical factors shaped the implementation of the JDC's aid programs. Just because the JDC wanted something–for example, the unification of Jewish welfare–did not guarantee that this would actually happen.

The study of the JDC's postwar programs also allows us to better understand the important shifts in the Jewish diaspora after the Holocaust and the creation of Israel. In the long term, the JDC helped provide an argument in favor of renewing European Jewish life. The organization supported a continued Jewish presence in certain places in Europe at a moment when the geopolitical situation was pushing European Jews to the West (the United States and Latin America) and to the East (British Mandate Palestine and later Israel). The very fact that the JDC invested its resources in postwar Europe, especially after 1948, is not surprising due to its historically lukewarm position on Zionism, but it is significant. After the creation of Israel, it could have abandoned its European programs in order to encourage emigration to the young country. This did not occur. Instead, the JDC affirmed the European branch of the diaspora by helping Jews who wanted to remain in those places where the JDC saw possibility.

Finally, one can step back and consider the many ways in which Jewish identity changed as a result of the Holocaust. In this liminal moment of mourning and recovery, postwar Jewish welfare became a new site for the expression of Jewish identity, bringing together the religious and the secular in a common project and allowing for new modes of communal cohesion that cut across class, ideological, and religious divisions. It was JDC funding that fueled this vast expansion of Jewish welfare–short lived in Poland and Germany, more extensive in France and Hungary–providing a home, or at least some succor, for many Jews at this uncertain time.

---

[1] Maud S. Mandel, "Philanthropy or Cultural Imperialism? The Impact of American Jewish Aid in Post-Holocaust France," *Jewish Social Studies* 9.1 (2002), 53–94; Maud S. Mandel, *In the Aftermath of Genocide. Armenians and Jews in Twentieth Century France* (Durham: Duke University Press, 2003).

[2] Laura Hobson Faure, *Un "Plan Marshall Juif": La présence juive américaine en France après la* Shoah, 1944–1954 (Paris: Armand Colin, 2013, Editions le Manuscrit 2018); Laura Hobson Faure, *A "Jewish Marshall Plan:" The American Jewish Presence in Post-Holocaust France* (Bloomington: Indiana University Press, forthcoming).

[3] "Hungary after the German Occupation," USHMM, accessed March 28, 2019, https://encyclopedia.ushmm.org/content/en/article/hungary-after-the-german-occupation.

[4] Yehuda Bauer, *Out of the Ashes: The Impact of American Jews on Post-Holocaust Jewry* (Oxford: Pergamon Press, 1989), 14, 133–148; Kinga Frojimovics, "The Activity of the JDC in Hungary, 1945–1953," in *The JDC at 100. A Century of Humanitarianism*, ed. Avinoam Patt et al. (Detroit: Wayne State University Press, 2019), 421–438.

[5] Atina Grossmann, *Jews, Germans and Allies, Close Encounters in Occupied Germany* (Princeton: Princeton University Press, 2007); Veerle Vanden Daelen, *Laten We Hun Lied Verder Zingen: De Heropbouw van de Joodse Gemeenschap in Antwerpen na de Tweede Wereldoorlog (1944–1960)* (Amsterdam: Aksant, 2008); Avinoam J. Patt, *Finding*

Home and Homeland: Jewish Youth and Zionism in the Aftermath of the Holocaust (Detroit: Wayne State University Press, 2009); Tara Zahra, *The Lost Children: Reconstructing Europe's Families after World War II* (Cambridge, MA: Harvard University Press, 2011); Daniella Doron, *Jewish Youth and Identity in Postwar France: Rebuilding Family and Nation* (Bloomington: Indiana University Press, 2015).

6   Laura Hobson Faure and Veerle Vanden Daelen, "Imported from the United States? The Centralization of Private Jewish Welfare After the Holocaust: The Cases of Belgium and France," in *The JDC at 100. A Century of Humanitarianism*, ed. Avinoam Patt et al. (Detroit: Wayne State University Press, 2019), 280.

7   The data on JDC funding are derived from Bauer, *Out of the Ashes*, the population data from Bauer, *Out of the Ashes*, 4, 48; *The JDC at 100*, ed. Patt et al.

8   Bauer, *Out of the Ashes*, xviii.

9   Hobson Faure and Vanden Daelen, "Imported from the United States," 293.

10 Avinoam Patt and Kierra Crago-Schneider, "Years of Survival: JDC in Postwar Germany, 1945–1957," in *The JDC at 100,* ed. Patt et al., 364.

11 Bauer, *Out of the Ashes,* xviii.

12 Bernard Wasserstein, *Vanishing Diaspora: The Jews in Europe since 1945* (Cambridge, MA: Harvard University Press, 1996), 92.

13 As seen in the Slansky affair (1952) and the Doctors' Plot (1953).

14 Executive Committee Minutes, April 18, 1950, 249, France 1945–1954, JDC Archives, New York (JDC-NY).

15 American Jewish Joint Distribution Committee, Research Department, *J.D.C. Primer* (New York: American Jewish Joint Distribution Committee, 1945), France, 8. This percentage is based on a Jewish population numbering between 180,000 and 200,000 individuals.

16 Zahra, *The Lost Children;* Doron, *Jewish Youth and Identity.*

17 JDC Budget and Research Department Report no. 59, JDC Assistees in Europe and North Africa, November 10, 1948, Archives départementales de la Seine-Saint-Denis, Fonds David Diamant, 335J/115.

18 Erin Corber, "L'Esprit Du Corps: Bodies, Communities, and the Reconstruction of Jewish Life in France, 1914–1940" (PhD diss., Indiana University, 2013), 144–194.

19 Viktória Bányai, "The Impact of the American Jewish Joint Distribution Committee's Aid Strategy on the Lives of Jewish Families in Hungary, 1945–49," in *Jewish and Romani Families in the Holocaust and Its Aftermath,* ed. Kateřina Čapková and Eliyana R. Adler (forthcoming); Frojimovics, "The Activity of the JDC in Hungary," 421–438.

20 Doron, *Jewish Youth and Identity,* 118–161.

21 Bányai, "The Impact of the American Jewish Joint Distribution Committee's Aid Strategy."

22 Doron, *Jewish Youth and Identity,* 149.

23 Zahra, *The Lost Children,* 72.

24 In France they funded communist homes until 1953. See Laura Hobson Faure, "Shaping Children's Lives: American Jewish Aid in Post-World War II France (1944–1948)," *in Re-examining the Jews of Modern France: Images and Identities*, ed. Jonathan Zvi Kaplan and Nadia Malinovich (Leiden, Brill: 2016), 173–193.

25 Welfare Department Report #2, Report of Child Care Department, Office for France on developments from October 1946 to October 1948, April, 1949, 249, France 1945/54, JDC-NY.

26 Welfare Department Report #2; Frojimovics, "The Activity of the JDC in Hungary," 430–434.

27 Bányai, "The Impact of the American Jewish Joint Distribution Committee's Aid Strategy."

28 "Standards and Policies for Welfare Programs. Prepared for JDC Country Directors' Conference, April 5–11, 1948," 3–4, 4/11/1948, JDC Archives, Records of the Geneva Office of the American Jewish Joint Distribution Committee, 1945–1954, Folder FR.543, cited in Frojimovics,"The Activity of the JDC in Hungary," 431–432.

[29] I obtained this information when I presented my research to OSE Amicale, a group of former OSE children who continue to meet weekly at the OSE headquarters, October 20, 2014, as well as from a telephone interview with Armand Bulwa, March 9, 2015.

[30] Mandel, "Philanthropy or Cultural Imperialism? The Impact of American Jewish Aid in Post-Holocaust France," 54–55.

[31] Abraham Karp, *To Give Life. The United Jewish Appeal and the Shaping of the American Jewish Community* (New York: Schocken, 1981), 77–85.

[32] On her early work with the JDC see Zhava Litvac Glaser, "Laura Margolis and JDC Efforts in Cuba and Shanghai: Sustaining Refugees in a Time Catastrophe," in *The JDC at 100*, ed. Patt et al., 167–204.

[33] Emil Kerenji, "Rebuilding the Community: The Federation of Jewish Communities and American Jewish Humanitarian Aid in Yugoslavia, 1944–1952," *Southeast European and Black Sea Studies* 17.2 (2017): 257.

[34] Hobson Faure and Vanden Daelen, "Imported from the United States," 302–303; Vanden Daelen, *Laten We Hun Lied Verder Zingen*.

BIBLIOGRAPHY

Bányai, Viktória. "The Impact of the American Jewish Joint Distribution Committee's Aid Strategy on the Lives of Jewish Families in Hungary, 1945–49." In *Jewish and Romani Families in the Holocaust and Its Aftermath,* edited by Kateřina Čapková and Eliyana R. Adler (forthcoming). / **Bauer, Yehuda.** *Out of the Ashes: The Impact of American Jews on Post-Holocaust Jewry.* Oxford: Pergamon Press, 1989. / **Corber, Erin.** "L'Esprit Du Corps: Bodies, Communities, and the Reconstruction of Jewish Life in France, 1914–1940." PhD diss., Indiana University, 2013. / **Doron, Daniella.** *Jewish Youth and Identity in Postwar France: Rebuilding Family and Nation.* Bloomington: Indiana University Press, 2015. / **Frojimovics, Kinga.** "The Activity of the JDC in Hungary, 1945–1953." In *The JDC at 100. A Century of Humanitarianism*, edited by Avinoam Patt et al., 421–438. Detroit: Wayne State University Press, 2019. / **Glaser, Zhava Litvac.** "Laura Margolis and JDC Efforts in Cuba and Shanghai: Sustaining Refugees in a Time Catastrophe." In *The JDC at 100. A Century of Humanitarianism*, edited by Avinoam Patt et al., 167–204. Detroit: Wayne State University Press, 2019. / **Grossmann, Atina.** *Jews, Germans, and Allies: Close Encounters in Occupied Germany.* Princeton: Princeton University Press, 2007. / **Hobson Faure, Laura.** *Un "Plan Marshall Juif": La présence juive américaine en France après la Shoah, 1944–1954.* Paris: Armand Colin, 2013, Editions le Manuscrit, 2018. / **Hobson Faure, Laura.** "Shaping Children's Lives: American Jewish Aid in Post-World War II France (1944–1948)." In *Re-examining the Jews of Modern France: Images and Identities*, edited by Jonathan Zvi Kaplan and Nadia Malinovich, 173–193. Leiden, Brill: 2016. / **Hobson Faure, Laura.** A *"Jewish Marshall Plan:" The American Jewish Presence in Post-Holocaust France.* Bloomington: Indiana University Press, forthcoming. / **Hobson Faure, Laura** and **Veerle Vanden Daelen.** "Imported from the United States? The Centralization of Private Jewish Welfare After the Holocaust: The Cases of Belgium and France." In *The JDC at 100. A Century of Humanitarianism*, edited by Avinoam Patt et al., 279–314. Detroit: Wayne State University Press, 2019. / **Karp, Abraham.** *To Give Life. The United Jewish Appeal and the Shaping of the American Jewish Community.* New York: Schocken, 1981. / **Kerenji, Emil.** "Rebuilding the Community: The Federation of Jewish Communities and American Jewish Humanitarian Aid in Yugoslavia, 1944–1952." *Southeast European and Black Sea Studies* 17.2 (2017), 245–262. / **Mandel, Maud S.** "Philanthropy or Cultural Imperialism? The Impact of American Jewish Aid in Post-Holocaust France." *Jewish Social Studies* 9.1 (2002), 53–94. / **Mandel, Maud S.** *In the Aftermath of Genocide. Armenians and Jews in Twentieth Century France.* Durham: Duke University Press, 2003. / **Patt, Avinoam J.** *Finding Home and Homeland: Jewish Youth and Zionism in the Aftermath of the Holocaust.* Detroit: Wayne State University Press, 2009. / **Patt, Avinoam** and **Kierra Crago-Schneider.** "Years of Survival: JDC in Postwar

JDC staff member Morris Laub inspects JDC supplies
in a British DP camp in Cyprus, 1947. JDC Archives,
New York

Germany, 1945–1957." In *The JDC at 100. A Century of Humanitarianism*, edited by Avinoam Patt et al., 361–420. Detroit: Wayne State University Press, 2019. **/ USHMM.** "Hungary after the German Occupation." Accessed March 28, 2019. https://encyclopedia.ushmm.org/content/en/article/hungary-after-the-german-occupation. **/ Vanden Daelen, Veerle.** *Laten We Hun Lied Verder Zingen: De Heropbouw van de Joodse Gemeenschap in Antwerpen na de Tweede Wereldoorlog (1944–1960).* Amsterdam: Aksant, 2008. **/ Wasserstein, Bernard.** *Vanishing Diaspora: The Jews in Europe since 1945*. Cambridge, MA: Harvard University Press, 1996. **/ Zahra, Tara.** *The Lost Children: Reconstructing Europe's Families after World War II*. Cambridge, MA. Harvard University Press, 2011.

BUDAPEST
THE CITY OF SURVIVORS

KATA BOHUS

> They stood there, mouths agape, then called out my name, and old
> Steiner even embraced me just as I was, sweaty, in my cap and striped
> jacket. ... I had to answer the usual questions as to where, how, when,
> and what, then later I asked my questions and learned that other people
> really were now living in our apartment ... I asked "My father?"
> At that they clammed up completely.
>
> Imre Kertész[1]

At the end of the war, Hungary's Jewish population of 400,000[2] had been
reduced to about 180,000–200,000 survivors.[3] Though Budapest's Jewish
residents were forced into a ghetto during the last phase of the war, the rapid
advance of the Red Army prevented large-scale deportations from the city,
which was liberated in February 1945. The Jewish survival rate was above
50 percent in the capital, as opposed to a meager 20 percent in the provinces.
Thus, the majority of survivors in Hungary–about 120,000–140,000 persons
–lived in Budapest,[4] forming one of the largest remaining Jewish communities in
postwar Europe. The first Jewish congregations reestablished after the war were
also in the capital. They retained the prewar division between Neolog, Orthodox
and Status Quo branches,[5] but there were also some dramatic changes.

The postwar Jewish community in Budapest differed fundamentally from
the prewar one. Two thirds of the men between the ages of 20 and 60 had been
killed while in military labor service, whereas about half of the children and
women, and two thirds of those over 60 years of age survived.[6] Owing to the
particular historical development of the urban Jewish population, the majority
of survivors in the capital were assimilated and secularized. Because so many of
them were children, elderly, and single women, the postwar Jewish community
in the capital was in dire need of immediate aid.

Recognizing this need, the leadership of the Neolog and Orthodox communities of Budapest, together with the Hungarian Zionist Association (*Magyar
Cionista Szövetség*), formed an organization in March 1945, which came to be

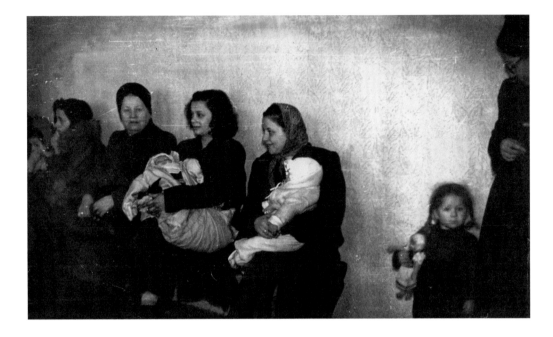

Mothers with their babies waiting for aid at the office
of the National Committee for Attending Deportees,
1945–1947. Photo: Sándor Bojár, Hungarian Jewish
Museum and Archives, Budapest

Survivors receive a warm meal at a soup kitchen,
1945–1947. Photo: Sándor Bojár, Hungarian Jewish
Museum and Archives, Budapest

Clothing aid distribution for survivors at the
National Committee for Attending Deportees, 1945–1947.
Photo: Sándor. Bojár, Hungarian Jewish Museum and
Archives, Budapest

known as the National Committee for Attending Deportees (*Deportáltakat Gondozó Országos Bizottság*, DEGOB). They also maintained the National Jewish Relief Committee (*Országos Zsidó Segítő Bizottság*), which oversaw the activities of the DEGOB. These and a number of other, smaller institutions working to bring home the deported and help survivors were all funded by the JDC, which paid special attention to Hungary.

After receiving alarming news from its representative in Budapest about the "catastrophic" situation of survivors in November 1945,[7] the JDC's New York leadership decided to prioritize Hungary as a destination for aid. Between 1945 and 1948, 23 to 27 percent of all JDC funds for Europe were allocated to Hungary.[8] In the period from 1945 to 1953, the organization's Hungarian aid program was the "most expensive project in the history of the Joint."[9] Besides providing direct material aid such as food packages and clothing, the JDC ran dozens of children's homes in Budapest alone,[10] along with soup-kitchens, healthcare institutions, and manufacturing workshops.

The financial help of the JDC was indispensable, but the rapid establishment of communal institutions under the direst circumstances was also the result of the survivors' own efforts. The Orthodox elementary school in Dob street opened a mere two weeks after the liberation of the Budapest ghetto and operated despite decimated teacher and student populations and the physical frailty of the survivors. "Many children have been absent for longer periods because of frostbite and skin problems due to vitamin-deficiency," one teacher wrote in an end-of-year report.[11] Despite all the hardships, the next academic year (1946/47) already saw eighteen Jewish elementary schools in Budapest. Of these, sixteen were funded by the JDC, of which ten were maintained by the Neolog and six by the Orthodox community. The other two were run by the Zionist Association. More than 2,000 children attended these schools.[12] Since most of these children had lost one or both parents, the schools provided a community in lieu of the families which had perished during the war.

Support for the Hungarian Zionist Association increased dramatically after the war. Besides their direct goal of furthering emigration to Palestine, the Zionists organized numerous social activities that brought thousands of young people into the movement. While the total national membership had numbered only 4,000–5,000 in the early 1930s, in 1948 the Association had more than 8,000 registered members in Budapest alone.[13] Despite this popularity, the Zionists' principal goal–to encourage emigration to Israel–was only partially achieved. About 50,000 surviving Jews left between 1945 and 1949,[14] but the majority stayed in Hungary.

The Rabbinical Institute and the Jewish Museum in Budapest swiftly reopened. The first postwar ordination of seven rabbis who had earned their degrees at the seminary took place in early 1946.[15] The institute played an important role in reorganizing Jewish education in Hungary. During the Cold War, it was the only remaining rabbinical institute in the entire Eastern Bloc. The collections of the Jewish Museum had survived the war in crates hidden in the cellars of the Hungarian National Museum. Restoration work on the building of the Jewish Museum was completed in 1947, and the first exhibit opened a year later.[16] Faced with the destruction wrought by the Shoah, the museum now focused principally on the preservation of Hungarian Jewish cultural heritage. Between 1945 and 1955, a great number of objects were incorporated in the museum's collection with the explicit goal of "allowing at least a few memories of the destroyed communities to become part of collective memory."[17]

However, these positive developments were inhibited and eventually cut short as the communists gradually gained power in Hungary. Helped by the Soviet occupiers, one-party communism was established in 1949, and Jewish institutions were subordinated to state control. The atheist state massively restricted religious activities. The three branches of the religious community were merged and Jewish schools were nationalized. The Hungarian Zionist Association was disbanded in 1949, and the activities of the JDC were banned two years later. Moreover, certain general anti-bourgeois policies pursued by the new regime affected Jewish survivors with particular intensity. For example, in 1951, when members of the so-called "exploiting classes" were compulsorily relocated from Budapest to provincial farms and villages throughout the country, about 40 percent of those transferred from the seventh district–an area where many Jews lived and owned small businesses–were Jewish survivors[18] who, having confronted the destruction of their communities and livelihoods, had managed to reestablish their lives here after the war.

The postwar history of the Jewish community in Budapest showcases how successful the joint effort of local survivors and foreign Jewish aid organizations could be in re-establishing Jewish communal life. However, many of the capital's secular and assimilated Jews did not participate in this reconstruction process. The following decades of communist restrictions on the expression of Jewish identities also prized many away from the religious community, which was further weakened by the wave of emigration following the failed revolution of 1956.[19] Despite these developments, a Jewish revival occurred after the fall of communism.

---

[1] Imre Kertész, *Fatelessness: A Novel*, translated by Tim Wilkinson (New York: Vintage International, 2004), 253–254.

[2] This number does not include the 50,000–90,000 Christians categorized as Jews by the Hungarian racial laws, who were living on the territory of what would become postwar Hungary. Nor does it include the Jewish population of territories that were annexed by Hungary in 1938 and 1940. Including these territories, the Jewish population under Hungarian jurisdiction amounted to about 800,000. See Tamás Stark, *Zsidóság a vészkorszakban és a felszabadulás után (1939–1955)* (Budapest: MTA Történettudományi Intézete, 1995), 54.

Group photo of a boys' first grade class on the courtyard of the Kazinczy Street Orthodox Center in Budapest, 1946–1947. Photo: Gyula Hámori, Fortepan, courtesy of Gyula Hámori, Budapest

Friends and family say goodbye to *mizrachim* leaving for British Mandate Palestine at Budapest Keleti Railway station, 1947. Photo: János Toronyi, Hungarian Jewish Museum and Archives, Budapest

3   Stark, *Zsidóság*, 41–47. Estimates of the number of survivors range from 140,000 to 260,000.

4   Stark, *Zsidóság*, 47. András Kovács refers to 144,000 survivors in Budapest. András Kovács, "Jews and Jewishness in Post-war Hungary," *Quest. Issues in Contemporary Jewish History* no. 1 (2010), 39.

5   In the second half of the nineteenth century, Hungarian Jewry split into three groups. The so-called Jewish schism reflected ideological differences between the Neolog and Orthodox movements. The Neolog community favored cultural integration into Hungarian society and moderate religious reform, which the Orthodox steadfastly opposed. The Status Quo group, which emerged a few years later, decided to ignore the split and did not align itself with either of these camps. For more details, see Jacob Katz, *A House Divided: Orthodoxy and Schism in Nineteenth-Century Central European Jewry*, translated by Ziporah Brody (Hanover, NH: Brandeis University Press, 1998).

6   Viktória Bányai, "The Impact of the American Jewish Joint Distribution Committee's Aid Strategy on the Lives of Jewish Families in Hungary, 1945–49," in *The Holocaust and its Aftermath from the Family Perspective*, ed. Eliyana Adler and Kateřina Čapková (New Brunswick: Rutgers University Press, forthcoming). I would like to thank Viktória Bányai for sending me her manuscript.

7   Yehuda Bauer, *Out of the Ashes. The Impact of American Jews on Post-Holocaust European Jewry* (Oxford: Pergamon Press, 1989), 136.

8   See Laura Hobson Faure's contribution to this volume and Bauer, *Out of the Ashes*, xviii.

9   Kinga Frojimovics, "Different Interpretations of Reconstruction: The American Jewish Joint Distribution Committee and the World Jewish Congress in Hungary after the Holocaust," in *The Jews are Coming Back. The Return of the Jews to their Countries of Origin after WWII*, ed. David Bankier (New York, Jerusalem: Berghahn, Yad Vashem, 2005), 280.

10 In 1947, there were 26 JDC-funded children's homes in Budapest. See Attila Novák, *Átmenetben. A cionista mozgalom négy éve Magyarországon (1945–1948)* (Budapest: Múlt és Jövő Kiadó 2000), 118–120.

11 Novák, *Átmenetben*, 63.

12 Novák, *Átmenetben*, 58.

13 Kovács, "Jews and Jewishness," 40.

14 Stark, *Zsidóság*, 94.

15 Moshe Carmilly-Weinberger, "One Hundred Years of the Seminary in Retrospect," in *The Rabbinical Seminary of Budapest 1877–1977*, ed. Moshe Carmilly-Weinberger (New York: Sepher-Hermon Press, 1986), 35.

16 Kinga Frojimovics, Viktória Pusztai, and Andrea Strbik, *Jewish Budapest. Monuments, Rites, History*, edited by Géza Komoróczy (Budapest: Central European University Press, 1999), 298.

17 Zsuzsanna Toronyi, "Egy budapesti kert történetei," *Korall* 11.41 (2010), 108.

18 I would like to thank Gábor Dombi for this information.

19 Between 20,000 and 30,000 Jews left Hungary at this point. Kovács, "Jews and Jewishness," 48.

Gyula Ortutay, representing the ruling communist
Hungarian Workers' Party, speaks at the Jewish
National Assembly, which marked the official merger
of the three branches of the Hungarian Jewish
religious community, 1950. Near the ornate *menorah*,
the portraits of three communist leaders adorn the wall:
Lenin, Stalin and General Secretary of the Hungarian
Workers' Party Mátyás Rákosi, 1950. Hungarian Jewish
Museum and Archives, Budapest

ÉVA SZEPESI
(BORN 1932)

Éva Szepesi was born into a middle-class Jewish family in Budapest as Éva Diamant. She was deported to Auschwitz in 1944 and liberated there by the Red Army. She was still only twelve years old. Her father, mother, and younger brother Tamás died during the Holocaust. Éva arrived in Budapest with a transport of survivors on September 18, 1945. There, she learned that two siblings of her father, uncle Imre and aunt Etel, as well as Imre's wife Olga had survived the war. She found the apartment of her parents looted by their neighbors, but she did manage to get back a few family photos. These became her most treasured possessions, keeping the memories of her lost family alive.

Upon her return to Budapest, Éva moved in with her uncle and his wife. She went back to school, found new friends, and joined a folk-dance group, but she did not talk about her wartime experiences. After finishing middle-school, she trained at a well-known Budapest salon to become a seamstress. She met her husband, Andor Szepesi, on a streetcar and they got married in 1951. Andor also came from a Jewish family, and was conscripted to do military labor service in the Hungarian Army during the war. The couple's first daughter, Judit, was born in 1952. In 1954, Andor was transferred to the Hungarian Foreign Trade representation in Frankfurt am Main as an accountant. Though Éva was reluctant to move to the "land of the perpetrators," they did finally establish a new, permanent home in Frankfurt. Their second daughter, Anita, was born there in 1964.

Éva Szepesi published a memoir about her wartime and postwar experiences in 2011. She is still living in Frankfurt today.

Éva Szepesi, 1949. Private collection,
Éva Szepesi, Frankfurt am Main

Éva with her husband Andor Szepesi and daughter Judit, 1952–1953. Private collection, Éva Szepesi, Frankfurt am Main

Éva Szepesi (then Diamant) with her family, first half of the 1940s. Lower row: Éva's mother Valéria, brother Tamás, Éva, and her father Károly. Upper row: Éva's two uncles, Oszkár and Zoltán. Only Éva survived the war and a few assorted photos were all that was left for her from her family's possessions. This family portrait is one of them. Private collection, Éva Szepesi, Frankfurt am Main

SÁNDOR SCHEIBER
(1913–1985)

Sándor Scheiber was born into a rabbinical family in Budapest. He himself studied to become a rabbi and was ordained at the Budapest Rabbinical Seminary in 1938. He also earned a doctorate in 1937. Until 1944, he was the rabbi of the Jewish community in Dunaföldvár, about 80 kilometers south of Budapest. He belonged to the Neolog branch of the Hungarian Jewish community. On March 19, 1944, when Germany invaded Hungary, he was in the capital and could not leave anymore. He was conscripted to do military labor service later that year. His mother died in his arms after being shot by a member of the Hungarian fascist Arrow Cross militia.

After the end of the war, he became a professor at the Rabbinical Seminary, where he taught literature and biblical studies. He then served as the institution's director from 1950 until his death. He was instrumental in ensuring that the seminary remained open throughout the communist era, when it was the only institution in Eastern Europe to train rabbis. Students arrived from all over the Eastern Bloc. In 1949, Scheiber also became an associate professor at the University of Szeged. As a scholar, he published extensively on topics related to Hungarian and Jewish folklore, and the history of Hungarian Jewry. He and his wife Lili had a daughter, Mária.

After the Second World War, Sándor Scheiber felt that it was his duty to serve the surviving Jewish community and the Rabbinical Seminary, to preserve the Judaica that remained after the destruction, and to pass on Jewish traditions. Thus, despite several tempting offers for positions from abroad, he remained in Budapest.

Sándor Scheiber, 1950. The portrait is from the large photo tableau commemorating the meeting of the Jewish National Assembly, which marked the official merger of the three branches of the Hungarian Jewish religious community. The merger, imposed by the ruling communist regime, provided the state authorities full political control over religious and community affairs. Hungarian Jewish Museum and Archives, Budapest

Scheiber's rabbinical ordination, 1938. Scheiber is standing, second from right. He came from a rabbinical family and shortly after this photo had been taken, became the rabbi of Dunaföldvár, a smaller town about 80 km from Budapest. Hungarian Jewish Museum and Archives, Budapest

PASSOVER 1946
THIS YEAR IN JERUSALEM

WERNER HANAK

Liberated Jewish men, women, and children were able to celebrate Passover (*Pesach*) for the first time again in Southern Italy in the spring of 1944 and in Poland in 1945. Yet the celebration of the holiday in 1946 was of unusual symbolic significance to Jewish survivors all over Europe. Since Pesach commemorates the liberation of the Jews from slavery in Egypt recounted in the Bible, it was particularly well suited to raise the issue of the Jews' future in Europe and beyond after their brutal persecution by the Nazis, and it gave the survivors an opportunity to express their hopes for the future.

This is borne out not only by the numerous photos that show the *seder* meals held on the eve of Pesach, be it in private households, community venues, or huge halls in the DP camps. In many of the *Haggadot* produced after liberation, the accounts of the exodus from Egypt also referenced the Shoah. In some cases, they even included practical instructions for making *aliyah* to Eretz Yisrael. The best-known ritual object from this period is arguably a seder plate which the JDC produced in huge numbers for the Jewish DPs. On it, the wish traditionally expressed at the end of the *seder*, "next year in Jerusalem," was changed to "this year in Jerusalem," signaling both how urgently change and better conditions were needed, as well as the intention of many survivors to leave Europe as soon as possible.

In 1946, Samuel Gringauz, who had survived a number of camps including Dachau, was the President of the Central Committee of Liberated Jews and thus the highest-ranking representative of the Jewish DPs in the U.S. occupation zone. In his preface to the *Pessach-Buch 5706/1946 (Pesach Book 5706/1946)* published in Marburg, he wrote: "It is as the remnant of our destroyed people, robbed of our freedom of movement, crushed by the lasting burden of Nazi oppression, and lacking spiritual and moral orientation that we celebrate." Yet he concluded his article with three optimistic exhortations: "Permitted by no one—we will go all the same. Led by no one—we will march all the same. Taught by no one—we will create all the same."[1]

In his contribution to the *Pessach-Buch 5706/1946*, Rabbi Leopold Neuhaus, who had returned to Frankfurt from Theresienstadt in 1945, suggested that the "edifying words" of the traditional *Haggadah* were questionable on this

"This year in Jerusalem" is the message on this light-blue glazed *seder* plate, which was produced on JDC initiative after the liberation of European Jews. The stamp on the back qualifies it as a "Product of the Organization of the Surviving Jews in the Diaspora in Germany," 1946–48. Jewish Museum Frankfurt occasion. The exhortation "you shall tell" could be understood as committing the entire *She'erit Hapletah* (the "Surviving Remnant") to "collect all the documents pertaining to our distress and persecution and create a large Jewish archive to preserve them for the future."[2] Yet he concluded by urging the survivors to focus on the future too. Despite their liberation, they had not yet gained their inner freedom. "Fog rises from the blood-drenched earth and obstructs the path towards, and the vision of, a better future."[3]

Rabbi Neuhaus moved to the U.S. in 1946, Samuel Gringauz in 1948.

[1] *Pessach Buch 5706/1946. Zum ersten Freiheits- und Frühlingsfest der Überreste Israels in Europa. Zusammengestellt und redigiert von Israel Blumenfeld*. Published by *The Jewish Review*, 1946, "by and for liberated Jews in Germany, Marburg/Lahn, U.S. Zone, Germany," 15.
[2] *Pessach Buch 5706/1946*, 199.
[3] *Pessach Buch 5706/1946*, 199.

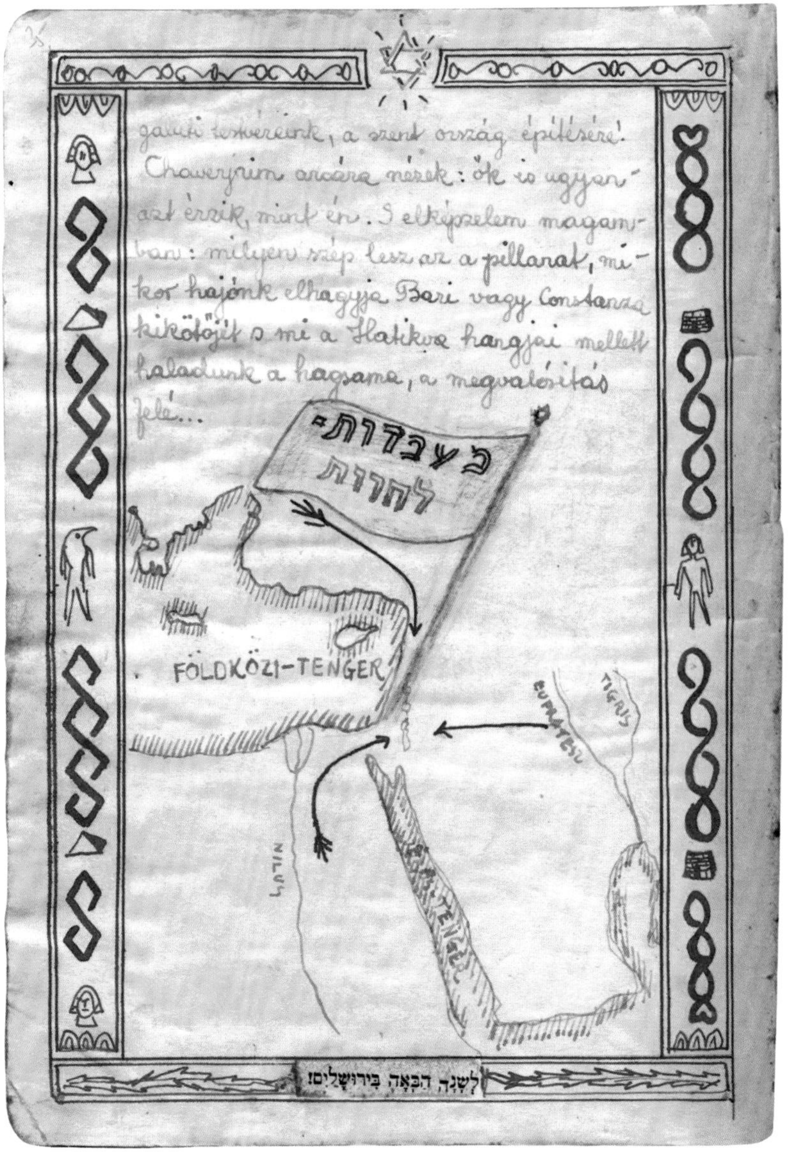

Handwritten Passover *Haggadah* of the Hashomer
Hatzair organization, Debrecen, Hungary, 1946–1948.
This *Haggadah* was published by the Hashomer
Hatzair left-wing Zionist youth organization in
Debrecen, Hungary. The illustration shows three
red arrows leading to Israel. The one coming from
the north symbolizes the desired *aliyah* to Palestine.
The text recommends the route across the Black Sea
town of Constanza and the Mediterranean port of Bari.
The other two arrows symbolize Jewish migration
through the desert after the flight from Egypt and the
return from Babylonian exile. The inscription on the
banner: "Born in slavery" emphasizes the overarching
theme of liberation. Hungarian Jewish Museum and
Archives, Budapest

Pessach Buch 5706/1946. Zum ersten Freiheits- und Frühlingsfest der Überreste Israels in Europa (Passover Book 5706/1946. For the First Liberation and Spring Festival of the Remnants of Israel in Europe). Compiled and edited by Israel Blumenfeld. Published by The Jewish Review, 1946, "by and for liberated Jews in Germany, Marburg/Lahn, U.S. Zone, Germany." Jewish Museum Frankfurt, Library

The first Passover *seder* in the Landsberg DP camp
in Bavaria, 1946. Photo: Zvi Kadushin, Beit Hatfutsot,
Tel Aviv, Zvi Kadushin Collection

Passover *seder* in the Schöneberg Town Hall in Berlin for members of the Jewish community and the Allied Forces, 1946. Photo: Gerhard Gronefeld, Deutsches Historisches Museum, Berlin

Survivors' Haggadah, Munich 5706/1946, arranged and designed by Yosef D. Sheinson (1907–1990) with seven woodcuts by Miklós Adler (1909–1965). Private collection Benjamin Soussan, Kirchzarten, Germany. The so-called *Survivors' Haggadah* had been completed in Munich for Passover which started on April 15, 1946. It was intended as a supplement to the traditional Passover narrative by integrating the recent persecution and murder of European Jews into the images and words of traditional Passover texts. Yosef D. Sheinson, a survivor from Lithuania and then a resident of the Landsberg DP camp, assembled traditional and contemporary texts. He also selected seven recently completed woodcuts by the Hungarian artist Miklós Adler, with scenes from concentration camps. For the texts, Sheinson himself created graphic frames in which he combined images of persecution (see on the next double page: a swastika over a supposedly dead prisoner at the bottom right) with the future ideal landscape of *Eretz Yisrael* (oranges, olives, grapes and a sickle with ears of wheat in the upper left).

הוצאת
ההסתדרות הציונית
האחידה ו,נָחָם" בגרמניה.

וואס זאל זײן גרעסער ווי
די וועלכע ליגט אין דעם
אלטן פעדאגאגישן
געבאט.
איז דען דא א ליטערא־
רישערע שאפונג, וועל־
כע דערצײט צו עקל צו
דער קנעכטשאפט, צו
פרײהײט ליבע, מער
ווי די געשיכטע פון
פארשקלאפונג און
יציאת מצרים ?
איז דען דא אן אלטע
דערינערונג, וואס זאל זײן
דער סימבאל פאר דער
געגנווארט און צוקונפט

בן - בנימין

שֶׁלֹּא אֶחָד בִּלְבָד עָמַד עָלֵינוּ לְכַלּוֹתֵינוּ

TAKING UP THE CAUSE OF THE JEWISH COLLECTIVE
JEWISH COMMUNISTS IN BERLIN'S SOVIET SECTOR DURING THE "INTERREGNUM" FROM 1945 TO 1950

PHILIPP GRAF

On September 12, 1948, the Lustgarten in the center of East Berlin—i.e., the park square between Berlin's cathedral, the forecourt of the imperial palace, the Spree Canal, and the Old Museum and long a preferred location for various political demonstrations—was the site of an enormous rally attended by tens of thousands of people. It marked the "Memorial Day for the Victims of Fascism" (hereafter: Memorial Day) organized annually in early September by the Association of Persecutees of the Nazi Regime (VVN).[1] A closer look at photos of the event reveals that there was more than meets the eye to what seemed like the sort of party-organized late-Stalinist mass commemoration typical of later years in the GDR. The main podium had been erected in front of the south-eastern façade of the Old Museum, which had been lavishly adorned with twenty-one large flags representing the nations that had fallen prey to Hitler. Among them, rather surprisingly given what we know about the subsequent character of these commemorative events, was Israel's flag with the Star of David (*Magen David*), displayed in a central position between its counterparts from Yugoslavia and Luxemburg.[2]

That the rally was an ambiguous affair was indicated not least by the oversized version of the VVN logo located right above the Israeli flag. It showed the organization's acronym on top of the red triangle that had designated political prisoners in the National Socialist concentration camp system. Against this backdrop, regardless of whether it was seen as a symbol of Judaism or of Israeli sovereignty, this unproblematic, matter-of-fact presentation of the Jewish

National Memorial of the GDR in Buchenwald.
View of the "street of nations" with some of the
18 pylons. Photo: Wittig, Allgemeiner Deutscher
Nachrichtendienst–Zentralbild, Bundesarchiv,
Bild 183-56769-0008

Commemoration at the Lustgarten (Memorial Day
for the Victims of Fascism) on September 12, 1948.
Photo: Abraham Pisarek, Deutsche Fotothek, SLUB
Dresden

emblem seems all the more counter-intuitive. Following the establishment of the GDR in 1949, a similarly prominent and equitable presentation of the *Magen David* would have been inconceivable away from the Jewish community and a handful of monuments. As a self-styled antifascist state, the GDR refused to take any responsibility for the crimes perpetrated by the National Socialists and was, consequently, unwilling to fulfill Jewish claims to restitution and compensation. Moreover, it officially subordinated the fate of the Jews in the pantheon of communist commemoration. It is no coincidence that Jews no longer featured in the design of the central memorial inaugurated in 1958 on the site of the former Buchenwald concentration camp, which subsequently shaped the memorialization of National Socialism in the GDR. In contrast to the rally at the Lustgarten ten years earlier, none of the eighteen pylons erected along the so-called "street of nations" to represent the home countries of the camp's prisoners was assigned to Israel or the more than 11,000 Jews killed in Buchenwald.[3]

The chronicler of the remarkable rally on September 12, 1948 to whom we owe the images in question was the Jewish photographer Abraham Pisarek (1901–1983) who found himself at the Lustgarten that day in his capacity as a photojournalist employed by the Soviet Military Administration (hereafter: SMAD).[4] Working for the SMAD's newspaper, *Tägliche Rundschau*, he regularly reported on current events. For example, he also shot the iconic photo of the handshake with which Wilhelm Pieck and Otto Grotewohl sealed the merger of the Communist and Social Democratic parties to form the Socialist Unity Party (SED) on April 22, 1946. Yet a closer look at his oeuvre in the immediate postwar period, which, alongside his reporting on current events, also encompassed theater photography and portraits, indicates a consistent interest in Jewish themes. Not only did he document the life of the Jewish community of Berlin, focusing on days of remembrance, the Purim ball, and similar occasions, and include Jewish personalities from East Berlin among the subjects of his sought-after portraits. There are also plenty of traces of Jewish life in the photos commissioned by the SMAD. For example, he also took the equally poignant photo showing the staff of Berlin's Jewish Hospital among the crowds flocking to the first VVN Memorial Day rally held in Berlin on September 14, 1946.[5] This suggests that Pisarek, when taking photos at the Lustgarten on September 12, 1948, consciously captured the way in which the Israeli flag had been granted equal status among its counterparts, since he was quite aware of the significance of what he saw and its wider implications.

Given Pisarek's past, his attention to these issues was hardly surprising. He had survived the Holocaust in Berlin thanks to his non-Jewish spouse and owed his life to the resistance of the "Aryan" wives who had taken part in the so-called "Rosenstraße Protest" to prevent their husbands' deportation. He was one of several thousand survivors who, along with former camp inmates, people who had survived in hiding, and political returnees, formed the core of the German-speaking Jewish community in Berlin, which comprised roughly 7,000 souls after the war. They were joined by about the same number of Jewish DPs from Eastern Europe who had been stranded in Berlin on their way to the U.S. occupation zone.[6] Among his peers–with their various backgrounds, stories of survival, and political convictions–Pisarek stood out as a communist. He was, in other words, affiliated with a political movement hardly known for its great interest in, let alone compassion for, the fate of the Jews. Strictly speaking, Jewishness and communism were mutually exclusive concepts. To be sure, Jews could subscribe to communism, as demonstrated by hundreds of them between the wars. However, by turning to communism they committed themselves to abandoning all those traits characterized as "Jewish" and no longer attaching any importance to their Jewish origin.[7]

Yet at this time, there were still quite a few Jews in the SED and the circles associated with it in East Berlin who, as in Pisarek's case, stood up for Jewish causes. They included the economist Siegbert Kahn (1909–1976) who in 1948 published an undogmatic analysis of antisemitism with the party publisher Dietz;[8] the former Auschwitz prisoner Julius Meyer (1909–1979) who negotiated with the SED for the Association of Jewish Communities in the Soviet occupation zone (SBZ), whose chairman he was;[9] and the party's in-house counsel Leo Zuckermann (1908–1985) who had been in exile in Mexico and whom the party leadership commissioned in the winter of 1947–48 to prepare draft legislation for restitution procedures in the SBZ.[10] With the possible exception of Meyer, they saw themselves as communists in the first instance and only then as men with a Jewish family background. Even so, the experience of Nazi rule had convinced them that Jews had suffered a distinct fate that needed to be taken into consideration in the construction of postwar society. The particular experience of a specific form of persecution left a mark on their primarily universalist concept of equality. As Pisarek's photographs indicate, this was a concern which, in marked contrast to subsequent developments, still enjoyed some resonance during this "interregnum."[11]

THE "GERMAN PREDICAMENT"

For the time of its existence, the German-speaking communist movement had not tended to show any great interest in the "Jewish question." The few publications that discussed it from the vantage of the party, such as Otto Heller's 1931 polemic, *Der Untergang des Judentums* (*The Demise of Jewry*), interpreted antisemitism as a symptom of the social question, which the introduction of socialism would render obsolete. They categorically denied that the Jews formed a

Siegbert Kahn (1909–1976), 1951. After having
returned from exile in the UK in 1946, Kahn worked
in the Central Secretariat of the SED. In 1949, he
became head of the German Economic Institute.
In 1948 he wrote a publication of nearly 100 pages
entitled *Antisemitismus und Rassenhetze. Eine
Übersicht über ihre Entwicklung in Deutschland*
(*Antisemitism and Racial Incitement. A Summary
of their Development in Germany*). Bundesarchiv,
Bild Y 10–346/00

national collective.[12] Yet in 1948, the economist Siegbert Kahn, who had returned from exile in the UK, decided to outline some original considerations on the matter in a publication of nearly 100 pages entitled *Antisemitismus und Rassenhetze. Eine Übersicht über ihre Entwicklung in Deutschland (Antisemitism and Racial Incitement. A Survey of their Development in Germany)*. Following his return to Germany in August 1946, he joined the staff of the Central Secretariat of the SED before switching over to head the German Economic Institute in 1949. He too propagated the implausible thesis that antisemitism was a "diversionary tactic," skilfully deployed by the powers that be to channel the social and economic "dissatisfaction of the masses" towards the Jews. Even so, he did modify the communist theory of antisemitism in some respects. For instance, he criticized Stalin's contention that the Jews did not constitute a nation.[13] To be sure, he nominally affirmed this claim and included the obligatory footnote referencing Stalin. Yet he qualified this affirmation, adding that the Jews in Palestine now had "the right [...] to their own national development." He also referred to the claim for restitution, making the case for the return of, or payment of compensation for, stolen Jewish assets. For him, this was not only a necessary social welfare measure but also a "moral obligation." Unusually for a communist whose principal concern is the welfare of the collective, he singled out the fate of Jews and emphasized the importance of meeting their specific needs. Given the tragedy that had befallen (German) Jewry, Kahn took it for granted that socialist society had a particular responsibility for its Jewish citizens. They should neither be compelled to assimilate nor prevented from "developing their own Jewish culture."[14]

At the time, numerous (not only Jewish) returnees and survivors in the Soviet occupation zone were engaged in a broadly based debate, conducted in commentary and fiction, on the radio and in film, designed to make sense of recent events by elucidating what was termed the "German predicament" (*Deutsche Misere*). Friedrich Meinecke's *Die deutsche Katastrophe* (*The German Catastrophe*) epitomized similar debates in the western occupation zones. Kahn saw his publication as a contribution to this debate. Its participants sought to ascertain how Hitler's ascendancy had been possible by scrutinizing German history and culture.[15] One of the best-known proponents of this approach in the SBZ was the Jewish journalist Alexander Abusch, a party loyalist who had been in exile in Mexico. Following his return in July 1946, he took charge of the Cultural League as its secretary and of the resurrected journal, *Weltbühne*, as its editor in chief. In his bestseller, *Irrweg einer Nation* (*An Errant Nation*), he described Hitler's regime as the culmination point of a dialectical struggle between progressive-democratic and reactionary forces. What had begun in the Peasant Wars of the sixteenth century ultimately resulted in the Nazi dictatorship because the bourgeoisie was consistently indecisive.[16] Despite Abusch's critical observations, he remained a loyal party cadre. For his study focused squarely on the socialist future, which, it was assumed, would arrive as a matter of course, provided one eliminated the causes of "fascism." Kahn, who also wanted his book to be regarded as a "contribution to the critical examination of our intellectual heritage," was exceptional insofar as his vision of the future took account of the Jewish experience. Presumably, the annihilation of the Jews was one of the reasons for the soul-searching of all those concerned with the "German predicament." Yet very few of them actually made it their point of departure and explicitly discussed it as Kahn had.[17]

The available sources do not indicate why Kahn was ahead of his contemporaries in taking the fate of the Jews seriously.[18] Kahn, who was born in Berlin in 1909, was basically a poster boy for communism. He had become part of the KPD's innermost circle in 1929 when he joined the so-called "M-Apparatus," the party's clandestine intelligence service. Tasked with further illegal activities when the Nazis came to power, he was arrested in November 1933, charged with "conspiracy to commit treason," and given a prison sentence of just under three years. Yet, following his release, his path deviated from that of most of his comrades. Until he fled to Prague in 1938, he worked for the Jewish community in Berlin and then, for a short while, for a Jewish refugee committee in Czechoslovakia. As a Jew, he did not have many options when it came to earning his keep, and it seems highly likely that, as a communist, his relationship to these jobs was purely instrumental. Even so, it would seem that they impressed on him how significant antisemitism was to Nazi ideology. They provided him with first-hand, indeed with personal, intimate knowledge of the ways in which the fate of the Jews differed from that of other (political) victims of persecution, including himself. This insight was presumably reinforced once he fled to the UK in 1939. There, he joined the leadership of the exiled KPD group around Jürgen Kuczynski. Many of its members were young Jewish émigrés. In contrast to the members of the "Ulbricht Group" in Moscow, their exile in Britain offered them a space to reflect critically, encouraged by the anti-German sentiments of much of the British public, on the Germans' crimes and the support of the German population for the Nazis.[19] In that context, Kahn continued to insist that it was impossible to understand National Socialism without taking into account the "gruesome drama" in which "six million people were slaughtered just because they were Jews."[20]

REPRESENTATION

It was still possible to publish a fairly unorthodox book like that of Siegbert Kahn in East Berlin in 1948 because, at the time, party discussions of the Jewish experience had not yet been marginalized to the extent they subsequently were in the GDR. Initially, May 8, 1945 really placed the survivors of the prisons, concentration camps, and death marches on the same par. They had a common advocate in the VVN, which, until 1949–50, also interceded, as a matter of course, on behalf of the Jewish victims of persecution. Given the numbers, this was hardly surprising. In May 1946, there were 4,600 people in Berlin who had been persecuted by the Nazis for political reasons, but more than 10,000 Jewish victims of Nazi persecution.[21] Among the forty members of the VVN's Central Board for the SBZ were no fewer than ten Jews.[22] It was no coincidence that Heinz Galinski (1912–1992), who later served as Chairman of the Jewish Community of West Berlin and the Central Council of Jews in Germany, was, in his capacity as Deputy Chairman of the VVN in Berlin, the official host of the aforementioned Memorial Day event at the Lustgarten. Until it was closed down by the authorities in 1953, the VVN's monthly, *Unser Appell*, renamed *Die Tat* in 1949, dealt with Jewish topics in virtually every issue; among these were widespread antisemitism, the fact that restitution was not forthcoming, and developments in Israel.[23]

Central to these activities in East Berlin was the SED member Julius Meyer who, like Galinski, had survived Auschwitz.[24] Although the fact that he had been a *kapo* in Auschwitz drew some criticism, by the early 1950s he held no fewer than five influential positions concerned with the pursuit of Jewish interests.[25] Beginning in October 1945, he was in charge of the department created specifically for "victims of the Nuremberg Laws" within the Main Office for Victims of Fascism run by the municipal authorities in Berlin. In December 1945, he was elected to the board of the Jewish Community of Berlin, where he took responsibility for social affairs. Over time, he was also elected to the board of the VVN and served as president of the Regional Association of Jewish Communities in the SBZ (and later the GDR), which, moreover, he represented in the directorate of the Central Council of Jews. Meyer thus emerged as one of the most prominent advocates of Jewish causes in the SBZ. Before the war, Meyer had shown little interest in things Jewish. A professional leatherworker, he had joined the KPD in 1930. His professional development was rudely cut short in 1938, when he was drafted as a slave laborer and forced to work, *inter alia*, in road construction. Following his arrest and deportation to Auschwitz in February 1943, he eventually became a *kapo*, supervising the road construction and canalization detail. After his liberation, he initially worked as commissioner for fruit, vegetables, and potatoes with Berlin's food agency but left this position to take up the aforementioned role with the municipality. As Meyer later recalled, he had decided to devote himself to the struggle for the equal recognition of the Jewish victims and, by extension, for the concerns of the Jewish collective. For he had been told, when he first visited the social welfare office for former concentration camp inmates shortly after his arrival in Berlin, that, "as a Jew, he was not a victim of fascism."[26]

In East Berlin, the nonpartisan VVN was initially a natural ally in this quest. The SED's interference notwithstanding, many of its members, having shared similar experiences, were willing to listen when the rights and claims of the Jewish victims of Nazi persecution were at stake.[27] When the SMAD stated in February 1948 that denazification was over and done with, precipitating the reintegration of numerous former fellow travellers into society, many in the VVN were disappointed. They were equally disconcerted that restitution legislation had not been forthcoming. Nevertheless, the association was increasingly drawn into the emerging Cold War system conflict. In the western occupation zones, the VVN was viewed with suspicion and denounced as an outpost of the SED. Consequently, in September 1948, the Social Democratic Party (SPD) banned its members from joining the VVN. As the conflict escalated, the SPD organized its own Memorial Day rally outside the Reichstag (i.e., in West Berlin), which the SED promptly denounced as a "fascist" event.[28] Opinions on the VVN were also split within Berlin's Jewish community, which urged its officers to exercise caution when it came to taking on political roles. While Galinski acted on his increasing unease in December 1948 by resigning his position in the VVN, and thereafter focusing exclusively on his role within the Jewish community, the communist Meyer–whether out of conviction or not–stuck with the SED for the time being.[29]

RESTITUTION

All the efforts undertaken in those years to see Jewish claims given their due culminated in debates concerning restitution and compensation, which likewise were taking place in East Berlin. There had long been calls from the VVN and others in the SBZ to finally regulate the claims of the victims of Nazi persecution, not least because such regulations seemed to be imminent in the western occupation zones. In September 1947, when attempts to introduce joint regulations for all four occupation zones had irrevocably failed, the SED, feeling under pressure to act, commissioned the German Labor and Welfare Administration directed by Paul Merker (1894–1969) and Helmut Lehmann (1882–1959) to prepare draft legislation. This presented Merker with the opportunity to finally translate into legislation the convictions he and his close collaborator, the Jewish legal scholar Leo Zuckermann, had developed while in exile in Mexico. The émigré group led by Merker had publicly stated that restitution would have to be made for the crimes perpetrated against the Jews and acknowledged that the demand to establish a Jewish state in Palestine was justified.[30] Now back in Germany, they had to take various restrictions into account. On the one hand, the requirements of the new socialist economic order had to be considered. Major enterprises in the key industries, banks, and insurances, including former Jewish businesses, had already been nationalized and could no longer be given back. On the other hand, concessions had to be made to the sensibilities of the party leadership, given that it presumably did not want Jewish concerns to feature prominently in its dealings with the general population. Hence, a law dealing exclusively with issues of restitution would have been doomed from the outset. Merker and Zuckermann tried to circumvent this problem by merging proposals concerning the issue they had been commissioned to address together with draft regulations for a pension scheme to benefit victims of Nazi persecution in general. The integration of the issue of restitution was facilitated by first placing the victims of "racial" and political persecution on a par and applying the same regulations to them. Only then, in the second part of the draft, did they suggest that those "whose assets were expropriated between January 30, 1933 and May 8, 1945 on the grounds of their race, religion, ideological orientation, or political opposition to National Socialism" should have their assets returned to them or, should this not be possible, be offered compensation.[31] The draft ultimately envisaged a so-called "small solution," focusing primarily on the restitution of "Aryanized" small businesses and real estate properties in the SBZ.[32] Even so, given some 55,000 assets, its implementation would have interfered with the sensitive property regime in postwar East Germany in a fairly substantial way. At its meeting on January 26, 1948, the SED's Central Secretariat nevertheless approved the proposal. With his draft, Zuckermann had aligned himself fairly closely with individuals and positions that should have been anathema to a communist. Its thrust overlapped to a considerable degree with the approach we now think of as underpinning Jewish postwar claims in crucial ways, an approach articulated from 1944 onwards by the likes of Nehemiah Robinson in the U.S. and Siegfried Moses in Palestine who called for restitution to be made, or compensation offered, for the assets expropriated from Jews all over Europe.[33]

These demands were predicated on the assumption that the Jews formed a collective with a claim to restitution in its own right. This claim ensued from the specificity of the National Socialists' attempt to get hold of all Jews worldwide for no other purpose than to murder them. As an unintended consequence, this distinct form of persecution had resulted in their retrospective elevation to a quasi-national collective.[34] For all their ideological differences with Zionists like Robinson and Moses, the news of the indiscriminate murder of the Jews had led Merker and Zuckermann, while still exiled in Mexico, to develop a similar approach. They too acknowledged that the communists were persecuted because they had fought against the Nazis while the Jews were murdered for no other reason than that they were Jews.[35] Having previously distanced himself from his

Dr. Leo Zuckermann, between 1947 and 1950.
Zuckermann returned from Mexican exile in 1947
and worked in the Central Secretariat of the SED.
He became head of the foreign policy commission
of the SED board in 1949, and co-authored the constitution of the GDR. After the Slánský trial, he was
denounced as a Zionist agent in 1952, fleeing the
GDR to France, and then to Mexico. Photo: Abraham
Pisarek, Deutsche Fotothek, SLUB Dresden

Jewishness, not least by joining the KPD in 1928, Zuckermann had in a sense reconnected with his Jewish origins when confronted with the Holocaust. In this vein, the SED's draft legislation of 1947–48 revealed that the Jewish self-perception as a people was gaining widespread traction on account of the genocide–in this case, significantly, in Berlin's Soviet sector.

In combination with the proposed welfare provision, the implementation of the draft legislation on restitution would have amounted to a serious signal from the party leadership, underscoring its determination to reverse, or at least ameliorate, the consequences of "Aryanization." One can only imagine what this might have meant in the long-term for the Jewish experience in the GDR and relations between the authorities, the Jewish community, and the State of Israel. It would seem that Zuckermann too saw the draft legislation as something akin to a cornerstone for Jewish life in a socialist German state. At the same time, his approach also pitted him against the symbolic ban imposed on postwar Germany by international Jewish organizations. They took it for granted that, after the catastrophe of the Holocaust, Jews had no future in the country of the perpetrators.[36]

Yet as we know, none of this came to pass. While the draft was approved by the Soviets with only minor amendments in the autumn of 1948, it was not then referred to the East German federal states for consultation. The failure to do so resulted from initial reservations in the judicial administration that it might create a problematic precedent and from the Soviet Union's reversal of its position regarding the Middle East in the course of 1948 and 1949. Just days before the creation of the GDR on October 7, 1949, the Central Committee hastily issued a decree that merely regulated the legal status of the VVN (including those persecuted on racial grounds) while abandoning the stipulations concerning the issue of restitution.[37] This was never rectified in the GDR, and the issue was not resolved until 1990, when it was addressed in the Two Plus Four Agreement and the Unification Treaty.

THE WINDOW OF OPPORTUNITY CLOSES

Hence, the emergence of a newly won collective Jewish self-understanding after Auschwitz, one of the most important features of the post-1945 "interregnum," was also in evidence in the Soviet occupation zone, where it was even articulated by Jewish communists within the SED. It has often been assumed that the Soviet sphere of influence was a no man's land in this respect (with the exception of a few countries, primarily Poland where much of the catastrophe had unfolded). Yet evidently such efforts to see the specifically Jewish experience of the Second World War given its legal, political, and intellectual due were also undertaken in those Central and East European states which were in the process of being homogenized as "people's democracies." However, such efforts were able to continue only for as long as the Soviets tolerated them. For attentive observers, then, it became evident within weeks of the rally at the Lustgarten mentioned at the outset that the party's position had begun to shift. On October 3, the party's flagship daily, *Neues Deutschland*, published an article by Ilya Ehrenburg, one of the most prominent Soviet Jews, which had previously appeared in *Pravda*. In it, Ehrenburg publicly took leave of the Soviet leadership's concessions of recent years. Following the German aggression against the Soviet Union in 1941, those leaders had facilitated the establishment, on Stalin's suggestion, of the Jewish Antifascist Committee. Its principal task had been to mobilize support for the Red Army in the western hemisphere, but it also contributed substantially to the revival of a collective Jewish self-understanding among Soviet Jews. Seven years later, one of that committee's figureheads now reverted to insisting that Soviet Jews should focus exclusively on the wellbeing of their "Socialist homeland," the Soviet Union. This was a clear indication that overly positive references to Israel and any kind of distinct Jewish self-understanding would henceforth be taboo.[38] On the face of it, Ehrenburg's article was a response to the deterioration in Soviet-Israeli relations that followed Golda Meir's visit to Moscow in September 1948. It also has to be seen against the backdrop of the dramatic changes in global politics in the course of that year. Following the coup in Czechoslovakia in February, Yugoslavia's withdrawal from the Soviet Bloc in March, and the Berlin Crisis in June, the Cold War was now well and truly underway. This had considerable consequences for the policies of the Communist Party of the Soviet Union and her sister parties, including, in this case, the SED.

The VVN's annual rallies at the Lustgarten were likewise affected by this change of course. In 1949, the rally was still largely similar to those in previous years, and the flag with the *Magen David* again featured in a prominent position. However, the following year, the rally's character changed considerably. On September 10, 1950, Memorial Day was marked by a peace rally organized jointly by the VVN and the *Fédération internationale des anciens prisoniers politiques* (FIAPP), the umbrella organization of Europeans who had fought in the resistance movements against Nazi Germany. Its motto, "United Front for World Peace, Against War and Fascism," clearly indicated a radically changed focus, leaving little space for Jewish concerns. Not only did the event focus exclusively on the victims of *political* persecution by the Nazis; it was also deployed as a propaganda tool in the Cold War conflict of systems. From then on, warnings about possible future conflicts displaced the specificity of the previous war. At this point, Berlin's official Jewish community had already withdrawn from the spectacle. As Galinski noted in a speech, the community had "deliberately" decided to hold its own ceremony in the Pestalozzistraße Synagogue in order "to ensure that our dead are not misappropriated at other rallies to score political points."[39]

The central commemorative events at the Lustgarten were abandoned in 1951. By this time, the protagonists determined to see the Jewish experience given its due whom we have met in the course of this chapter had fallen silent. Leo Zuckermann and Julius Meyer hastily fled the GDR given the strong antisemitic overtones of the party purge carried out in the winter of 1952–53. Given their earlier engagement, they would likely have fallen prey to a show trial had they stayed. Abraham Pisarek withdrew from political photojournalism, moved to West Berlin, and henceforth focused on the rather less controversial field of theatre photography. Only Siegbert Kahn continued his career in the SED, but he no longer commented on Jewish issues in any official capacity. As Director of the German Economic Institute, he now undertook traditional orthodox-Marxist analyses of imperialism. The "interregnum" of the years between 1945 and 1950 that had permitted the articulation of Jewish interests on a more or less equal footing, even in East Germany, was finally over.

[1] "Das wahre Berlin steht im Weltlager des Friedens," *Neues Deutschland* no. 214, September 14, 1948, 1.

[2] See http://www.deutschefotothek.de/documents/obj/88930567/df_pk_0000488_033, accessed September 6, 2018.

[3] Wolfgang Emmerich, "Buchenwald," in *Encyclopedia of Jewish History and Culture Online*, accessed June 14, 2019. http://dx.doi.org/10.1163/2468-8894_ejhc_COM_0124; Karin Hartewig, *Zurückgekehrt. Die Geschichte der jüdischen Kommunisten in der DDR* (Cologne: Böhlau, 2000), 476–481.

[4] See Abraham Pisarek, *Jüdisches Leben in Berlin/Jewish Life in Berlin, 1933–1941*, edited with an essay by Joachim Schlör (Berlin: Edition Braus, 2012); Inge Unikower, *Suche nach dem gelobten Land. Die fragwürdigen Abenteuer des kleinen Gerschon* (Berlin: Verlag der Nation, 1978).

[5] See http://www.deutschefotothek.de/documents/obj/88930388, accessed September 6, 2018.

[6] Atina Grossmann, "Rabbi Steven Schwarzschild's Reports from Berlin, 1948–1950," *Leo Baeck Institute Year Book* 60 (2015), 237–242.

[7] *Dark Times, Dire Decisions. Jews and Communism*, ed. Dan Diner and Jonathan Frankel. Studies in Contemporary Jewry, vol. 20 (Oxford: Oxford University Press, 2005).

[8] Siegbert Kahn, *Antisemitismus und Rassenhetze. Eine Übersicht über ihre Entwicklung in Deutschland* (Berlin: Dietz, 1948).

[9] Karin Hartewig, "Meyer, Julius," in *Wer war wer in der DDR? Ein Lexikon ostdeutscher Biographien*, ed. Helmut Müller-Enbergs et al. Accessed September 6, 2018. https://www.bundesstiftung-aufarbeitung.de/wer-war-wer-in-der-ddr-%2363%3B-1424.html?ID=2314.

[10] Leo Zuckermann, "Die Bedeutung des VdN-Gesetzes," *Unser Appell* no. 7, May 15, 1948, 1.

[11] Dan Diner, "Zwischenzeit 1945 bis 1949. Über jüdische und andere Konstellationen," *Aus Politik und Zeitgeschichte* 65.16–17 (2015), 16–20.

[12] Otto Heller, *Der Untergang des Judentums. Die Judenfrage, ihre Kritik, ihre Lösung durch den Sozialismus* (Vienna, Berlin: Verlag für Literatur und Politik, 1931).

[13] Joseph V. Stalin, "Marxism and the National Question," in Joseph V. Stalin, *Works*, vol. 2 (Moscow: Foreign Languages Publishing House, 1953), 308–309, 312–313.

14 Kahn, *Antisemitismus und Rassenhetze*, 8, 88, 90–91.

15 See Hartewig, *Zurückgekehrt*, 442–460.

16 Alexander Abusch, *Irrweg einer Nation* (Berlin: Aufbau, 1946).

17 Paul Merker, *Deutschland – Sein oder Nicht Sein*, 2 vols. (Mexico City: El libro libre, 1944/45).

18 Hartewig, *Zurückgekehrt*, 449–452. See also, Bernd-Rainer Barth, "Kahn, Siegbert," in *Wer war wer in der DDR?* Accessed September 6, 2018. https://www.bundesstiftung-aufarbeitung.de/wer-war-wer-in-der-ddr-%2363%3B-1424.html?ID=1619.

19 For these discussions, see, for example, the monthly journal, *Freie Tribüne*, which was published in London from 1939 to 1946.

20 Kahn, *Antisemitismus und Rassenhetze*, 7.

21 Elke Reuter and Detlef Hansel, *Das kurze Leben der VVN von 1947 bis 1953* (Berlin: edition ost, 1997), 95.

22 "Der Zentralvorstand der VVN für die sowjetische Besatzungszone," *Unser Appell* no. 5, March 20, 1948, 7.

23 Hans-Erich Fabian, "Israel – die Heimat eines Volkes," *Unser Appell* no. 11–12, September 9, 1948, 23; Hans Mayer, "Auschwitz," *Unser Appell* no. 15, December 1, 1948, 5–7; "Almosen statt Wiedergutmachung," *Die Tat* no. 2, February 16, 1949, 7; "Unser Kommentar zum Harlan-Prozeß," *Die Tat* no. 9, May 4, 1949, 3.

24 Andreas Weigelt, "'Der zionistische Agent Julius Meyer und seine Auftraggeber…' Julius Meyer (1909–1979)," in *Zwischen Bleiben und Gehen. Juden in Ostdeutschland 1945 bis 1956. Zehn Biographien*, ed. Andreas Weigelt and Hermann Simon (Berlin: edition berlin, 2008), 73–129.

25 Weigelt, "Julius Meyer," 77.

26 Quoted in Weigelt, "Julius Meyer," 78.

27 Hartewig, *Zurückgekehrt*, 373–386.

28 "Wieder Reichstagsbrandstifter," *Neues Deutschland* no. 211, September 10, 1948, 1.

29 Weigelt, "Julius Meyer," 86.

30 Paul Merker, "Hitlers Antisemitismus und wir," *Freies Deutschland* 1.12 (1942), 9–11.

31 Gesetz über die Rechtstellung der Verfolgten des Naziregimes (VdN-Gesetz), SAPMO DY 30/IV 2/2027/31, Bl. 67–78.

32 Jan Philipp Spannuth, Rückerstattung Ost. Der Umgang der DDR mit dem „arisierten" Eigentum der Juden und die Rückerstattung im wiedervereinigten Deutschland (Essen: klartext, 2007), 164–166, 204.

33 Nehemiah Robinson, *Indemnification and Reparations. Jewish Aspects* (New York: Institute of Jewish Affairs, 1944); Siegfried Moses, *Die jüdischen Nachkriegs-Forderungen* (Tel Aviv: Bitaon, 1944).

34 Dan Diner, "Restitution," in *Enzyklopädie jüdischer Geschichte und Kultur*, vol. 5. (Stuttgart, Weimar: Metzler, 2014), 202–209.

35 Paul Merker, "Hitlers Antisemitismus und wir"; Leo Zuckermann, "Restitution und Wiedergutmachung," *Weltbühne* no. 17, April 27, 1948, 430–432.

36 See Dan Diner, "Banished: Jews in Germany after the Holocaust," in *A History of Jews in Germany since 1945. Politics, Culture, and Society*, ed. Michael Brenner (Bloomington: Indiana University Press, 2019), 7–53.

37 "Anordnung zur Sicherung der rechtlichen Stellung der anerkannten Verfolgten des Naziregimes." *Zentralverordnungsblatt Teil I, Amtliches Organ der Deutschen Wirtschaftskommission und ihrer Hauptverwaltungen sowie der Deutschen Verwaltungen für Inneres, Justiz und Volksbildung* no. 89, October 14, 1949, 765–766.

38 Ilya Ehrenburg, "Die Sowjetunion, der Staat Israel und die Lösung der 'jüdischen Frage'. Anlässlich eines Briefes," *Neues Deutschland* no. 231, October 3, 1948, 3. The text was published in English as "Answer to a Letter," *Jewish Life* (June 1949), 25–27.

39 Quoted in Weigelt, "Julius Meyer," 81.

Commemoration at the Lustgarten (Memorial Day
for the Victims of Fascism) on September 12, 1948.
Photo: Gerhard Gronefeld, Deutsches Historisches
Museum, GG 375/22

BIBLIOGRAPHY

Abusch, Alexander. *Irrweg einer Nation.* Berlin: Aufbau-Verlag, 1946. / "Almosen statt Wiedergutmachung." *Die Tat* no. 2, February 16, 1949, 7. / **Barth, Bernd-Rainer.** "Kahn, Siegbert." In *Wer war wer in der DDR? Ein Lexikon ostdeutscher Biographien*, ed. Helmut Müller-Enbergs et al. Accessed September 6, 2018. https://www.bundesstiftung-aufarbeitung.de/wer-war-wer-in-der-ddr-%2363%3B-1424.html?ID=1619. / **Diner, Dan.** "Restitution." In *Enzyklopädie jüdischer Geschichte und Kultur*, vol. 5. Stuttgart, Weimar: Metzler, 2014, 202–209. / **Diner, Dan.** "Zwischenzeit 1945 bis 1949. Über jüdische und andere Konstellationen." *Aus Politik und Zeitgeschichte* 65.16–17 (2015), 16–20. / **Diner, Dan.** "Banished: Jews in Germany after the Holocaust." In *A History of Jews in Germany since 1945. Politics, Culture, and Society*, ed. Michael Brenner. Bloomington: Indiana University Press, 2019, 7–53. / **Diner, Dan,** and **Jonathan Frankel,** eds. *Dark Times, Dire Decisions. Jews and Communism* (Studies in Contemporary Jewry, vol. 20). Oxford: Oxford University Press, 2005. / **Ehrenburg, Ilya.** "Die Sowjetunion, der Staat Israel und die Lösung der 'jüdischen Frage'. Anlässlich eines Briefes." *Neues Deutschland* no. 231, October 3, 1948, 3. / **Emmerich, Wolfgang.** "Buchenwald." in *Encyclopedia of Jewish History and Culture Online*, accessed June 14, 2019. http://dx.doi.org/10.1163/2468-8894_ejhc_COM_0124. / **Fabian, Hans-Erich.** "Israel–die Heimat eines Volkes." *Unser Appell* no. 11–12, September 12, 1948, 23. / **Grossmann, Atina.** "Rabbi Steven Schwarzschild's Reports from Berlin, 1948–1950." *Leo Baeck Institute Year Book* 60 (2015), 237–242. / **Hartewig, Karin.** *Zurückgekehrt. Die Geschichte der jüdischen Kommunisten in der DDR.* Cologne: Böhlau, 2000. / **Hartewig, Karin.** "Meyer, Julius." In *Wer war wer in der DDR? Ein Lexikon ostdeutscher Biographien*, ed. Helmut Müller-Enbergs et al. Accessed September 6, 2018. https://www.bundesstiftung-aufarbeitung.de/wer-war-wer-in-der-ddr-%2363%3B-1424.html?ID=2314. / **Heller, Otto.** *Der Untergang des Judentums. Die Judenfrage, ihre Kritik, ihre Lösung durch den Sozialismus.* Vienna, Berlin: Verlag für Literatur und Politik, 1931. / **Kahn, Siegbert.** *Antisemitismus und Rassenhetze. Eine Übersicht über ihre Entwicklung in Deutschland.* Berlin: Dietz, 1948. / **Mayer, Hans.** "Auschwitz." *Unser Appell* no. 15, December 1, 1948, 5–7. / **Merker, Paul.** "Hitlers Antisemitismus und wir." *Freies Deutschland* 1.12 (1942), 9–11. / **Merker, Paul.** *Deutschland – Sein oder Nicht Sein*, 2 vols. Mexico City: El libro libre, 1944/45. / **Moses, Siegfried.** *Die jüdischen Nachkriegs-Forderungen.* Tel Aviv: Bitaon, 1944. / **Pisarek, Abraham.** *Jüdisches Leben in Berlin/Jewish Life in Berlin, 1933–1941*, edited with an essay by Joachim Schlör. Berlin: Edition Braus, 2012. / **Reuter, Elke,** and **Detlef Hansel.** *Das kurze Leben der VVN von 1947 bis 1953.* Berlin: edition ost, 1997. / **Robinson, Nehemiah.** *Indemnification and Reparations. Jewish Aspects.* New York: Institute of Jewish Affairs, 1944. / **Spannuth, Jan Philipp.** *Rückerstattung Ost. Der Umgang der DDR mit dem „arisierten" Eigentum der Juden und die Rückerstattung im wiedervereinigten Deutschland.* Essen: klartext, 2007. / **Stalin, Joseph V.** "Marxism and the National Question." In Joseph V. Stalin, *Works*, vol. 2. Moscow: Foreign Languages Publishing House, 1953, 300–381. / **Unikower, Inge.** *Suche nach dem gelobten Land. Die fragwürdigen Abenteuer des kleinen Gerschon.* Berlin: Verlag der Nation, 1978. / "Unser Kommentar zum Harlan-Prozeß." *Die Tat* no. 9, May 4, 1949, 3. / "Das wahre Berlin steht im Weltlager des Friedens." *Neues Deutschland* no. 214, September 14, 1948, 1. / **Weigelt, Andreas.** "'Der zionistische Agent Julius Meyer und seine Auftraggeber...' Julius Meyer (1909–1979)." In *Zwischen Bleiben und Gehen. Juden in Ostdeutschland 1945 bis 1956. Zehn Biographien*, ed. Andreas Weigelt and Hermann Simon. Berlin: edition berlin, 2008, 73–129. / "Wieder Reichstagsbrandstifter." *Neues Deutschland* no. 211, September 10, 1948, 1. / "Der Zentralvorstand der VVN für die sowjetische Besatzungszone." *Unser Appell* no. 5, March 20, 1948, 7. / **Zuckermann, Leo.** "Restitution und Wiedergutmachung." *Weltbühne* no. 17, April 27, 1948, 430–432. / **Zuckermann, Leo.** "Die Bedeutung des VdN-Gesetzes." *Unser Appell* no. 7, May 15, 1948, 1.

BERLIN (EAST)
THE CITY OF JEWISH COMRADES

ERIK RIEDEL

> The creation of a democratic Germany presents German Jews with
> a new opportunity and new hope that they will be able to fight side
> by side with the progressive forces in Germany too.
>
> Wilhelm Pieck in December 1947[1]

Of the roughly 160,000 Jews who lived in Berlin in 1933, approximately 8,000
were still alive at the end of the war. Most of them had escaped deportation
thanks to their "privileged mixed marriages" to non-Jewish spouses. Some 1,900
Jews from Berlin had survived in various camps and somewhere between 1,400
and 1,700 of those hiding in Berlin were still alive when the Red Army liberated
the city.[2]

As soon as the last remaining German commander in Berlin had capitula-
ted, on May 2, 1945, the Soviet Military Administration in Germany (*Sowjetische
Militäradministration in Deutschland*, SMAD) began to restore the functions of
administration and infrastructure, including public transport. By the end of May,
the Soviet commander of the city had appointed a new municipal authority, the
Magistrat, as well as the requisite civil servants, most of whom were members
of the Communist Party. Hence, when the western Allies arrived in Berlin in
July 1945 and took over the parts of the city they had been assigned at the Yalta
Conference, a functioning administration was already in place. Berlin was now
governed jointly by the four Allied commanders in the city.

The Jewish community in Berlin likewise began to resume its activities
within weeks of the war ending. Alongside its religious life, it focused primarily on providing assistance for the survivors and the East European Displaced
Persons (DPs) streaming into the city. Initially, the impact of the division between
the eastern and western halves of the city was negligible. Although the blockade
of 1948-49 intensified tensions between east and west, separate Jewish communities were not established until 1953.

Kosher butcher shop "for Jewish customers only,"
Berlin, 1947. Photo: Fritz Eschen, Deutsche Fotothek
SLUB Dresden

Front door with a yellow star and provisional name plate
(Emil Israel Blumenfeld), 1947. The Star of David was
perhaps a silent protest against the fact that Jews were
not recognized in the Soviet occupation zone as a distinct
group among "Victims of Fascism." Photo: Fritz Eschen,
Deutsche Fotothek SLUB Dresden

However, the division of the city into four sectors did have one important, more or less immediate effect: many communist and socialist Jews who returned from exile after the war intentionally headed for East Berlin in order to participate in the creation of a new society there. Most of them were secular in orientation and not members of the official Jewish community. For all that, they sought to integrate into the emerging socialist society. Their Jewish background, however, did occasionally cause problems even before Stalin unleashed his antisemitic campaigns of the early 1950s.[3] "In certain social and political contexts, the biographies of Jewish communists and the persecution their families had endured surfaced and infringed on political and ideological narratives and taboos."[4]

COMMUNITY AND PARTY

The Soviet occupation zone, which would go on to become the GDR, understood itself as being fundamentally antifascist in orientation, as the "other" Germany which derived its legitimacy from the persecution suffered by National Socialism's political opponents and their resistance. However, this emphasis on political persecution and resistance led to a marginalization of other victim groups, including the Jews. As early as July 15, 1945, the official Jewish community felt the need to appeal to the occupation authorities:

> We therefore request that our liberators grant us the assistance they
> promised us. In particular, we request for it to be arranged that the
> Jews who a) were imprisoned in concentration camps, b) had to go
> into hiding when pursued by the Gestapo, c) were compelled to wear
> the Yellow Star, as well as their wives and children, are treated as victims
> of National Socialism and receive the same status, in every respect,
> as the Victims of Fascism.[5]

Immediately after the war, those recognized as "Victims of Fascism" (*Opfer des Faschismus*, OdF) received vital benefits like additional food rations. At first, only those who had engaged in active resistance were granted this status by the relevant committees. Only from October 1945 onwards, following a heated public debate, were the victims of "racial" persecution also included in this category. However, a distinction was now introduced between "Victims of Fascism" and "Fighters against Fascism," placing the latter in a privileged position.[6]

The status of the Jewish Victims of Fascism and the related issues of compensation and restitution illustrate the potential for conflict that existed between the official Jewish community and the communist regime from the outset. The

Soviets refused the restitution of property confiscated by the National Socialist state. Given the large number of exiled Jews who lived in capitalist countries, it was feared that this would weaken the emerging socialist order. Although the SED, the communist party that would govern the GDR from 1949 onwards, in fact approved compensation legislation, the law was not ratified after the GDR had been established in 1949.[7]

On the other hand, Jewish community officials were appointed to administrative positions, for example, in the municipal authority's committee for Victims of Fascism, where Heinz Galinski, Julius Meyer, and a number of other officials worked for the department dealing with the fallout from the Nuremberg Laws. One should not think of this simply as a form of instrumentalization by the regime since these community officials made a serious attempt to use their position within organizations such as the Association of Persecutees of the Nazi Regime (*Vereinigung der Verfolgten des Naziregimes*, VVN) to advance the causes of the Jewish community. In the immediate postwar years, then, Jewishness and socialism did not necessarily seem to be incompatible in East Berlin. Indeed, a number of Jews held important positions within the regime. Among them were Alexander Abusch, who was a member of SED's party executive and headed one of the departments of the Cultural League (*Kulturbund*), and Leo Zuckermann, who went on to serve as chief of staff to the GDR's first president, Wilhelm Pieck, and who coauthored the GDR's constitution.

DISPLACED PERSONS AND RETURNEES

Numerous DPs arrived in Berlin as soon as the war ended. Three DP camps were established in the city's western sectors: Mariendorf and Schlachtensee (Düppel) in the American sector and Wittenau in the French sector. In November 1946, roughly 7,800 DPs lived in these camps.[8] Until 1948, Berlin was the single most important gateway for Jewish DPs coming to Germany. There were no DP camps in the Soviet sector, and the two transit camps initially established by the Jewish community in the districts Mitte and Pankow were closed again in early 1946.[9]

Most of the Jewish DPs were either survivors of the concentration camps or East European Jews who had fled the advancing Germans and survived in the Soviet Union. At this time, they were fleeing the increasing antisemitism in Eastern Europe epitomized by the pogrom in Kielce in July 1946. In addition, in the summer of 1947, some 300 Jews who had originally lived in Berlin returned to the city from Shanghai.[10]

The fact that the Jewish community supported Jewish refugees from the People's Republic of Poland and the Soviet Union created tensions with the

Julius Meyer (left) with Heinz Galinski at the "Memorial
Day for the Victims of Fascism" at Berlin's Lustgarten,
1948. Photo: Abraham Pisarek, Deutsche Fotothek
SLUB Dresden

Soviet Military Administration. Some of the community's officials supported the *Bricha*, those organizations that were helping Jews from the socialist states in Eastern Europe migrate to the western occupation zones so they could move to Palestine from there. The Soviet authorities responded by arresting some of the community's officials. The former chairman, Erich Nelhans, and Fritz Katten, a member of the community's executive board, were arrested, charged at Soviet military courts with anti-Soviet activities and with abetting the treason of Soviet citizens, and given long prison sentences. After two years in captivity, Nelhans died in a Soviet camp. Katten was released in 1956 and allowed to move to West Germany.[11]

When tensions between the western Allies and SMAD escalated in the summer of 1948, the Soviets blockaded Berlin. All roads, railway lines, and waterways leading to the western sectors were closed off to both passengers and goods. Given this precarious situation, the western Allies closed the DP camps in the city in September 1948. While supplying West Berlin via the so-called airlift (*Luftbrücke*), American and British aircrafts evacuated the DPs to West Germany.

EXODUS

The situation of the Jewish organizations became increasingly difficult from 1948 onwards. The blockade of Berlin and the creation of the State of Israel, followed by the establishment of separate West and East German states, were the most obvious milestones in this process of escalation. Zionism now became a bogeyman, and the contacts Jewish community officials maintained with international aid organizations such as the JDC were presented as forms of collaboration with capitalist forces abroad, or even as instances of espionage on behalf of western powers. In early 1953, the conflict culminated in the flight of some 600 Jews, including many members of the various official Jewish communities' executive boards. The Jewish community in East Berlin continued to dwindle in subsequent years and, for the longest time, it went without a rabbi of its own. By 1989, the community had no more than 250 members.[12]

[1] Press statement by SED chairman Wilhelm Pieck, December 3, 1947, in response to the recommendation of the UN General Assembly to partition Palestine, Bundesarchiv Berlin, Stiftung Parteien und Massenorganisationen der DDR, DY 30/IV 2/4/Bd. 112, Bl. 377, cited in Andreas Weigelt, "Leo Zuckermann (1908–1985)," in *Zwischen Bleiben und Gehen. Juden in Ostdeutschland 1945 bis 1955. Zehn Biographien*, ed. Andreas Weigelt and Simon Hermann (Berlin: edition berlin, 2008), 216.

[2] See Gabriel E. Alexander, "Berlin," in *Encyclopedia of the Holocaust*, ed. Israel Gutman et al. (New York: Macmillan, 1990), 202; Atina Grossmann, *Jews, Germans, and Allies: Close Encounters in Occupied Germany* (Princeton: Princeton University Press, 2007), 88, 303.

Arrival of Jewish returnees from Shanghai in the
Teltower Damm transit camp in Berlin-Zehlendorf,
1947. Photo: Henry Ries, © Henry Ries / Deutsches
Historisches Museum, Berlin

A cargo plane approaching Tempelhof airport
during the Berlin airlift, 1948. Photo: Henry Ries,
© Henry Ries / Deutsches Historisches Museum, Berlin

[3] After 1948, several party purges were carried out in the communist parties in Stalin's sphere of influence. These purges took an openly antisemitic turn at the end of 1952 and also led to a series of measures against alleged "Zionist agents" in the GDR. See Karin Hartewig, *Zurückgekehrt. Die Geschichte der jüdischen Kommunisten in der DDR* (Cologne: Böhlau, 2000), 315–386; Angelika Timm, *Hammer, Zirkel, Davidstern. Das gestörte Verhältnis der DDR zu Zionismus und Staat Israel* (Bonn: Bouvier, 1997), 98–126.

[4] Karin Hartewig, *Zurückgekehrt,* 106.

[5] Archiv der Stiftung Neue Synagoge Berlin – Centrum Judaicum, CJA, 5A1, 0045, Bl. 43/45.

[6] Angelika Timm, *Hammer, Zirkel, Davidstern,* 51–53.

[7] On this, see Philipp Graf's contribution to this volume.

[8] Grossmann, *Jews, Germans, and Allies*, 120.

[9] Arolsen Archives. International Center on Nazi Persecution: Verzeichnis der DP-Lager, accessed June 14, 2019, https://dpcampinventory.its-arolsen.org/uebersicht-zonen/berlin-westsektoren/dp-camps. In addition, the Jewish community ran a children's home in the district of Niederschönhausen from 1945 to 1952, which housed many DP children (though it was not exclusively for them).

[10] Georg Armbrüster, "Das Ende des Exils in Shanghai. Rück- und Weiterwanderungen nach 1945," in *Exil Shanghai 1938–1947. Jüdisches Leben in der Emigration*, ed. Georg Armbrüster et al. (Teetz: Hentrich & Hentrich, 2000), 190–191.

[11] Andreas Weigelt, "Fritz Katten (1898–1964)," in *Zwischen Bleiben und Gehen,* ed. Andreas Weigelt and Simon Hermann, 55–74; Andreas Weigelt, "Erich Nelhans (1899–1950)," in *Zwischen Bleiben und Gehen,* ed. Andreas Weigelt and Simon Hermann, 131–161.

[12] "Von Komitees in Besatzungszonen zum zentralen Dachverband. Die Geschichte des Zentralrats der Juden in Deutschland," Zentralrat der Juden in Deutschland, accessed June 14, 2019, https://www.zentralratderjuden.de/der-zentralrat/geschichte/.

JULIUS MEYER
(1909–1979)

Julius Meyer was born in Krojanke (West Prussia) in 1909. In 1930, having trained as a leather worker, he joined the communist party (KPD). He moved to Berlin in 1935, where he was arrested in February 1943. He was imprisoned in a number of concentration camps, including Auschwitz and Ravensbrück. The National Socialists murdered 83 of his relatives, including his wife and children.

From 1945 until 1953, he sat on the executive board of the official Jewish community in Berlin, serving as its chairman after 1946, and was president of the regional association (*Landesverband*) of Jewish communities in the Soviet occupation zone after 1947. In addition, Meyer was in charge of the department dealing with the repercussions of the Nuremberg Laws under the auspices of the municipal authority's committee for Victims of Fascism (*Opfer des Faschismus*, OdF) in Berlin. He also served on the board of the Association of Persecutees of the Nazi Regime (*Vereinigung der Verfolgten des Naziregimes*, VVN), a group which he likewise represented in the GDR's parliament (the *Volkskammer*).

Meyer was particularly interested in ensuring that Jews who had suffered persecution were compensated and officially recognized as "Victims of Fascism." In January 1953, as the impact of the antisemitic campaigns of Stalin's final years was increasingly felt in the GDR and elsewhere, he fled to West Berlin to avoid a scheduled interrogation. He had been denounced as a Zionist with numerous contacts in the West. Meyer then moved to Brazil, where he died in 1979. When applying for restitution in West Germany, his claim was initially rejected because of his membership in the SED and because he had been a deputy in the *Volkskammer*.

Julius Meyer celebrating *Pesach* with Jews from Berlin and soldiers of the four occupation powers in Schöneberg's Town Hall, 1946, Photo: Gerhard Gronefeld, © Gerhard Gronefeld/Deutsches Historisches Museum, Berlin

Julius Meyer at the commemoration in the Funkhaus under the theme "Kristallnacht", Berlin 1946. Photo: Abraham Pisarek, Deutsche Fotothek SLUB Dresden

Shabbat at the Meyers with American soldiers, 1945. Photo: Gerhard Gronefeld, © Gerhard Gronefeld/ Deutsches Historisches Museum, Berlin

ANNA SEGHERS
(1900–1983)

Anna Seghers was born into a traditional Jewish family in Mainz in 1900 as Anna (Netty) Reiling. In 1925, she married the Hungarian sociologist László Radványi. She published her first book, *Revolt of the Fishermen of Santa Barbara*, in 1928 under the pseudonym Anna Seghers. That same year, she also joined the communist party (KPD). She left the official Jewish community in 1932.

In 1934, Seghers fled to France. As the Germans advanced, she escaped first to the southern part of France not occupied by the Germans and eventually made it to Mexico. It was there that she found out about the genocide perpetrated against European Jewry, leading her to discuss the Jewish heritage of her family in two autobiographical essays. In 1944, the film version of her novel *The Seventh Cross*, starring Spencer Tracy, brought her international fame.

Seghers returned to Germany in 1947. She initially lived in West Berlin and joined the SED. That same year, she received Germany's most prestigious literary award, the Georg Büchner Prize. In April 1948, she visited the Soviet Union along with other artists. Although initially appalled at the conditions in Germany, Anna Seghers maintained her faith in the possibility of creating a better and more just world based on socialist principles.

She eventually moved to East Berlin in 1950 where she was appointed to the German Academy of Arts as one of its founding members. The following year, she received the National Prize of the GDR and travelled to China. She was the President of the East German Authors' Association (*Schriftstellerverband*) from 1952 to 1978. When she died in 1983, she was given a state funeral in the Academy of Arts and interred in the Dorotheenstädtische Friedhof, a cemetery in the heart of Berlin where many famous personalities are buried.

Anna Seghers outside her first home following her return from exile, a hotel near the Wannsee in West Berlin, April 27, 1947. Photo: Allgemeiner Deutscher Nachrichtendienst, Federal Archives, Germany

Anna Seghers receives one of the first certificates of appointment from Wilhelm Pieck at the ceremonial opening of the Academy of Arts of the GDR, March 24, 1950. Photo: Rudolph, Federal Archives, Germany

Provisional residence permit for Netty Radvanyi (Anna Seghers), dated July 26, 1947, issued by the aliens' branch of the Berlin police department. Citizenship is marked as "Mexico," under residence "Bln. [Berlin] -Wannsee, Am Landwerder 5." Akademie der Künste, Anna-Seghers-Archiv

PHOTOGRAPHERS IN BERLIN

ERIK RIEDEL

In the immediate postwar years, a number of remarkable photographers were working in Berlin. Their images are not only exceptional historical documents but also illustrate the backdrop against which photographers captured Jews and Jewish motifs in their photos at the time.

Abraham Pisarek (1901–1983) had been close to the communist party during the Weimar years and worked for a number of publications including the *Arbeiter-Illustrierte-Zeitung*. Under the Nazi regime, he could work only in the orbit of the Jewish community. He was the sole photographer accredited with the Jewish Cultural League in Berlin and with the five Jewish newspapers licensed to appear until 1941. Subsequently, he was assigned to forced labor but avoided deportation thanks to his "privileged mixed marriage" to a non-Jewish woman. In the Soviet occupation zone, Pisarek was employed as a press photographer and then especially as a theater photographer.[1]

Henry (originally Heinz) Ries (1917–2004) fled to the U.S. in 1937–38. In the Second World War, he joined the U.S. Air Force, where he trained as a specialist in aerial photography. He eventually returned to Berlin, the city of his birth, with the American occupation forces. While working for the U.S. army, he covered the Nuremberg Trials of major war criminals, events in postwar Berlin, as well as the fate of the 4,500 refugees on board the Exodus, a ship that the British forced to return to Europe after it had reached the coast of Palestine. Ries' book of photos portraying the defeated German population, *German Faces*, became a bestseller in the United States.[2]

Gerhard Gronefeld (1911–2000) worked as a war reporter for the propaganda battalion of the Wehrmacht. Though not Jewish, in the immediate postwar years he created several series of photos documenting Jewish life in Berlin. These included photo essays for various papers and magazines as well as private photographs. For example, he shadowed Julius Meyer, a member of the community's executive board, and his family for several years. In the 1950s, Gronefeld specialized in animal photography.[3]

Jewish community building in Rosenstraße, after 1945.
Photo: Abraham Pisarek, Deutsche Fotothek, SLUB
Dresden. The community center was destroyed during
an air raid. It was here that the Rosenstraße Protests
took place in which hundreds of women in "mixed
marriages" managed to prevent their husbands'
deportation in 1943.

Fritz Eschen (1900–1964) worked as a freelance journalist for various agencies, beginning in 1928. Following his expulsion from the Reich Association of the German Press in late 1933, he was reduced to occasional commissions from American agencies, which he could not publish under his name. Like Pisarek, he too was arrested and assigned to forced labor, only to avoid deportation and survive in Berlin thanks to a "privileged mixed marriage." After the war, Eschen was a freelance photo journalist for various papers and magazines in Berlin.[4]

Eva Kemlein (1909–2004) worked as a science and travel photographer. Under the Nazi regime she made ends meet as a laborer, working at a number of places including Siemens. To escape deportation, she and her partner went underground in 1942. They had to switch hideouts more than 30 times. When they were finally liberated, they had been hiding in a basement in the district of Schöneberg. After the war, Kemlein worked for the newly established *Berliner Zeitung* and became a cross-border commuter, living in West Berlin but working in East Berlin. As a theater photographer, she documented all the important productions on East Berlin's stages.[5]

[1] See Kerstin Delang et al., "Pisarek, Abraham," Deutsche Fotothek, accessed August 5, 2019, http://www.deutschefotothek.de/documents/kue/90011828.

[2] Henry Ries, *Ich war ein Berliner. Erinnerungen eines New Yorker Fotojournalisten* (Berlin: Parthas, 2001); Henry Ries, *Berlin: Photographien 1946–1949* (Berlin: Nicolai, 1998); Henry Ries, *Photographien aus Berlin, Deutschland und Europa 1946–1951* (Berlin: Berlinische Galerie, 1988).

[3] Winfried Ranke, *Deutsche Geschichte kurz belichtet. Photoreportagen von Gerhard Gronefeld 1937–1965* (Berlin: Nicolai, 1991).

[4] See "Eschen, Fritz," Deutsche Fotothek, accessed August 5, 2019, http://www.deutschefotothek.de/documents/kue/90023707.

[5] See *"Berlin lebt auf!" Die Fotojournalistin Eva Kemlein*, ed. Anna Fischer and Chana Schütz (Berlin: Hentrich & Hentrich, 2016); Eva Kemlein and Ingeborg Pietzsch, *Eva Kemlein. Ein Leben mit der Kamera* (Berlin: Edition Hentrich, 1998).

Return of Berlin Jews from Shanghai, 1947.
Photo: Henry (Heinz) Ries, © Henry Ries / Deutsches
Historisches Museum, Berlin. The spontaneity
of the photo is clearly demonstrated by the raw
emotions it captures.

Reunion of two Jewish concentration camp survivors,
1945. Photo: Gerhard Gronefeld, © Gerhard Gronefeld
/ Deutsches Historisches Museum, Berlin. This photo
was taken in August 1945 for the article "Dem Leben
wiedergegeben" (Back to Life), in which the *Deutsche
Volkszeitung* presented some examples of the fates
of Jewish survivors. As a closer look at the clothing
of those portrayed reveals, the images were carefully
staged.

Two young women reading the paper on a bench which,
as stipulated by the sign above, had been prohibited
to Jews, Berlin, 1945. Photo: Fritz Eschen, Deutsche
Fotothek, SLUB Dresden. The photo illustrates that the
traces of Nazi ideology by no means simply disappeared
after the war. While swastikas were promptly removed
from public buildings, traces of the recent persecution
were initially overlooked in less prominent locations.

Black market on Friedrichstraße, Berlin 1945.
Photo: Eva Kemlein, Stiftung Stadtmuseum Berlin,
reproduction: Friedhelm Hoffmann. The black market
as an important part of Berlin's post-war lifestyle was
captured by theater photographer Eva Kemlein. She
had survived the persecution in hiding in Berlin.

ON THE RECONSTRUCTION OF JEWISH CULTURE
IN GERMANY'S AMERICAN OCCUPATION ZONE

TAMAR LEWINSKY

In 1949, the renowned photographer Chim (David Seymour) captured a street scene in Munich. Taken in Möhlstraße, a street in a once grand and exclusive residential area in the Bogenhausen neighborhood, the photograph shows a kiosk in a wooden shack squeezed between a kosher restaurant and a one-story dry goods store. A large billboard above the kiosk's sales window reads (in Yiddish): "Jew! Only Buy Your Paper Here! And, In So Doing, Support The Jewish National Fund." Beneath the teasers with top news stories and poorly pasted Yiddish posters one can recognize the three letters KKL–*Keren Kayemet LeIsrael*–on the detachable shutters.

The photograph reveals a more than merely documentary interest in Möhlstraße and its Jewish infrastructure. As David Szymin, Chim had grown up among the Yiddish and Hebrew books of his father, a well-respected Jewish publisher in Warsaw,[1] and with his photo he tells the story of the destruction of a previously flourishing culture. Taken only a few months after the photographer finally found out for certain what had happened to his parents–they too had been murdered–this is one of the few photos by Chim that incorporates a Jewish motif.[2]

Far from just chronicling the measure of destruction wrought upon Jewish life in Germany, Chim's image of the wooden shack displays all the characteristics of Jewish culture in postwar occupied Germany: it was temporary in nature, inevitably improvised, Zionist in orientation, and predominantly Yiddish. Indeed, by the time he took the photo, little of that culture was left. Following the creation of the State of Israel and the loosening of immigration rules in the U.S. the year before, most of the DPs had left the U.S. occupation zone. This also held true for the small group of journalists, historians, authors, actors, mu-

Möhlstraße, Munich, 1949. On the kiosk in the middle, the Yiddish sign says: "Jew! Only Buy Your Paper Here! And, In So Doing, Support The Jewish National Fund." The original title of the photo was "Milch-strasse." Photo: Chim (David Seymour), Jewish Museum Berlin

sicians, and artists, as well as the considerably larger group of laypeople. All of those involved had facilitated the short-lived revival of Jewish culture in, of all places, Germany.

This transitional culture had begun to flourish four years earlier but had its roots in the years of persecution. Just three weeks after the liberation of Buchenwald, as the war was still ongoing, a Yiddish paper was published at the camp in early May 1945. It bore the programmatic title *Tkhies hameysim* (*Resurrection of the Dead*) and was created by former prisoners who had secretly held classes for the children in Buchenwald. They wanted their paper to mark the beginning of a new press that would pass on the legacy of Jewish culture.[3]

Two months later, *Nitsots* (*Spark*) began to appear. Established in the Lithuanian city of Kaunas by members of a Zionist youth organization, the Hebrew periodical had initially been published under Soviet occupation. Following the German invasion in the summer of 1941, it was continued in the ghetto until the editors were deported to southern Germany. There, they produced a further seven issues under the unimaginable conditions of life in one of Dachau's subsidiary camps. The first issue following their liberation was published at the Upper Bavarian Benedictine monastery of St. Ottilien. A fluke of history had now turned the monastery into a DP hospital and the nucleus of Jewish self-organization in the American occupation zone.[4]

Survivors of Dachau also laid the foundation stone for the regular Yiddish press. On October 12, 1945, the first issue of *Undzer veg* (*Our Way*) came out in Munich. It was, as the header stated, the official paper of the Central Committee of the "liberated Jews in the German diaspora." Apart from one substantial interruption, it was published once or twice a week until 1950 in print runs of up to 20,000 copies.[5] And outside the former capital of the National Socialist movement, periodicals of varying format and quality emerged in numerous DP camps dotted all over the occupation zone. Their editors were motivated by the desire to satisfy, at least in part, the hunger for information and reading material among the survivors stranded in Germany. By the time the DP camps were dissolved, more than one hundred papers and magazines had been published.[6]

This is all the more remarkable, given the technical conditions under which the first papers were produced. Like *Nitsots* and *Tkhies hameysim*, most of the local papers published in the U.S. occupation zone had to be painstakingly written and copied by hand. The Yiddish typewriter that the founders of the Yiddish paper *Undzer lebn* (*Our Life*) in Berlin had at their disposal was a rare luxury indeed. This time of scarcity and inevitable improvisation led to a unique episode in the history of Yiddish publications: Given the dearth of Hebrew printers' type (which is also required for Yiddish texts), many of the papers were printed in Latin script following Polish orthography.[7]

From 1947 onwards, virtually all the local periodicals were superseded by the Zionist party press. Under the influence of emissaries from Palestine and the already politicized Polish refugees who flooded into the U.S. zone of occupation in large numbers, especially after the bloody pogrom in Kielce, the political spectrum within the DP community became more diverse. The unitary Zionist party formed at the outset of the self-organization process was now replaced by a number of Zionist groups that largely corresponded to the parties in the *Yishuv* and published their own papers for their respective supporters. These papers were produced in Munich. It was there, especially in Möhlstraße, that not only the occupation authorities, the aid organizations, and the institutions of Jewish self-organization, but also the Zionist parties had set up their offices. The city on the Isar thus emerged as the DPs' unofficial capital. Its buzzing center in Bogenhausen became the port of call for the thousands of Jews in the city and the DPs in the refugee facilities in the greater Munich area, some 75,000 people in all.[8]

The content of the party papers largely corresponded to that of their eponymous Hebrew sister papers in the *Yishuv*. Often, articles were transferred more or less unchanged. Its political reporting aside, the party press in Germany, like its local predecessors, was also characterized by the central role it allotted to history, art, and literature. The feature pages consisted of articles about Jewish history, excerpts from East European Yiddish literature, specialist articles, short stories, and memoirs. By closely merging journalistic and didactic goals, they sought to contribute to the education of the DPs.[9]

Yiddish played a crucial role in this context. It was not only the most common linguistic denominator within the heterogeneous refugee community but it also positioned the DPs, many of whom had enjoyed only a rudimentary education due to the war, within a specific cultural tradition. To be sure, the Zionist parties would much rather have undertaken their political and cultural activities in Hebrew. Yet, much like the socialist Zionists of the interwar years, they had been compelled by the incompatibility of ideal and reality to take a pragmatic stance. Officially, then, the DPs subscribed to the pre-war notion that Yiddish was the language of the present and Hebrew the language of the future. Only once the DPs had grasped the basics would it be possible to proceed to educate them in accordance with the precepts of Jewish nationalism and Zionism.[10]

From the outset, the feature pages of this press also offered a forum to literary authors. In part, the presentation of literary texts, whether created by DPs or taken from the canon of classical Jewish or world literature in translation, reflected a longstanding tradition in Yiddish periodical publishing. The Yiddish press, whether in Poland, Lithuania, or the U.S., had traditionally included texts of this kind in every issue. It nevertheless seems paradoxical that the Zionist press in Germany both made use of Yiddish and effectively acted as a midwife to the publication of newly created Yiddish literary texts at a time when the

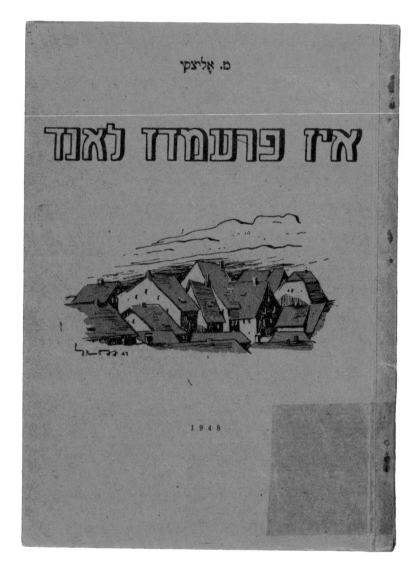

The poetry book *In fremdn land (In a Foreign
Country)* by Mates Olitski (1915–2008). This book,
published in Eschwege in Hesse in 1947, focuses on
the encounter between displaced persons and the
foreign and hated country of Germany. Olitski had
survived in the Soviet Union and returned to Poland
in 1946; from there, he went to the American zone of
Germany. Johann Christian Senckenberg University
Library, Goethe University, Frankfurt

Yiddish language and literary tradition were subject to harsh criticism in the *Yishuv*. There Yiddish was routinely denounced as the shameful tongue of the diaspora.[11]

Over time, some of the short stories and poems that had first appeared in the DP press also came out in book form. By the time the DP camps were dissolved, some thirty volumes of poetry and prose had been published in the U.S. occupation zone. Quite a few of them appeared with small party publishers originally established to supply the DPs with basic political texts.[12]

Some of the writers–mostly men, for female voices are missing from nearly all cultural activities in the DP camps–had already published in the 1930s. Others only began to write after the war. Either way, during their sojourn in Germany all of them grappled with the Holocaust, the war years, and their current situation. Writing to articulate their own personal experiences, they created a literary corpus reflecting the consequences of the persecution and annihilation of European Jewry across its full geographical range–from Dachau to Samarkand. Their poems and short stories treated all aspects of East European Jewry's experiences from the interwar period up to that time. Consistently negotiating the line between wartime and postwar literature, their works arguably amount to the earliest contributions to Holocaust literature.

How to approach the recently endured catastrophe with literary techniques was hotly debated by the members of the Writers' Association, which had been established as one of numerous professional organizations. Transpiring long before Adorno's famous contention that it was barbaric to write poetry after Auschwitz, these discussions hinged on purely aesthetic issues. Benjamin Harshav, who had survived the war in the Urals and was barely nineteen when he was able to publish his first volume of poetry in Munich, and who went on to become a professor of literature, subsequently recalled that "assimilated German Jews in the comfort of American universities could afford to say: How can you write poetry after Auschwitz? *Yidishe yidn* knew that you can, always could, and have to."[13]

An untitled poem by Shloyme Vorzogers who, like many of his colleagues, had survived the Second World War in the Soviet Union, may illustrate how Yiddish authors sought to find an adequate form:

> Too soon–to forget this shock,
> Too deep–to close, mend, and heal,
> There's no language–for this ordeal,
> No apt measure–to take stock.
> Nor is there–a name…
> Ev'ry word–blasphemy——
> Oh, give me strength, God–to stay silent.[14]

Yet the desire to write also had the potential to blur the lines between literature and witnessing. This distinction between fiction and memory was of immediate relevance to the DPs since historical commissions in the American occupation zone had begun in the autumn of 1945; their work was to create as accurate and comprehensive a record as possible of the events that would later be subsumed under the heading of the Shoah or the Holocaust. For the time being, they were referred to, in Hebrew, as the *Khurban* or, in Yiddish, the *Khurbn* (Destruction).[15] Soon after the establishment of the Historical Commission in Munich, its director, Israel Kaplan, following the imperative to collect and document, appealed to the Jewish public, listing the range of documents DPs could contribute to facilitate the recording of their traumatic history.[16]

Initial results of the work to that point were already presented in the inaugural, 36-page issue of the historical journal, *Fun letstn khurbn* (*On the Most Recent Destruction*), which appeared in August 1946. It included essays by the editors on the activities and goals of the commission, a bibliography, and a progress report, the first part of a study on the ghetto in Vilna, a selection of eyewitness accounts, poems written during the Holocaust, National Socialist documents, as well as photographs. In addition, Kaplan presented an initial selection of expressions used in the ghettos and concentration camps, a veritable secret language, which he later published in book form as *Dos folks-moyl in natsi-klem* (*Folk Expression under the Nazi Yoke*).[17]

It was the journal's declared goal to animate the DPs to play their part in documenting the Holocaust with their recollections, documents, and museum-worthy objects. After all, where might one more successfully gather such material, if not in the DP camps? As Israel Kaplan remarked at the Conference of the Historical Commissions in Germany in 1947, every DP had history on the tip of his tongue: "All one needs is an ear. Let us collect and preserve!" In the DP camps, the survivors lived together and were able to compare their recollections. Once their community was dissolved, it was rather more difficult to tap into this pool of collective experience.[18]

In practice, it was not always easy to persuade the DPs to participate. The historical commissions therefore initiated a systematic campaign to appeal to the survivors' moral conscience. Alongside the calls to submit material that were published in their journal, they also placed ads in the press on a regular basis, and circulated posters and flyers, appealing to the DPs to contribute to this national documentation project. In 1947, the Central Historical Commission in Munich announced an art competition for the design of a publicity poster.[19] There were two winners. One of them was the young artist Pinchas Schwarz (who later Hebraized his name to Shaar). His design, which was printed in color and displayed in the offices of the commission on Möhlstraße and various DP camps, shows the torso of a dead man. A scroll unfurled across his chest bears

Poster that says: "Helft shraybn di geshikhte fun
letstn khurbn" (Help write the history of the recent
destruction), Pinkas Schwarz, Munich, 1947.
This poster won a graphic design competition announced by the Jewish historical commissions
in the American zone of Germany. The poster was
designed to encourage survivors to collect and
share their memories and documents about survival.
Jewish Museum Berlin

the first words of the biblical book of Esther: "It happened in the days…" A quill and ink are on hand to continue the narrative of persecution and liberation into the present. The main text, in large letters, reads: "Help us write the history of the most recent destruction."

The history of the image is no less remarkable than its emotive force. The naked torso was based on the photograph of a man who had died of starvation and that was taken by Mendel Grossman, a photographer in the ghetto in Łódź. Grossman and Schwarz were close friends and, on the eve of the war, had collaborated on a number of projects. When their deportation from the ghetto was imminent, they hid tens of thousands of negatives, several hundred prints, and the Leica Grossman had used to document Jewish life and suffering in Łódź. Grossman did not survive the war, but Schwarz returned to Łódź after his liberation and was able to salvage some of the prints. Among them was the image he used for the design of the poster.[20]

Along with ten other artists, Schwarz belonged to a group that had established its own section within the Writers' Association. Their work was impeded by the scarcity of painting and drawing materials. More unusual supplies, such as a substantial amount of plaster for the creation of a bust of Herzl, were particularly hard to come by. The preparations for a planned art exhibition in Munich therefore had to be made far in advance. In the autumn of 1948, five artists (one of them female) were finally able to present a total of 165 works of various genres in the municipal Lenbachhaus gallery. The works exhibited by Schwarz included models for stage sets he had designed for Yiddish theaters in the DP camp in Feldafing and in Munich. One of the reviewers noted his many talents but complained that he was spreading himself too thin. Yet this could hardly be avoided given the small number of artists involved in these various activities of the DP community.[21]

Feldafing was the site of the first purely Jewish DP camp and home to the "Amkho" dramatic society whose founding members initially rehearsed in a basement room. They created a wide-ranging revue merging stage dialogues, lines from songs, and stories they recalled in new ways. They had to reconstruct the texts from memory, with few suitable props at their disposal, and often the actors had no more theater experience than the audience. It would therefore have been difficult to produce anything other than this sort of often loosely connected succession of skits. Yet their revue also offered a distant echo of the Yiddish cabaret that had combined song and dance, satirical sketches, and skits to great success in interwar Poland. There were roughly sixty such amateur societies in the western occupation zones. Many of the smaller groups performed scenes created by the celebrated acting duo Dzigan and Schumacher and the Ararat and Azazel cabarets. Yet they also produced their own shows, satirizing novel topics including life in the DP camps.[22]

The Yiddish theater in Munich was a professional ensemble initially established in Lower Silesia by actors who had studied with the renowned Shlomo Mikhoels and managed to survive in the Soviet Union. The *Bricha* movement had transferred them, along with some of the props, to Germany. In Munich they were joined by other professional actors. Under the artistic leadership of Israel Becker and Aleksander Bardini, the ensemble's program also sought to meet didactic goals. They performed both plays from the classical Yiddish repertoire and new productions. Since the DPs had little experience of attending theater performances, the ensemble organized a companion program of lectures, discussions, and literary events when it went on tour. There were even plans to establish a theater academy with its own curriculum to train amateur actors, but the undertaking ultimately did not come to fruition.[23]

In 1947, the troupe performed the Holocaust drama *Ikh leb* (*I am alive*) by Moyshe Pintshevsky. There was good reason for opting for a play that focused on the death camps. Polish Jews who had been repatriated from the Soviet Union now formed the majority of the DPs in the American occupation zone. Many of them had only begun to grasp the extent of the catastrophe on their return, and the play was meant to help them do so. In a private letter, Lucy Schildkret (who, as Lucy Dawidowicz, went on to become a well-known historian), offered an account of her conversation with the director and one of the performances in Munich: "[T]hey do not know what the death camps were like … Because of this, this particular play was put on. A sort of 'Lest we Forget' idea. The theatre itself, a rather famous German building, was packed; at least 1000 people, I would estimate; possibly more. Much weeping and sobbing throughout."[24]

The performances of the amateur drama societies in particular frequently combined theater and music. There had always been a close nexus between Yiddish theater and music, whether in Poland, the U.S., or Argentina. When an amateur choir began to rehearse in the DP camp in Feldafing at the same time as the Yiddish theater, it was taken for granted that the singers would also participate in the first drama production. On the night, the conferencier, Avrom Yoakhimovitsh, introduced them as the "first Yiddish choir in Bavaria."[25]

Given how few professional musicians there were among the DPs, the emergence of the Central Committee's Representative Orchestra was all the more remarkable. It toured throughout the American occupation zone with its repertoire of classical and Jewish music as well as Hebrew and Yiddish folk songs, and even performed with Leonard Bernstein in 1948. Its first concert took place within weeks of Germany's liberation, on May 27, 1945, in St. Ottilien. It was the first cultural event organized for DPs in Germany. Alongside a number of Military Government and UNRRA representatives, the audience comprised some 800 survivors residing in St. Ottilien or one of the other DP camps established in the vicinity of the liberated concentration camps. The event officially began with Grieg's *Triumphal March*. This was followed by a moving, trailblazing speech on the self-organization of the liberated Jews by the physician and future chair of their Central Committee, Zalman Grinberg. The concert then continued with two pieces by Bizet, Grieg's *Solveig's Song*, and several Jewish folk songs.[26]

The singer at the concert was Henia Durmaschkin who continued to perform with the orchestra in subsequent years. Her sister, the pianist Fania Durmashkin, also joined the small ensemble. Along with some of their fellow musicians, they had belonged to the orchestra in the Kaunas Ghetto led by their brother, the composer Wolf Durmashkin, who was later murdered in a camp. Henia Durmashkin performed both folk songs and songs from the ghetto. Two of the latter featured at a concert held for members of the International Military Tribunal and attendees of the Nuremberg Trials in the city's opera house. Its stage had repeatedly been used for the propagation of National Socialist propaganda, and the musicians staged their performance as an emotive appeal to the world's conscience. They wore striped uniforms and presented themselves as an "Ex-Concentration Camp-Orchestra."[27]

Following the establishment of the State of Israel in 1948, the DP camps were gradually shut down. With considerable irony, the DPs referred to this process as one of "liquidation." In this chaotic period, most of the cultural activities were discontinued. In 1949, the professional associations closed down and their members no longer received funding. To be sure, the artists and cultural workers had likewise hoped for an end to the DPs' limbo. Yet while the archive of the Historical Commission was brought to Israel, a substantial part of what had been integral to Jewish culture in postwar Germany was simply abandoned. The inventory of the Representative Theater, for example, was dumped in a back yard on Möhlstraße. As a mark of black humor, someone attached a poster for one of the ensemble's most successful productions, *Di hofenung* (*Hope*), to the props that had been so carelessly thrown away.[28]

The hopes of the cultural workers that they might be able to continue their artistic activities full-time after emigrating were rarely fulfilled. In many cases, we have lost all trace of those who, under difficult circumstances, had taken it upon themselves to preserve the remnants of an extinguished culture. It is owing to them that the transitory Jewish DP community, with its shared experiences and memories, was able to recover a measure of normality and cultural authority.

The St. Ottilien Ex-Concentration Camp-Orchestra
performs a concert in Munich, wearing striped
concentration camp uniforms, 1945–1946. The letters
at the front of the stage read "Am Yisrael Chai"
(The People of Israel Lives). United States Holocaust
Memorial Museum, Washington D.C., courtesy
of Sonia Beke

Purim in the Feldafing DP camp, 1946–1948. Jewish
DPs dressed up as Hitler and Goebbels, pretend to
beg for money. During the holiday of Purim, Jews celebrate their people's deliverance from the hands of
Haman, an official in ancient Persia, who wanted to kill
all the Jews in the Empire. Haman was often portrayed
as Hitler during celebrations in the postwar period.
United States Holocaust Memorial Museum,
Washington D.C., courtesy of Allen Rezak

Yiddish theater in the Feldafing DP camp, 1947–1948.
A performance of the play *Tevye*, based on Sholem
Aleichem's short stories about a pious Jewish
dairyman in Tsarist Russia. The photo is from the
collection of actress Leah Fischer (third from right).
United States Holocaust Memorial Museum,
Washington D.C., courtesy of Leah Zynger Fisher-Lee

1 Derived from his surname (Szymin), the photographer adopted the pseudonym Chim while living and working in Paris in the 1930s. He moved to New York in 1939 where he co-founded the Magnum Photo Agency after the war. When he was naturalized in the U.S. in 1943, he took the official name David Robert Seymour.

2 Cynthia Young, "We Went Back. Photographs from Europe 1933–1956 by Chim," in *We Went Back. Photographs from Europe 1933–1956 by Chim*, ed. Cynthia Young (Munich: Prestel, 2013) 46–47; Roger Cohen, "Actual Responsibility," *We Went Back*, ed. Cynthia Young, 56–58.

3 "Fun der redaktsye," *Tkhies hameysim* no. 1, May 4, 1945, 6; Yechiel Szeintuch, "'Tkhies hameysim'–ha-iton ha-rishon shel she'erit ha-peleta ve-orcho," *Chulyot* 10 (2006), 191–218.

4 Shlomo Shafir, "Ha-'Nitsots' she-lo kava," *Kesher* 9 (1991), 52–57; Ayin-Yud, "Mi-hektograf le-linotip," *Nitsots* no. 13 (80) (11 July 1947), 1–2; Zeev W. Mankowitz, *Life between Memory and Hope. The Survivors of the Holocaust in Occupied Germany* (Cambridge: Cambridge University Press, 2002), 30–31.

5 Tsemach Mosche Tsamriyon, *Ha'itonut shel she'erit hapeleta beGermania ke-bitui le-va'ayo-teha.* (Tel Aviv: Irgun She'erit hapeleta, 1970), 95.

6 Tamar Lewinsky, *Displaced Poets. Jiddische Schriftsteller im Nachkriegsdeutschland, 1945–1951* (Göttingen: Vandenhoeck & Ruprecht, 2008), 33–34.

7 Lewinsky, *Displaced Poets*, 35–36.

8 Lewinsky, *Displaced Poets*, 147–150. Anna Holian, "Die Möhlstraße und der Wiederaufbau jüdischen Wirtschaftslebens in Nachkriegsdeutschland," *Münchner Beiträge zur Jüdischen Geschichte und Kultur* 12.1 (2018), 23–34.

9 Lewinsky, *Displaced Poets*, 147–150.

10 Ezra Mendelsohn, *On Modern Jewish Politics* (New York: Oxford University Press, 1993), 30, 57; Tamar Lewinsky, "Kultur im Transit. Osteuropäisch-jüdische Displaced Persons," *Osteuropa* 8–10 (2008), 268–270.

11 Tom Segev, *One Palestine Complete* (New York: Metropolitan Books, 2000), 263–269.

12 Lewinsky, *Displaced Poets*, 68–69.

13 Benjamin Harshav, "Erinnerungsblasen," in *Unterbrochenes Gedicht. Jiddische Literatur in Deutschland 1944–1950*, ed. Tamar Lewinsky (Munich: Oldenbourg, 2011), VIII.

14 Shloyme Vorzoger, *Zayn. Lider* (Munich: Nayvelt, 1948), 35.

15 On this, see Elisabeth Gallas's contribution to this volume.

16 Laura Jockusch, *Collect and Record! Jewish Holocaust Documentation in Early Postwar Europe* (New York: Oxford University Press, 2012), 128–129; Israel Kaplan, "Zamlen un fart-seykhenen!" *Unzer veg* no. 12, December 21, 1945, 3.

17 *Fun letstn khurbn* 1 (1946); Israel Kaplan, *Dos folks-moyl in natsi-klem. reydenishn in geto un katset* (Munich: Tsentrale historishe komisye, 1949).

18 Jockusch, *Collect and Record*, 140. The quotation is from: Israel Kaplan, *In der tog-teglekher historisher arbet. Fortrag gehaltn af dem tsuzamenfor fun di historishe komisyes.* Munich: Tsentrale historishe komisye, 1947, 24.

19 Jockusch, *Collect and Record*, 141–145.

20 Pinchas Shaar, "Mendel Grossman. Photographic Bard of the Lodz Ghetto," in *Holocaust Chronicles. Individualizing the Holocaust Through Diaries and Other Contemporaneous Personal Accounts*, ed. Robert Moses Shapiro (Hoboken, N.J.: KTAV, 1999), 131–132, 134. Grossman's sister took the negatives and the camera to Palestine where they were lost in the turmoil of the Israeli War of Independence. The original print is now held by Yad Vashem.

21 Artists' Association to Philipp Auerbach, January 28, 1948, YIVO RG 294.2, Folder 1348; Correspondence of the Artists' Section with the Bavarian Ministry of the Interior, March 11, 1948, YIVO RG 294.2, Folder 1348; Minutes of the Writers' Association for April 21, 1947 and May 29, 1947, YIVO RG 294.2, Folder 1343; *Oysshtelung fun yidishe kinstler* (Munich: [Central Committee of the liberated Jews in the US occupation Zone, Cultural Affairs Department], 1948); Hans Eckstein, "Ausstellung jüdischer Künstler," *Süddeutsche Zeitung* no. 114, December 11, 1948, 2.

22 Avrom Yoakhomovitsh, "Vi azoy s'iz antshtanen der dram.-krayz 'amkho'," *Ilustrirter yoyvl-zhur-nal*, ed. Dram. krayz „Amcho" baym yidishn arbeter-komitet in Feldafing (Feldafing, 1946), 16.
23 Norbert Horovits, "Yidish teater in der sheyres hapleyte," in *Fun noentn over*, vol. 1 (New York: Congress for Jewish Culture, 1955), 114–117; Jacqueline Giere, "Wir sind unterwegs. Aber nicht in der Wüste. Erziehung und Kultur in den jüdischen Displaced Persons-Lagern der amerikanischen Zone im Nachkriegsdeutschland 1945–1949" (PhD diss., Goethe University Frankfurt, 1993), 198.
24 Lucy Schildkrecht, letter of November 17, 1946, American Jewish Historical Society P-675, box 55, folder 3. Cf. Lewinsky, *Displaced Poets*, 166–167.
25 Shteynman, "Di antshteyung un tetikayt fun khor," *Ilustrirter yoyvl-zhurnal*, 10. L. Fingerhut, "Nokhn khurbn," *Ilustrirter yoyvl-zhurnal*, 8.
26 Mankowitz, *Life between Memory and Hope*, 30–31; Angelika Königseder and Juliane Wetzel, *Lebensmut im Wartesaal. Die jüdischen DPs (Displaced Persons) im Nachkriegs-deutschland* (Frankfurt a. M.: Fischer, 1994), 81–85; Yoysef Gar, "Bafrayte yidn," in *Fun noentn over*, vol. 3 (New York: Congress for Jewish Culture, 1957), 186–187; "Programme of the Liberation-concert. Hospital for political ex-prisoners in Germany in St. Ottilien," accessed November 9, 2018. http://dphospital-ottilien.org/concert/.
27 Bret Werb, "'Vu ahin zol ikh geyn?': Music Culture of Jewish Displaced Persons," in *Dislocated Memories: Jews, Music, and Postwar German Culture*, ed. Tina Frühauf and Lily E. Hirsch (New York: Oxford University Press, 2014), 87–88; Wolf Durmashkin Award, accessed June 18, 2019, https://wdc-award.org/?page_id=2; Jewish Ex-Concentration Camp Orchestra program. Archive of the Jewish Museum Berlin, Inv.-Nr. 2015/367/1.
28 M. Volf, "A sheyres-hapleyte tog-bukh," *Naye yidishe tsaytung* no. 5, December 8, 1950.

BIBLIOGRAPHY

Ayin-Yud. "Mi-hektograf le-linotip." *Nitsots* no. 13 (80) (11 July 1947), 1–2. / **Cohen, Roger.** "Actual Responsibility." In *We Went Back. Photographs from Europe 1933–1956 by Chim*, ed. Cynthia Young, 53–59. Munich: Prestel, 2013. / **Eckstein, Hans.** "Ausstellung jüdischer Künstler." *Süddeutsche Zeitung* no. 114, December 11, 1948, 2. / **Fingerhut, L.** "Nokhn khurbn." *Ilustrirter yoyvl-zhurnal*, ed. Dram. krayz „Amcho" baym yidishn arbeter-komitet in Feldafing, 8. Feldafing, 1946. / "Fun der redaktsye." *Tkhies hameysim* no. 1, May 4, 1945, 6. / *Fun letstn khurbn* 1 (1946). / **Gar, Yoysef.** "Bafrayte yidn." In *Fun noentn over*, vol. 3, 77–188. New York: Congress for Jewish Culture, 1957. / **Giere, Jacqueline.** "Wir sind unterwegs. Aber nicht in der Wüste. Erziehung und Kultur in den jüdischen Displaced Persons-Lagern der amerikani-schen Zone im Nachkriegsdeutschland 1945–1949." PhD diss., Goethe University Frankfurt, 1993. / **Harshav, Benjamin.** "Erinnerungsblasen." in *Unterbrochenes Gedicht. Jiddische Litera-tur in Deutschland 1944–1950*, ed. Tamar Lewinsky. Munich: Oldenbourg, 2011. VII–IX. / **Holian, Anna.** "Die Möhlstraße und der Wiederaufbau jüdischen Wirtschaftslebens in Nachkriegs-deutschland." *Münchner Beiträge zur Jüdischen Geschichte und Kultur* 12.1 (2018), 23–34. / **Horovits, Norbert.** "Yidish teater in der sheyres hapleyte." In *Fun noentn over*, vol. 1, 113–182. New York: Congress for Jewish Culture, 1955. / **Jockusch, Laura.** *Collect and Record! Jew-ish Holocaust Documentation in Early Postwar Europe*. New York: Oxford University Press, 2012. / **Kaplan, Israel.** "Zamlen un fartseykhenen!" *Undzer veg* no. 12, December 21, 1945, 3. / **Kaplan, Israel.** *In der tog-teglekher historisher arbet. Fortrag gehaltn af dem tsuzamenfor fun di historishe komisyes*. Munich: Tsentrale historishe komisye, 1947. / **Kaplan, Israel.** *Dos folks-moyl in natsi-klem. reydenishn in geto un katset*. Munich: Tsentrale historishe komisye, 1949. / **Königseder, Angelika, and Juliane Wetzel,** *Lebensmut im Wartesaal. Die jüdischen DPs (Displaced Persons) im Nachkriegsdeutschland*. Frankfurt a. M.: Fischer, 1994. / **Lewinsky, Tamar.** *Displaced Poets. Jiddische Schriftsteller im Nachkriegsdeutschland, 1945–1951.* Göttingen: Vandenhoeck & Ruprecht, 2008. / **Lewinsky, Tamar.** "Kultur im Transit. Osteuropäisch-jüdische Displaced Persons." *Osteuropa* 8–10 (2008), 265–277. / **Mankowitz, Zeev W.** *Life between Memory and Hope. The Survivors of the Holocaust in Occupied*

Germany. Cambridge: Cambridge University Press, 2002. **/ Mendelsohn, Ezra.** *On Modern Jewish Politics.* New York: Oxford University Press, 1993. **/** *Oysshtelung fun yidishe kinstler.* Munich: [Central Committee of the liberated Jews in the US occupation zone, Cultural Affairs Department], 1948. **/** "Programme of the Liberation-concert. Hospital for political ex-prisoners in Germany in St. Ottilien." Accessed November 9, 2018. http://dphospital-ottilien.org/concert/. **/ Segev, Tom.** *One Palestine Complete.* New York: Metropolitan Books, 2000. **/ Shaar, Pinchas.** "Mendel Grossman. Photographic Bard of the Lodz Ghetto." In *Holocaust Chronicles. Individualizing the Holocaust Through Diaries and Other Contemporaneous Personal Accounts*, ed. Robert Moses Shapiro, 125–140. Hoboken, NJ: KTAV, 1999. **/ Shafir, Shlomo.** "Ha-'Nitsots' she-lo kava." *Kesher* 9 (1991), 52–57. **/ Shteynman.** "Di antshteyung un tetikayt fun khor." *Ilustrirter yoyvl-zhurnal*, ed. Dram. krayz „Amcho" baym yidishn arbeter-komitet in Feldafing, 10. Feldafing, 1946 **/ Szeintuch, Yechiel.** "'Tkhies hameysim'—ha-iton ha-rishon shel she'erit ha-peleta ve-orcho," *Chulyot* 10 (2006), 191–218. **/ Tsamriyon, Tsemach Mosche.** *Ha'itonut shel she'erit hapletah beGermania ke-bitui le-va'ayoteha.* Tel Aviv: Irgun She'erit hapeleta, 1970. **/ Volf, M.** "A sheyres-hapleyte tog-bukh." *Naye yidishe tsaytung* no. 5, December 8, 1950. **/ Vorzoger, Shloyme.** *Zayn. Lider.* Munich: Nayvelt, 1948. **/ Werb, Bret.** "'Vu ahin zol ikh geyn?': Music Culture of Jewish Displaced Persons." In *Dislocated Memories: Jews, Music, and Postwar German Culture*, ed. Tina Frühauf and Lily E. Hirsch, 75–98. New York: Oxford University Press, 2014. **/ Yoakhomovitsh, Avrom.** "Vi azoy s'iz antshtanen der dram.-krayz 'amkho'." *Ilustrirter yoyvl-zhurnal*, ed. Dram. krayz „Amcho" baym yidishn arbeter-komitet in Feldafing, 16. Feldafing, 1946 **/ Young, Cynthia.** "We Went Back. Photographs from Europe 1933–1956 by Chim." In *We Went Back. Photographs from Europe 1933–1956 by Chim*, ed. Cynthia Young, 31–51. Munich: Prestel, 2013.

THE KATSET-TEATER
"CONCENTRATION CAMP THEATER" IN THE BERGEN-BELSEN DP CAMP

WERNER HANAK

A few years ago, the Jewish Museum in Frankfurt was given a photo album as a permanent loan. The photos depict performances of the *Katset-Teater* (*Katset* as in KZ, the German acronym for concentration camp), a Yiddish theatre project established in 1945 in the Bergen-Belsen DP camp. Some of them are printed on photographic paper produced by Agfa, an enterprise belonging to the I.G. Farben conglomerate. On closer inspection, it was established that the photos are, for the most part, original prints. The commemorative album itself, however, was compiled at a later date. This is evident not least from two stamps on the photographs. One refers in English to the "Concentration Camp Theater of the Central Jewish Committee of Bergen Belsen," suggesting it was addressed to an international audience. The other, on the back of one of the photos, provides an Israeli address for the man who founded the theater, Sami Feder. Yet he only arrived in Israel in 1962.

Sami Feder was born in the Upper Silesian town of Zawiercie in 1909. After the First World War, he joined his grandfather in Frankfurt am Main where he completed his secondary school education. In Frankfurt, he mingled with Polish Jewish exiles and became increasingly interested in Yiddish language, literature, and theater. Having moved to Berlin, where he collaborated with important figures in the world of theater at large such as Erwin Piscator, he played an increasingly professional role in Yiddish theater groups.[1]

In 1945, after twelve years as a prisoner in a number of concentration and forced labor camps, Feder was liberated in Bergen-Belsen. There he established a theater group for both professional and talented lay actors, together with a range of people with whom he had already cooperated during their imprisonment, including Sonia Boczkowska. Before gaining access to the relevant literature again, they had initially reconstructed plays, songs, and poems from memory. Between the summer of 1945 and 1947, they offered ten cabaret programs and 47 theater performances.[2] The photos in the album primarily cover the first two cabaret programs performed in September 1945 and February 1946, respectively. The performances offered the survivors not only access to some of the Yiddish classics but also a first opportunity to work through what they had just survived. Those involved in this theater work were particularly keen to expose the so-called "infiltrees"–those who had survived in the Soviet Union and, following their repatriation to Poland, fled to the American and British occupation zones from 1946 onwards–to documentary theater programs comprising material from the ghettos and the concentration and death camps.

¹ See Sophie Fetthauer, *Musik und Theater im DP-Camp Bergen-Belsen. Zum Kulturleben der jüdischen Displaced Persons 1945–1950* (Neumünster: von Bockel, 2012), 222.
² See Yad Vashem, 0-70/31a: Sami Feder: Fartseykhenishn tsum togbukh, 1982, Bl. 11, quoted in Fetthauer, *Musik und Theater*, 242.

The later stamp of the *Katset-Teater*, Israel, 1960s. The *Katset-Teater* of Bergen Belsen performed from the summer of 1945 until the summer of 1947. This stamp in English was created later. It shows two theater masks and a lyre surrounded by a barbed wire fence with "Katset-Teater" written in Hebrew letters on the gate. The gate represents the image of a camp barrack.

Katset-Teater in the Bergen-Belsen DP Camp, album with fotos from 1946/47, compiled in Israel after 1962. Jewish Museum Frankfurt, permanent loan from a private collection, Frankfurt am Main

```
"Mama, ich habe angst!... angst!...

"Schweig mein Kind. Die Türe wird sich öffnen ,
  die Sonne wird wieder aufgehen, und wir werden
  frei sein."

                "Die Jagd Gottes" nach Emil Bernhard
```

Scene shot from *Der Goel (The Redeemer),* the first
cabaret program of the *Katset-Teater,* September 1945.
Der Goel is the first act from Emil Bernhard Cohn's
drama *Die Jagd Gottes (God's Hunt)* which
was published in the 1920s. Feder reconstructed the
dialogues for this performance from memory.
The text reads: "Mother, I am scared! ... scared ..."
"Be quiet, my child. The door will open, the sun will rise
again, and we will be free." Based on *God's Hunt* by
Emil Bernhard

Group photo of the *Katset-Teater* in front of
a concentration camp scene with the inscription
"One Louse–Your Death." The founder of the theatre
group Sami Feder is in the second row (third from left).
His future wife Sonia Boczkowska is sitting right next
to him, stage designer Berl Friedler directly below him
in the first row (third from left). *Katset-Teater* in the
Bergen-Belsen DP Camp, photos 1946/47, album after
1962.

Sonia Boczkowska in *Shikh* (*Shoes*), after the dramatized poem *Kh'hob gezen a barg ...* by Moses Schulstein. The set shows a mountain of shoes with the word "Majdanek" at the top. The mountain of shoes which, as the poem describes, is "higher than Mont Blanc and more sacred than Mount Sinai," is an early artistic expression of the legacies of the murdered Jews in the death camps. Not least because of the permanent exhibition in the Auschwitz-Birkenau State Museum, the mountain of shoes would become a well-known symbol of the Shoah.

*Di shvartse Sonya–Totenkolonne (Black Sonja–
The Death Convoy)*. This piece by Sami Feder about
partisans wanting to rescue a prisoner convoy brought
the barracks of the concentration camps on stage.

The dance act *The yid the eybiker vanderer* (*The Jew–
the Eternal Wanderer*) with Dolly Kotz, based on David
Pinski's one-act play from 1906. Moving through a
plastic map of Europe, the dancer brings the material
into the DPs' present.

FRAGMENTS FROM A LOST WORLD
THE RESCUE AND RESTITUTION OF JEWISH CULTURAL ASSETS IN THE POSTWAR PERIOD

ELISABETH GALLAS

The annihilation of European Jewry during the Second World War was accompanied by the systematic destruction of its culture and the transfer of cultural assets on an unprecedented scale. As they fled or were deported, Jews were forced to leave behind innumerable works of art, library holdings, archival documents, and ritual objects, which then were misappropriated, destroyed, or disappeared in state institutions and private homes. Only rarely were their owners able to take such possessions into exile with them or recover them after the war. In only a few years, the Nazis had obliterated the entire structure of Jewish material culture that had evolved in Europe over many centuries. As a result, Yiddish newspapers from Vilna are now found in New York, library collections from Berlin in Moscow, rabbinical writings from Breslau in Mexico City, community files from Vienna in Jerusalem, and silver candlesticks from Frankfurt in London.

However, this new topography of Jewish cultural assets is not only the result of the repeated theft of the objects in question during the war and the immediate postwar period, a process which can rarely be retraced precisely. Instead, it also results from the activities of Jews who devoted themselves to the rescue of Jewish cultural property immediately after the war. Given the pan-European scope of the crime, the history of the rescue of the remaining assets is also transnational and spans the entire continent. It was closely connected to the policies of the Allies and reflects the close cooperation between Jewish organizations and the occupation powers (especially the Americans), which shaped postwar Jewish life in crucial ways. The emerging Cold War played an important role in this history since cultural restitution and reconstruction policies, and their underlying legal regulations, differed considerably between East and West.

Jewish activists and organizations were nonetheless concerned with much more than the mere preservation of the identifiable remnants of a devastated

Jewish cultural life. Rather, the history of these rescue efforts reflects crucial questions about the possibility of Jewish life in Europe after the catastrophe and Jewish participants' differing visions of the future. These ranged from the reconstruction of a cultural infrastructure *in situ* to the comprehensive transfer of all moveable assets to the new centers of Jewish life outside Europe. Moreover, while some saw only Palestine/Israel as the center for the revival of Jewish culture, others placed great emphasis on renewal in the Jewish diaspora, especially in the United States. Their activities also shaped the formation of both individual and collective forms of Holocaust commemoration in crucial ways. As embodiments of a past that preserved the history of their former owners as well as the knowledge and traditions of European Jewry, the material remnants of the obliterated Jewish world played an important role in shaping the emerging Jewish memorial culture in Europe and beyond.

Major aspects of this massive cultural restructuring after 1945 can be illustrated particularly well by developments in two locations: Frankfurt am Main (and nearby Offenbach) and Prague. These two cities highlight, in particular, the processes of theft and restitution, and the conditions of reconstruction and a new beginning in Europe. Before the National Socialists took control, both cities had been centers of Jewish culture and education. Under Nazi rule, they featured prominently in the regime's pursuit of looting, and both played a key role in postwar restitution efforts.

FRANKFURT AND OFFENBACH

Frankfurt had for centuries been an important cultural, religious, and intellectual focal point for German and European Jews. Before the Second World War, the city was home to substantial Jewish collections of books, ritual objects, and art works, including the Jewish Antiquities Museum and the holdings of Aron Freimann and the city's official Jewish community (*Israelitische Religionsgesellschaft*). It is thus hardly surprising that Alfred Rosenberg's Institute for the Study of the Jewish Question, one of the most notorious Nazi institutions involved in the expropriation of Jewish cultural property, was established in Frankfurt in 1941. It soon held roughly half a million books and archival documents that had been stolen from all over occupied Europe and were used by Rosenberg's staff in pursuit of their antisemitic research.

On April 9, 1945, two members of the U.S. Army's so-called Monuments, Fine Arts, and Archives Unit, which had already begun to concern itself with the preservation of art works and historical monuments during the war, discovered a hidden repository containing hundreds of thousands of books and documents captured by Rosenberg's institute in the small town of Hungen in Hesse. The material had been brought there to protect it from the bombing raids on Frankfurt. Eyewitnesses described the desolate state of the scattered material, which had been exposed to the elements and repeatedly looted. We owe one of the first accounts of such repositories, including the one in and around Hungen, to the American journalist Janet Flanner who reported on war-ravaged Europe for the *New Yorker*:

> In a brick kiln in the town of Hungen [...] were hidden the most precious Jewish archives, tomes and synagogue vessels from all over Europe, including the Rosenthalian collection from Amsterdam and that of the Frankfurt Rothschilds. In the kiln, the repository for the Jewish material Rosenberg planned to use in his projected post-war academy, where anti-Semitism was to be taught as an exact science, priceless illuminated parchment torahs were found cut into covers for Nazi stenographers' typewriters or made up into shoes. Here, too, were thousands of Jewish identity cards, marked with a yellow "J," all that remained of Jews who had perished in Nazi crematories.[1]

Alluding to the spaces created in or near synagogues to store no longer usable sacred texts, the American military chaplain Rabbi Herman Dicker, who visited Hungen soon after the discovery of the repository, referred to the unsettling site as a *genizah*, albeit one with a "Nazi coloring."[2]

Around the same time, American soldiers secured the remaining holdings still stored in the building of Rosenberg's institute on Bockenheimer Landstraße in Frankfurt, which had been damaged by an air strike. These holdings comprised some 900 to 1000 boxes containing books from the Soviet Union, France, the Netherlands, Belgium, and Germany. In the summer of 1945, they were brought for safekeeping to Rothschild Palais on the Untermainkai, which had stayed largely intact and serves as the main building of the Jewish Museum in Frankfurt today.[3] Several vivid accounts have survived in which Jewish representatives sent to Frankfurt describe the temporary library established there. The American Jewish historian Koppel S. Pinson, for instance, who supervised the American Jewish Joint Distribution Committee's cultural and educational work with Jewish Displaced Persons in the U.S. occupation zone, recalled the haunting and lasting impression the depository made on him:

> Never in my life did I feel so small, so humble and spiritually so overawed as when, in Oct. 1945 I first walked into the former Rothschild library on Untermainkai in Frankfurt am Main and was face to face with all that was left of the cultural treasures of European Jewry. There they were, some 3 million books, looted

A page from the photo album of American-Jewish historian Koppel Pinson. The photos document the sorting of books in the former Rothschild Library in Frankfurt and in the Offenbach Archival Depot (OAD), 1945–1946. The Magnes Collection of Jewish Art and Life, University of California, Berkeley

Koppel Pinson (fourth from left) with his colleagues in front of the Rothschild Palais, where the Rothschild Library used to be, 1945–1946. Since 1988, the building houses the Jewish Museum Frankfurt. In Pinson's album, the photo was mistakenly labeled as taken in Offenbach. The Magnes Collection of Jewish Art and Life, University of California, Berkeley and ravaged from all over Europe and collected by Rosenberg, Himmler and Streicher [...]. There were books and manuscripts and incunabula from Kiev, Kharkov and Odessa all the way across Europe to the Channel Islands. These were all that were left of the great libraries, schools and academies of European Jewry. And as I gazed at these homeless and to this day still unclaimed books, I knew that European Jewry was finished. [...] All that remains are a few thousand persons, a few million books, and glorious memories.[4]

Sixty German civilians recruited by the American occupation authorities, among them a small number of librarians, worked at Rothschild Palais to preserve these holdings as best they could. The Prague-born journalist Robert Weltsch, who had initially fled to Palestine and moved to England after the war, was rather surprised, describing the collection as "probably [...] the largest Jewish library on earth."[5] Weltsch was one of many Jewish and non-Jewish reporters, journalists, social workers, and political representatives who visited war-ravaged Europe and Germany to assess and report on the situation, or to support various welfare organizations and the Allies in their reconstruction and relief efforts.

Rothschild Palais was, however, far too small to house all the salvaged material. Thus, in the course of 1945, the U.S. military administration created seven so-called Collecting Points throughout the U.S. occupation zone where the looted artifacts were gathered, identified, and prepared for restitution. The central collecting point for Jewish books and ritual objects was located in the city of Offenbach, near Frankfurt. It was established in the winter of 1945–46 on a site on the Main River, which had previously belonged to I. G. Farben, and operated from March 1946 as the Offenbach Archival Depot (OAD). All the books retrieved in Hungen and Frankfurt were brought to the OAD where they were stored, along with numerous other salvaged holdings, in the sizeable rooms of the five-story building. The OAD soon housed several million books and documents that had once belonged to some of the most prestigious Jewish institutions in Europe including the *École Rabbinique* in Paris, the Jewish Theological Seminary in Breslau, the *Collegio Rabbinico* in Rome, and the Yiddish Scientific Institute (YIVO) in Vilna, along with thousands of crates of books from private Jewish collections. The U.S. officials responsible for the OAD undertook enormous efforts to reverse the effects of the Nazis' campaign of theft. About two-thirds of the holdings were successfully identified and returned to the original institutions by OAD-accredited representatives from various countries who were frequently dispatched from national libraries and archives. Several collections were shipped back during 1946, especially to France, Belgium, the Netherlands and Italy.

Official and private documents of those concerned show that both the Americans in charge, who were often Jewish themselves, and Jewish survivors attached great symbolic importance to the return of looted Jewish libraries in envisioning the reconstruction of the Jewish cultural landscape in Europe. The OAD's leading staff members soon realized that the operation was about much more than the books' sentimental value. Lt. Leslie I. Poste, who was stationed at the OAD, was highly empathetic in highlighting this dimension: "These books and objects were what was left of the hundreds of Jewish institutions of learning, of Jewish communities, wiped out by the Holocaust of Hitlerism. Few can fathom the depth of the Jewish tragedy of which these remnants stood as a sad memorial."[6] In terms of the future handling of the material, he also noted that "[t]he depot operates as an American trusteeship for the millions of Jews destroyed by the Nazis."[7]

In fact, the issue of this trusteeship turned out to be altogether more complicated than suggested by Poste's account. The question of who should act as legal successor and pursue the Jews' collective interests was a matter of some controversy. Its resolution would determine the future of hundreds of thousands of objects in the OAD whose origins were unknown or to which neither their former owners nor their heirs could any longer lay claim. While books were returned to a significant number of reopened libraries or community facilities in Western Europe, no such institutions existed for many of the books held in Offenbach.

RESTORING JEWISH OWNERSHIP

A number of Jews in Europe, Palestine, and America concerned themselves with this issue. Their initiatives were eventually coordinated by the renowned historian Salo Wittmayer Baron in New York and under his leadership both established and younger scholars such as Horace Kallen, Cecil Roth, Gershom Scholem, and Hannah Arendt worked together to determine the fate of these collections. Baron had established a committee back in 1944 designed to advise the Allies on the issue of preserving Jewish cultural assets in Europe. To lay the groundwork for possible restitution claims, its members engaged in a comprehensive research project to document in detail all the major collections held by Jewish communities and institutions in Europe prior to the war. Led by Arendt, a group made up primarily of Jewish scholars who had fled to America collated all the available information to document the Jewish cultural landscape that had been irrevocably destroyed. Between 1946 and 1948, it published five "Tentative Lists" detailing Jewish library and archival holdings, publishers, journals, and educational institutions in twenty countries.[8]

Piles of unidentified books in the warehouse of the Offenbach Archival Depot, 1946. Yad Vashem, Jerusalem

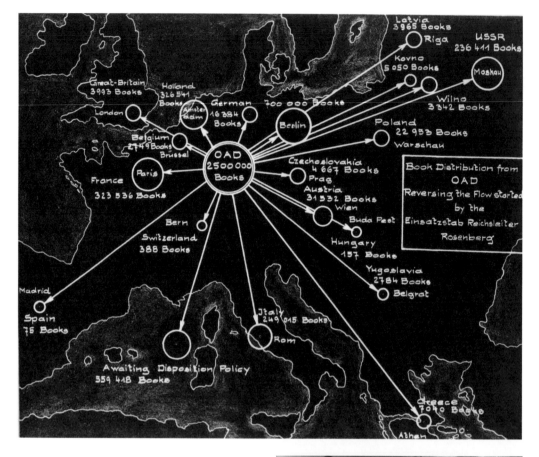

The diagram (1946–47) shows where the books collected in the Offenbach Archival Depot had come from and where they were supposed to be sent back. Eventually, most of the books found a new home either in the U.S. or in Israel. Yad Vashem, Jerusalem

Sorted books in the Offenbach Archival Depot, ready to be shipped back to the Soviet Union. Capt. Isaac Bencowitz (center), director of the OAD, with two Soviet restitution officers, 1946. Yad Vashem, Jerusalem

In the first instance, these lists were designed to record the extent of the destruction and the current state of the cultural institutions in question. Yet they offered much more. They presented the first systematic overview of the German looting of cultural assets and its significance in the overall context of the Nazis' policy of annihilation. In so doing, they provided an empirical basis for the concept of "cultural genocide" that the Jewish legal scholar Raphael Lemkin, who had fled to the U.S. from Poland, wanted the UN to include in its Genocide Convention.[9] Given the detailed nature of their bibliographical data and inventories, they also made a key contribution to the future field of provenance research. Ultimately, they formed a sort of textual archive of the Jewish culture which had been obliterated in Europe. Apart from a diverse range of Jewish cultural institutions, the lists also point to the political and religious structures at the time, to the range of languages used by Jews, as well as to the centers and peripheries of Jewish life faced with the challenges and contradictions of tradition and modernity.

Alongside their research, the members of the committee also developed political initiatives. As the number of ownerless cultural assets discovered by Allied soldiers in various locations grew, so did the urgency of creating a recognized Jewish trust that could claim and reutilize the material. It certainly could not be taken for granted that Jewish organizations would be able to claim possessions whose former Jewish owners could no longer do so themselves. The legal framework agreed upon in January 1946 on an intergovernmental basis at the Paris Conference on Reparation initially paid little attention to the claims of non-state actors (including victim groups). While restitution issues were not the only field affected by this approach, its impact was particularly pronounced in this context and of grave concern to Jewish observers the world over.

Above all, they were troubled by consequences of the international legal framework, two of which had already been in evidence in Offenbach. The first concerned the handing over of objects of Jewish provenance to non-Jewish institutions in Eastern Europe. In the summer of 1946, several thousand books predominantly owned by Jews were entrusted to the accredited representatives of the Soviet Union and Poland. It was highly unlikely that these books would be returned to Jewish institutions given that most Jewish communities in both countries had been destroyed, that the Soviets did not recognize a distinct form of Jewish victimhood, and that the German war of annihilation had devastated so much Jewish culture in the East. Consequently, it appeared that these holdings would be amalgamated in state collections and thereby almost certainly be lost to the Jewish world. Jewish envoys to the OAD repeatedly urged those responsible to refrain from sending objects of unambiguously Jewish provenance to Eastern Europe.

The second problem with the legal framework concerned the principle of *escheat*, which stipulated that the ownership of ritual objects and books of German Jewish provenance whose legitimate owners could not be identified would revert to the German (successor) state. This struck many Jewish observers as an intolerable prospect. To their minds, Germany had permanently forfeited its right to host, much less own, Jewish cultural assets.

To deal with these problems, Baron and his associates engaged in various endeavors to persuade the State Department and other relevant U.S. agencies that the existing restitution regulations needed to be changed. Their goal was the recognition of a representative organization legitimized to lay claim on behalf of the Jewish collective to all those assets which could not be returned to their rightful Jewish owners. In 1947, in collaboration with the most important Jewish organizations and institutions of the day, including the World Jewish Congress, the Jewish Agency, the Hebrew University in Jerusalem, and the Council of Jews from Germany, they established a non-profit corporation, which they called Jewish Cultural Reconstruction, Inc. (JCR). The JCR applied to be assigned the trusteeship for all those cultural assets in Europe to which their former Jewish owners or their heirs could no longer lay claim. It would take two years for the U.S. administration finally to agree to their request. Vigorous efforts had been made to find a joint solution for all four occupation zones, yet to no avail. Hence, in February 1949, an official agreement, valid only for the American occupation zone, was signed, recognizing the trusteeship of the JCR for all cultural assets that could not be returned directly to their former owners or their heirs. The agreement stipulated that the JCR would distribute the assets handed over to it on behalf of the Jewish people in order to strengthen Jewish cultural life worldwide.

While all this may sound rather legalistic and technical, it amounted to nothing short of a minor revolution in the field of Jewish politics. For decades, Jewish legal scholars had attempted to use the tools of diplomacy to ensure that the Jewish collective was legally recognized by the international community, despite the fact that it lacked a state or a territory of its own, The agreement with the JCR achieved this recognition through the back door, as it were, even if it was *ex negativo*, as a consequence of the Holocaust. Signed in Frankfurt, far from the big political stage, by three relatively unknown officials, this agreement recognized the Jewish people as an independent legal entity. Of all things, it was Jewish property, which had become ownerless as a result of the Nazis' policy of annihilation, that now precipitated the recognition of a collective Jewish claim in its own right.

Thanks to the "Frankfurt Agreement," the JCR was able to bring half a million books and several thousand ritual objects, more than half of them from the OAD, back into Jewish ownership between 1949 and 1952. Rarely were they returned to their former locations, most of them finding a new home elsewhere.

Although the members of the JCR frequently fought bitterly over where the material should best be sent, 40 percent generally went to Israel and 40 percent to the United States, while the rest was sent to various other countries, especially the United Kingdom. They certainly agreed among themselves that all the holdings should be removed both from Germany and the rest of continental Europe. That Jewish life should begin anew where one had attempted to fully eradicate it simply seemed inconceivable at the time. Hence, those responsible for the distribution sought to send the material to those locations where the largest numbers of refugees and survivors had found a safe haven.

This decision did lead to conflicts between the international envoys and those remaining Jews in Germany and other parts of Europe who were trying to reconstruct community life there. They wanted to use the books and ritual objects for their communities and put up (sometimes considerable) resistance to their being taken abroad. Yet Hannah Arendt, Salo Baron, and Gershom Scholem were convinced that community life would flourish neither in Germany nor in Eastern Europe, and that all the remaining Jews would sooner or later leave the countries in question. Consequently, they considered it too much of a risk to leave significant numbers of Jewish cultural assets behind. In any event, the subsequent development of Jewish community life in Germany proved their assumptions wrong, but this could hardly be foreseen in the late 1940s and early 1950s, and the fear prevailed that the remaining cultural assets might disappear yet again, this time possibly for good. Hence, the JCR frequently defied the wishes of local Jews. While Jewish communities in Western and Northern Europe were generally provided with the bare minimum required to sustain their activities, as many cultural assets as possible were taken out of Europe.

Where the best place might be for them was a matter of considerable controversy. The Israeli envoys argued emphatically that they should predominantly go to Israel. The leaders of the JCR, on the other hand, most of whom resided in America, acknowledged that the bulk of the material should go to Israel and Jewish institutions in North America, yet they also insisted that Jewish communities in Western and Northern Europe, South America, South Africa, and Australia should also benefit. In any event, material was sent to more than twenty countries.

PRAGUE, TEREZÍN, AND MIMOŇ

In Prague, the question of how best to deal with the salvaged Jewish cultural assets presented similar problems. While the political circumstances differed considerably, the situation was in many ways not unlike that in Offenbach. Only a fraction of the former Jewish population now lived in the area between the three relevant locations of Prague, Terezín, and Mimoň, but it was home to innumerable books and cultural assets previously owned by Jews. Here, too, the Nazis' frenzied collecting and unbridled rapacity had facilitated the survival of a substantial number of Jewish collections. These included some 100,000 books gathered in the former Czech capital, as one of European Jewry's most diverse and opulent cultural landscapes was being systematically dismantled. Following the German invasion, the National Socialists had turned the Jewish Museum established in Prague in 1906 into a depository for stolen assets with an exhibition space attached. It soon housed the cultural assets of numerous Jewish communities and individuals from all over Bohemia and Moravia.

In addition, two libraries had been established in the Theresienstadt concentration camp. At the time of the camp's liberation, there were some 180,000 books in the so-called Ghetto Library to which the prisoners had access. These books had previously belonged to a range of Czechoslovak communities, private households, and deportees. The special collection of the SS, which was established concurrently, held roughly 60,000 valuable Judaica and archival documents from all over Central and Eastern Europe. Lastly, the books looted by the Reich Main Security Office (RSHA) had been evacuated from Berlin to protect them from the air raids on the capital and brought to several palace sites in and around the small northern Bohemian town of Mimoň (Niemes in German). This collection contained further holdings from renowned Jewish libraries and institutions (including the Jewish community in Berlin and YIVO) as well as numerous private collections of considerable significance. Between 1945 and 1948, most of the looted Jewish cultural assets were brought to Prague and stored in the Jewish Museum, the University Library, and facilities belonging to the Jewish community. There their fate was to be determined.

The author and historian H. G. Adler, himself a survivor of Theresienstadt who had moved to England in 1947, was involved in the process of sorting and identifying the objects brought to the Jewish Museum. In a letter to his future second wife, Bettina Gross, he wrote: "An endless succession of storage facilities houses hundreds of thousands of books, ritual objects, images, and all manner of imaginable and unimaginable stuff. It will presumably take decades before [...] everything has been reviewed, inventoried, and processed. [...] Anyone with a sensitive nature can smell the Jewish suffering and Hitler's rage on these objects. We are administering a depressing estate."[10] A number of attempts were made to influence the way in which this "administering" was undertaken. The JCR had been alerted fairly early on to the assets evacuated to Bohemia by one of their informants, the Jewish classicist Ernst Grumach who had survived in Berlin and whom the RSHA had employed as a slave laborer in its library of stolen books. Yet, as it became increasingly clear that the Czechoslovak authorities were unwilling to cooperate with the JCR, it eventually had to withdraw. Its close ties to the U.S. apparently ruled out any constructive engagement.

The representatives of the Hebrew University fared somewhat better, not least because some of them, such as Arthur and Shmuel Hugo Bergman, originally hailed from Prague. As a result, they were at least given an opportunity to make their case for the wholesale transfer of the relevant collections to Jerusalem. Like their peers in Offenbach, they took it for granted that the local Jewish communities stood no chance of flourishing again, given the toll the National Socialist genocide had taken on them, not to speak of the increasing Soviet influence in, and the proceeding communist transformation of, the country. Gershom Scholem and his associates were convinced that in Israel, by contrast, the valuable holdings would contribute to the construction of the new country's culture and would assume an important function in processes of commemoration.

Yet the Hebrew University's representative also ran into trouble in the emerging new Czechoslovakia. Members of the local communities and museum workers, on the one hand, and the authorities and public educational institutions, on the other, opposed the export of cultural assets from the country, regardless of their provenance (since much of the material in question had not originated in the region anyway).

Still, one way or another, some 50,000 books from Prague eventually made their way to Israel. Together with the holdings sent by the JCR, they helped lay the foundation for the young country's educational institutions, especially the National Library in Jerusalem and thereby played a part in its nation-building efforts. The new beneficiaries of objects and books belonging to these "remnants saved from the conflagration" (as one contemporary source described them) often welcomed them enthusiastically and organized exhibitions and even celebrations (in some instances) to mark their arrival.[11]

BOOKS AND MEMORY

The symbolic significance attributed to the rescuing of books for Jewish life after the Holocaust can hardly be overstated. It resulted from the high value placed on the written word and books in Jewish tradition, on the one hand, and from the closely related, frequently drawn analogy between the fate suffered by human beings and books during the Holocaust, on the other.

Since late antiquity, the Torah had served diaspora Jews, among other things, as a substitute for the common territory they lacked, a substitute that connected the various Jewish communities the world over. This connectedness did not draw on a formally constituted common political space but on a common textual canon which preserved and interpreted the sacred law along with the collective's shared history. In the modern era, this reverence was increasingly extended beyond the strictly canonical texts and to some extent secularized as well. For many, not just a particular canon but books in general now constituted a common, albeit textual territory. The devastation and systematic looting of numerous Jewish libraries by the Germans before and during the war was therefore seen as integral to the war of annihilation conducted against the Jews, as an assault on the intellectual foundations of their existence. Against this backdrop, the postwar rescue of those library holdings which were recoverable was considered a crucial contribution to the renewed appropriation of Jewish history and its continuity. Indeed, it was regarded as a guarantee for the continued existence of the Jewish collective itself.

Numerous Jewish contemporaries specifically identified the depot in Offenbach as a location where these issues were tangible in their material form. The subsequent Holocaust historian Lucy S. Dawidowicz, who worked at the OAD for several months in 1947 in order to identify the looted holdings of the YIVO stored there, articulated the dramatic effect the site had on her. She described the OAD as a "mortuary of books."[12] The mountains of books stacked there symbolized the remnants of Europe's Jewish civilization and were, for Dawidowicz, a daily reminder of the Jews who had once owned them but were now dead. Yet the books not only recalled the past; in a way, they also vouched for the fact that those who had been murdered had once existed. Numerous eyewitnesses suggested that the rescue of the books was in some sense a substitute for the rescue of the victims that had never transpired. It opened up the prospect of a future for the Jewish collective, and it facilitated a specific form of commemoration of those who had been murdered by partially transcending the anonymity of their killing by the Nazis. Not unlike gravestones, they served to commemorate their murdered owners and the annihilated sites of Jewish cultural life. The rescued books made a material contribution to the preservation of Jewish culture, knowledge, and tradition. They were inscribed with the history of their desolation and theft, often quite literally. For many of the books bore the ex libris of their former owners, the markings of the Nazi looting units and research institutions, the stamp of the OAD, and the logo of the JCR. Yet they were also meant to help facilitate the new beginning of Jewish existence wherever they went. The history of the rescue of these assets thus reflects an extraordinary struggle for probity and justice, and for remembrance and recognition. It was undertaken in Europe immediately after the war, in the face of considerable adversity, by Jewish survivors, scholars, and political envoys determined to contribute actively to the postwar order and to influence the shape of Jewish life after the catastrophe in both its old and new locations.

---

[1]   Janet Flanner, *Men and Monuments* (London: Hamilton, 1957), 295–296.
[2]   Herman Dicker, "The Genizah of Hungen, Germany." The National Library of Israel, Jerusalem, Library Papers, Arc 4°793/288/6.

3 Leslie I. Poste, "The Development of U. S. Protection of Libraries and Archives in Europe During World War II" (PhD diss., University of Chicago, 1958), 333–339.

4 Koppel S. Pinson, "Commencement Address to Gratz College," June 17, 1947, 2–3. Stanford University Libraries, Special Collections, Jewish Social Studies Papers, M0670, BOX 4, Correspondence M–S, 1947–1965, Folder: Pinson Personal.

5 Robert Weltsch, "Besuch in Frankfurt," *Mitteilungsblatt des Irgun Olej Merkaz Europa*, January 11, 1946, 10.

6 Leslie I. Poste, "Books Go Home from the Wars," *Library Journal* 73.21 (1948), 1702.

7 Poste, "Books Go Home," 1703.

8 Research Staff of the Commission on European Jewish Cultural Reconstruction, "Tentative List of Jewish Cultural Treasures in Axis-Occupied Countries," *Jewish Social Studies* 8.1 (1946), supplement; "Tentative List of Jewish Educational Institutions in Axis-Occupied Countries," *Jewish Social Studies* 8.3 (1946), supplement; "Tentative List of Jewish Periodicals in Axis-Occupied Countries," *Jewish Social Studies* 9.3 (1947), supplement; "Addenda and Corrigenda to Tentative List of Jewish Cultural Treasures in Axis-Occupied Countries," *Jewish Social Studies* 10.1 (1948), supplement; "Tentative List of Jewish Publishers of Judaica and Hebraica in Axis-Occupied Countries," *Jewish Social Studies* 10.2 (1948), supplement.

9 Raphael Lemkin, *Axis Rule in Occupied Europe: Laws of Occupation, Analysis of Government, Proposals for Redress* (Washington: Carnegie Endowment for International Peace, Division of International Law, 1944), esp. 84–85. A specific clause concerning cultural genocide was not included in the Genocide Convention agreed upon by the United Nations in 1948.

10 H. G. Adler to Bettina Gross, January 11, 1946, Deutsches Literaturarchiv Marbach, Bestand A: Adler, Hans Günther. Cf. also, H. G. Adler, "Die Geschichte des Prager jüdischen Museums," *Monatshefte* 103.2 (2011), 161–172. This previously unpublished text was written in 1947.

11 Schalom Ben-Chorin, "Ausstellung geretteten Kulturgerätes im Jerusalemer Bezalel Museum," *Der Weg. Zeitschrift für Fragen des Judentums* 5.31 (1950), 4.

12 Lucy S. Dawidowicz, *From that Place and Time. A Memoir, 1938–1947* (New Brunswick: Rutgers University Press, 2008), 316.

BIBLIOGRAPHY

Adler, H. G. "Die Geschichte des Prager jüdischen Museums." *Monatshefte* 103.2 (2011), 161–172. **/ Ben-Chorin, Schalom.** "Ausstellung geretteten Kulturgerätes im Jerusalemer Bezalel Museum." *Der Weg. Zeitschrift für Fragen des Judentums* 5.31 (1950), 4. **/ Dawidowicz, Lucy S.** *From that Place and Time. A Memoir, 1938–1947.* New Brunswick: Rutgers University Press, 2008. **/ Flanner, Janet.** *Men and Monuments.* London: Hamilton, 1957. **/ Lemkin, Raphael.** *Axis Rule in Occupied Europe: Laws of Occupation, Analysis of Government, Proposals for Redress.* Washington: Carnegie Endowment for International Peace, Division of International Law, 1944. **/ Poste, Leslie I.** "Books Go Home from the Wars." *Library Journal* 73.21 (1948), 1699–1704. **/ Poste, Leslie I.** "The Development of U. S. Protection of Libraries and Archives in Europe During World War II." PhD diss., University of Chicago, 1958. **/** Research Staff of the Commission on European Jewish Cultural Reconstruction. "Tentative List of Jewish Cultural Treasures in Axis-Occupied Countries." *Jewish Social Studies* 8.1 (1946), supplement. **/** Research Staff of the Commission on European Jewish Cultural Reconstruction. "Tentative List of Jewish Educational Institutions in Axis-Occupied Countries." *Jewish Social Studies* 8.3 (1946), supplement. **/** Research Staff of the Commission on European Jewish Cultural Reconstruction. "Tentative List of Jewish Periodicals in Axis-Occupied Countries." *Jewish Social Studies* 9.3 (1947), supplement. **/** Research Staff of the Commission on European Jewish Cultural Reconstruction. "Addenda and Corrigenda to Tentative List of Jewish Cultural Treasures in Axis-Occupied Countries." *Jewish Social Studies* 10.1 (1948), supplement. **/** Research Staff of the Commission on European Jewish Cultural Reconstruction. "Tentative List of Jewish Publishers of Judaica and Hebraica in Axis-Occupied Countries." *Jewish Social Studies* 10.2 (1948), supplement. **/ Weltsch, Robert.** "Besuch in Frankfurt." *Mitteilungsblatt des Irgun Olej Merkaz Europa*, January 11, 1946, 9–10.

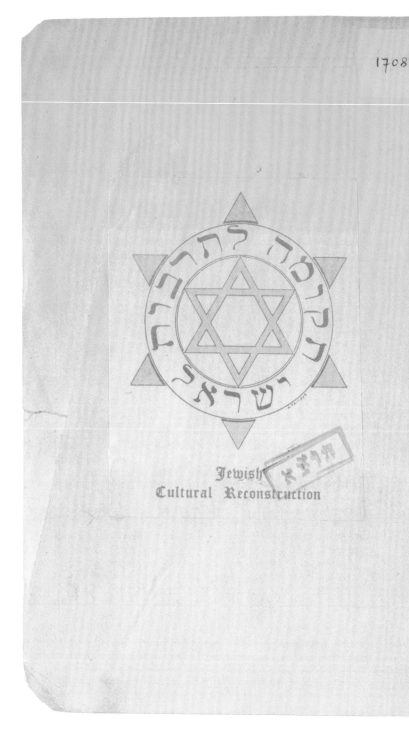

1708

Jewish
Cultural Reconstruction

Das jüdische Bekenntnis als Hinderungsgrund bei der Beförderung zum preußischen Reserveoffizier (The Jewish Confession as a Hindrance in the Promotion to Prussian Reserve Officer) by Max I. Loewenthal, Berlin, 1911.
A book from the Offenbach Archival Depot with various stamps, including that of the Jewish Cultural Reconstruction Inc. (JCR). Michael Krupp Collection, Jewish Museum Frankfurt

Das jüdische Bekenntnis als Hinderungsgrund bei der Beförderung zum preußischen Reserveoffizier.

Im Auftrage

des Verbandes der Deutschen Juden

dargestellt

von seinem Generalsekretär

Dr. Max I. Loewenthal.

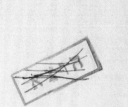

Berlin 1911.

Druck von H. S. Hermann.

RESCUE ATTEMPTS
THE HUNGARIAN JEWISH MUSEUM AND JEWISH CULTURAL HERITAGE AFTER 1945

KATA BOHUS

The genocide perpetrated against European Jewry was preceded and accompanied by the systematic confiscation and theft of Jewish property, including art and cultural objects, in Nazi Germany and the countries it occupied. After the war, many heirless Jewish cultural works and artifacts were discovered and the question arose: who is entitled to them?

At first, it was not self-evident at all that Jewish organizations could lay claim to heirless Jewish property. In the American occupation zone of Germany, the Jewish Cultural Reconstruction Inc. (JCR)—established in 1947 as an American Jewish initiative—succeeded in transferring the bulk of the Jewish assets found there to the United States and Israel. As a result, for example, many objects from the prewar holdings of the Frankfurt Museum of Jewish Antiquities ended up in overseas collections.

In Eastern Europe, under the control of the Red Army, many heirless Jewish cultural assets were found in Prague, but restitution became possible only after the collapse of communism four decades later. Nevertheless, in some places in and outside of the Soviet influence zone, Jewish museums and local Jewish institutions took on the task of saving what could still be saved of the local and national Jewish heritage. One such institution was the Jewish Museum in Budapest, Hungary. In September 1945, the museum contacted every single Jewish community in the country with a request to "find and temporarily store every possible remaining memory and document" of the prewar Jewish communities, and to inform the museum about them.[1] As a result, a great many objects were collected by the museum in the first decade after the Shoah.

In August 1955, the Museum sent two rabbinical students to visit Jewish communities in southern and central Transdanubia. They collected data, documents, and other artifacts that carried information about the past of the communities, the destruction caused by fascism, and the situation at the time. The

Inside view of the former study hall (*beit midrash*) of
the synagogue in Bonyhád, 1955. The photo was taken
by two rabbinical students from Budapest, entrusted by
the Jewish Museum there to collect information about
what remained of the smaller Jewish communities in
the Transdanubian region. Hungarian Jewish Museum
and Archives, Budapest

remaining Hungarian Jewish historical heritage was considered not only a source of knowledge, but an all-important carrier of the only traces of its murdered owners.

[1] "Survey of the Hungarian Jewish Museum and Archives of the remaining assets of Jewish communities, September 1945. National Office of Hungarian Israelites," *MAKOR–Magyar Zsidó Levéltári Füzetek* no. 7 (2010): *Zsidó közösségek öröksége*, 29.

Ledger book (*pinkas*) of the Jewish community of Kaba, Hungary, 1967–1910. The community donated the book to the Hungarian Jewish Museum in 1949. From the prewar Jewish community of about 250 people in Kaba, only 25 survived the war. Even though they reestablished the community, it ceased to exist in 1956 as all the members had moved away. Hungarian Jewish Museum and Archives, Budapest

FRANKFURT AND ZEILSHEIM
AMERICA IN GERMANY

MORITZ BAUERFEIND

> We cannot assume that there are Jews who feel drawn to Germany.
> The odor of corpses, of gas chambers and of torture chambers lies in
> the air here. Yet in fact a few thousand Jews do still live in Germany.
> […] This remnant of Jewish settlement should be liquidated as soon
> as possible. […] Germany is no place for Jews.
>
> Robert Weltsch, 1946

Between 1945 and 1948, there were two centers of Jewish life in the Frankfurt region. In Zeilsheim, a working-class area to the west of the city, the U.S. occupation forces established a camp predominantly for East European Jewish Displaced Persons (DPs) who had migrated to the U.S. occupation zone. Since its inhabitants were never entirely segregated from the surrounding population, there was not only contact but also conflict. The destruction wrought by the war on downtown Frankfurt was staggering, and even more so on its Jewish institutions. Jews had once made up five percent of the overall population of the city; in no other metropolitan area of Germany had their share been so substantial. Of the 29,000 Jews who once resided in Frankfurt, slightly more than half had managed to emigrate.[1] No more than 200 had survived the National Socialist regime of terror within the city itself.

All that notwithstanding, some of these survivors embarked on the tentative reconstruction of the city's once prominent Jewish community. Their efforts initially centered on Frankfurt's Ostend ("East End"). There, survivors who had predominantly returned from the Theresienstadt camp created an infrastructure for themselves in the vicinity of the synagogue on Baumweg and of the former Jewish hospital. One of the returnees was Dr. Leopold Neuhaus, the last surviving rabbi who had served the city's (now extinguished) community.

These two groups, the DPs in Zeilsheim and the German Jews in downtown Frankfurt, only really came into closer contact once the DP camp had been closed down, at which time some of its inhabitants, either individually or as families, moved from Zeilsheim to the city center. The merger of the two eventually produced the Jewish community that resides mainly in Frankfurt's Westend today.

ZEILSHEIM

Starting in August 1945, it was predominantly Polish Jews, fleeing from a new series of pogroms perpetrated by non-Jewish Poles, and driven by the knowledge that Poland had been turned into a "huge Jewish cemetery," who migrated to the U.S. occupation zone in Germany. After their arrival, many were placed in DP camps. By 1947, there were 157,000 of them in the U.S. occupation zone, of whom roughly 110,000 had come with the mass exodus from Poland.[2] They hoped that it would be easier for them to move on from there to the U.S. or Palestine. Within six months of its establishment, the camp in Zeilsheim was home to a constantly changing population of roughly 3,000 DPs.[3] Just how many DPs passed through the camp, officially known as the "Jewish Assembly Center Zeilsheim," can no longer be determined with any certainty. The assumption is that the vast majority, some 70 percent of them, were Polish Jews; Jews from Hungary (six percent) and Czechoslovakia (four percent) formed the second and third largest contingents.[4]

The first 185 inhabitants of the DP camp, survivors from Buchenwald and Bergen-Belsen, were housed in barracks previously used for the slave laborers of the chemical enterprise Farbwerke Höchst (formerly, I. G. Farben). Yet, in view of the ongoing influx of DPs, these were soon filled to capacity. Zeilsheim was a pilot project in that from the outset, the military administration attempted to ensure that only Jewish DPs were housed there. The common practice elsewhere was to group DPs by their countries of origin. Nonetheless, U.S. military authorities were soon pressured into providing other accommodations as a result of the ensuing chaos and the Harrison Report's (politically motivated) exaggerated portrayal of those Jews who were still interned in camps and behind barbed wire even after the war. To that end, 200 houses belonging to the works estate of the nearby chemical factory (formerly I.G. Farben) were confiscated and allotted to the DPs. Along with the continuing influx from eastern Europe, especially of refugees who had been repatriated to Poland after having survived the war in the Soviet Union, the high birth rate in Zeilsheim presented a considerable challenge. In the first half of 1946, 80 births and 150 additional pregnancies were registered in the camp. At the time, the rate of roughly 700 infants born each week of 1947 to Jewish mothers in the U.S. occupation zone was the highest of any Jewish community worldwide.[5]

Entrance gate of the Zeilsheim DP camp, IRO Assembly Center 557, 1947–48. Photo: E.M. Robinson, United States Holocaust Memorial Museum, Washington D.C., courtesy of Alice Lev

With the generous support of aid organizations such as the UNRRA and the JDC, most of the Jewish DPs were gradually able to move beyond mere survival, albeit with various difficulties. They began to rebuild their lives, find partners, and start families. Even in 1948, the JDC still maintained a staff of 560 in the U.S. occupation zone in order to support the remaining Jewish DPs. By that time, given the establishment of the State of Israel and the easing of the immigration regime in the U.S., their number had decreased from 165,000 in April to 30,000 in September.[6] In the postwar years, American Jews collected almost $200 million to assist the Jewish DPs.[7] From October 1945 until the summer of 1947, the JDC's team in Zeilsheim was run by Sadie Sender, a U.S. citizen.

Despite the universal scarcity, general insecurity, and constant changes, the DP camp was able to support a range of schools, professional training centers, cultural institutions, political parties, sports associations, etc. From late 1945 on, a total of 1,151 DPs completed training as tinsmiths, plumbers, car mechanics, hatters, photographers, mold makers, chauffeurs, dental technicians, and others.[8] In cooperation with the aid organizations, the camp's culture administration ran an education center for adults that offered language courses and lectures on history, religion, culture, and hygiene. In the summer of 1946, there were 50 patients in the camp hospital, most of whom were suffering from tuberculosis. As noted in the press, the first kosher kitchen in a German DP camp was created in Zeilsheim. For its part, the camp newspaper reported on social events and prominent visitors such as David Ben-Gurion and Eleanor Roosevelt. There were a number of such visitors, given that the camp was close to the Frankfurt headquarters of the U.S. occupation forces. Following on the heels of its Munich counterpart, *Unzer veg*, the Zeilsheim paper, *Undzer Mut*, first appeared on December 20, 1945. It was renamed *Untervegs* in April 1946, serving as the central periodical for the DP camps in Hesse. Until December 1947, 45 issues were circulated in print runs of 7,500 copies.[9] Whether engaged in religious, political, athletic, or educational activities, the overarching goal of the DPs' self-administration was to prepare the inhabitants of the camp for their future lives.

Considering that here (as elsewhere), it was impossible to segregate the camp's inhabitants from the local population, a range of contacts and various forms of barter developed. The local press tended to portray the camp as the regional epicenter of black market dealings. German observers suggested that the latter were the outflow of "Jewishness and Russian thinking" that had even succeeded in seducing virtuous Germans.[10] Taking into account the aid they received from various institutions, Jewish survivors had a certain amount of "start-up capital" at their disposal, which many non-Jewish Germans resented. At the same time, the American military authorities preferred to engage in business transactions with the Jews, given that they were not implicated in the Nazis' crimes. Writing in the *Frankfurter Rundschau* on August 18, 1947, the journalist Arno Rudert suggested that the illegal trade was in fact a logical consequence of the prevailing scarcity. He concluded that his contemporaries might want to "moderate their moralizing about life in the DP camp."[11]

By reducing the issue of the camps to the question of commercial activities within them, the majority society avoided giving any further consideration to the DPs' difficult situation or its causes. Instead, non-Jewish Germans justified their own participation in the black market with their desperate personal situation, yet regarded that of the unknown other as a crime. In his memoirs of the postwar years, the Frankfurt-based writer Valentin Senger has offered an account of the extent to which the U.S. military authorities and communal institutions were embroiled in the payment of bribes.[12] It is also worth noting that non-Jews continued to live in Zeilsheim.[13]

For some of the time, Frankfurt's Lord Mayor and its police chiefs joined in the smear campaign against the DPs, all the while suggesting that they did so in order to prevent a renewed eruption of the antisemitism that was still latent. Presumably, major disturbances were preempted by the presence of the American military.

Following the founding of the State of Israel and the easing of U.S. immigration restrictions in 1948, it was decided to close the camp down, and the remaining 2,000 to 2,500 inhabitants had to leave Zeilsheim by November 16. While most of them were sent to other camps, 200 were granted permission to move to downtown Frankfurt.[14]

DOWNTOWN FRANKFURT

When Frankfurt was liberated on March 29, 1945, fewer than 200 Jews were still alive in the city. Like August Adelsberger, the first administrator of what remained of the community, most of them had survived thanks to their "mixed marriages." As early as April and May, Adelsberger facilitated the return of survivors from Buchenwald, followed in June and July by some 300 former members of the community from Theresienstadt.[15] A further 650 German Jews returned to the city in late August, among them the prewar community's rabbi, Dr. Leopold Neuhaus. By that time, the U.S. commander in Frankfurt had already established the Jewish Welfare Center. This first communal institution in the city was run by members of the prewar community and located in a former kindergarten. Beginning on May 15, regular religious services took place there, and survivors were supplied with the absolute necessities. When the High Holidays came around in the autumn of 1945, the community was also able, with support from the municipal authorities and the JDC, to celebrate

Polish-Jewish family (or families) in the Zeilsheim DP camp. It is undeterminable when exactly this photograph was taken, and it has been described in literature both as a picture of people arriving in 1946, and leaving in 1948. Since the photo shows several generations, it seems reasonable to assume that they were originally from Poland, survived in the Soviet Union, returned to Poland after the war only to flee from there towards the American zone of Germany around 1946. Institute for the History of Frankfurt

The first children born in the Zeilsheim DP camp, 1946.
Yad Vashem, Jerusalem

services in the Westend Synagogue again. The interior of the synagogue, once the centerpiece of the prewar community, had been vandalized during the November Pogrom of 1938, but the building itself was still intact.

Neuhaus and his peers prioritized the reconstruction of the prewar community and managed to get the municipal authorities to return some of the prewar community's property. The aforementioned kindergarten, located in the city's Ostend, where Jews had traditionally left a strong mark, came to serve as the first seat of the community's provisional administration. In November 1945, another crucial communal institution was inaugurated when an old people's home—needed because of the advanced age of many of the survivors returning from Theresienstadt—was established in the former Jewish hospital. The Americans also ordered former Nazis to clean up the Jewish cemeteries in the city's Nordend district. The community nonetheless continued to be dependent on support from aid organizations and the authorities. With the help of small loans, individual members of the community began opening shops in the wooden shacks near the central location of Hauptwache.

In a 1947 New Year's speech, the Social Democratic Lord Mayor, Walter Kolb, called on the survivors and exiles from Frankfurt to return from their dispersal throughout the world. He was presumably the only German mayor to do so. Non-Jews in particular criticized his initiative, fearing that the returnees would receive preferential treatment. In fact, the U.S. military administration had to force the municipal authorities to fund and put in place memorial stones at the locations of the three destroyed synagogues. They were installed there in September 1945. Elsewhere in the world, how the non-Jewish German population treated the survivors was seen as a touchstone for the strength of Germany's democratic convictions.[16] Yet, aside from official events, few showed any empathy for those who had recently been persecuted. Conversely, Jewish organizations also viewed the community in Frankfurt as one that would soon cease to exist, given that a rebirth of Jewish life after the Shoah seemed inconceivable in the land of the perpetrators.

Along with the reconstruction of the community, the city also became home to a substantial number of foreign Jews settling in various parts of town from 1946 onwards. They were supported by the Committee of Liberated Jews in Frankfurt and developed their own rudimentary communal structures. Even though the number of East European Jews living outside of Zeilsheim grew considerably, the city's community made no effort to accommodate them. Dr. Neuhaus nonetheless recognized soon enough that it was illusory to pick up where the prewar community had left off, and he left for the U.S. in 1946. His counterparts on the Committee, Dr. Leon Thorn and Uri Bluth, continued to develop their own religious institutions, which likewise contributed to a situation in which the predominantly Polish DPs and the German returnees lived alongside each other but maintained little mutual contact. While the number of German returnees reached 850 by April 1949, the group's age structure seriously threatened its continued existence, given the disproportionate number of older members.

THE MERGER

The West German currency reform of June 1948 eventually made this duplication of Jewish communal structures–those of the DPs, on the one hand, and the German survivors, on the other–unaffordable. The official community was better off in terms of its real-estate holdings but weaker in terms of its infrastructure and access to aid. In the end, the merger took the form of the Committee disbanding and its 1,073 members individually joining the reestablished community. Moreover, it was stipulated that German Jews would continue to dominate the community's boards.[17] The merger was confirmed by a newly created joint board on April 24, 1949, thereby launching the postwar community that still exists today. Dr. Wilhelm Weinberg, who had already held the post since 1948, was appointed as the community's first rabbi. Frustrated by the difficult conditions on the ground, however, he too emigrated in 1951. Only in the figure of his successor, Isaak Emil Lichtigfeld, did a new era of continuity begin for the community. To be sure, it would still be a long time until the famous suitcases under the bed were unpacked. And the long struggle for individual restitution had only just begun. Despite that, the sojourn in the "waiting room" was finally over.

Previously, the duplication of structures had characterized Jewish life in Germany's American capital. Only once the DP camp had closed and numerous families and individuals had moved from Zeilsheim to downtown Frankfurt, did the two groups begin to interact in earnest and eventually merge to form today's Jewish community, which is centered principally in Frankfurt's Westend. Especially for those who had previously lived in Zeilsheim, life in Germany did not really begin until this point.

---

[1] Jim Tobias, *Zeilsheim. Eine jüdische Stadt in Frankfurt* (Nuremberg: ANTOGO, 2011), 19.

[2] Tobias, *Zeilsheim*, 41–45.

[3] On the official camp statistics of the YIVO and JDC, see Tobias, *Zeilsheim*, 127. However, given the number of DPs whose papers were incomplete or whose stay in the camps remained undocumented, these figures hardly present the full picture.

[4] Tobias, *Zeilsheim*, 7.

[5] Tobias, *Zeilsheim*, 70.

[6] Atina Grossmann and Tamar Lewinsky, "Part One: 1945–1949: Way Station," in *A History of Jews in Germany since 1945: Politics, Culture, and Society*, ed. Michael Brenner (Bloomington: Indiana University Press, 2018), 132.

U.S. military authorities raid the Zeilsheim DP camp on March 24, 1948. The raids were attempts to contain the black market. German Press Agency, Frankfurt am Main

Raid in the Zeilsheim DP camp, August 7, 1948. The U.S. military police discovered a grocery store in the basement of a house. German Press Agency, Frankfurt am Main

[7] Tobias, *Zeilsheim*, 35.

[8] Florian Ritter, "Das 'Displaced Persons'-Lager in Frankfurt am Main/Zeilsheim," in *Wer ein Haus baut, will bleiben. 50 Jahre Jüdische Gemeinde Frankfurt am Main. Anfänge und Gegenwart*, ed. Georg Heuberger (Frankfurt a. M.: Societäts-Verlag, 1998), 112.

[9] Tobias, *Zeilsheim*, 82–83.

[10] From the letter of a Catholic priest from Frankfurt to the Bishop of Limburg, quoted in Tobias, *Zeilsheim*, 106.

[11] Quoted in Ritter, "'Displaced Persons'-Lager," 115.

[12] Valentin Senger, *Kurzer Frühling* (Frankfurt a. M.: Fischer, 2011), 145–160.

[13] Laura J. Hilton, "The Reshaping of Jewish Communities and Identities in Frankfurt and Zeilsheim in 1945," in *We Are Here: New Approaches to Jewish Displaced Persons in Postwar Germany*, ed. Avinoam Patt and Michael Berkowitz (Detroit: Wayne State University Press, 2010), 194–226.

[14] "50 Jahre Jüdische Gemeinde: Bilddokumentation," in *Wer ein Haus baut, will bleiben. 50 Jahre Jüdische Gemeinde Frankfurt am Main. Anfänge und Gegenwart*, ed. Georg Heuberger (Frankfurt a. M.: Societäts-Verlag, 1998), 55.

[15] Alon Tauber, *Zwischen Kontinuität und Neuanfang. Die Entstehung der jüdischen Nachkriegsgemeinde in Frankfurt a. M. 1945–1949* (Wiesbaden: Kommission für die Geschichte der Juden in Hessen, 2008), 28.

[16] The term "touchstone" was first introduced in this context by John McCloy, the American High Commissioner in Germany. See Atina Grossmann, *Jews, Germans, and Allies: Close Encounters in Occupied Germany* (Princeton: Princeton University Press, 2007), 255.

[17] Grossmann, *Jews, Germans, and Allies*, 120–122.

Members of the Jewish community in Frankfurt
am Main commemorate the destroyed synagogue at
Börneplatz on March 20, 1946. The Imperial Cathedral
of Saint Bartholomew is standing in the background,
among the ruins of the bombed city. German Press
Agency, Frankfurt am Main

ROSA ORLEAN
(BORN 1927)

Rosa Orlean was born into a bourgeois family in Kraków in 1927. She was twelve when the Germans invaded Poland, and she spent her entire adolescence in various ghettos and camps, including Auschwitz. After her liberation in 1945, she joined a group of young women who managed to make their way to a location held by the American military, then returned to Kraków. Once there, she and her aunt witnessed an attack on their hostel, and as a result, she could no longer imagine living in Poland. Following a number of stops along the way, she eventually arrived in the DP camp in Frankfurt-Zeilsheim, where she found her sister, the only other member of her immediate family who had survived.

In the three years spent in the camp, she worked for the UNRRA (United Nations Relief and Rehabilitation Administration) administration. She also met her husband there. As a young woman, she enjoyed the proximity to the big city and regularly went dancing with other survivors in downtown Frankfurt. Yet life in the DP camp was difficult and characterized by insecurity and hopelessness. Rosa Orlean and her future husband therefore intended to move to the U.S. However, Rosa was diagnosed with lung disease and they were both refused entry to the United States Hence, when the camp was closed in 1948, she and her fiancé married and started a family in Frankfurt.

The move from the "waiting room" in Zeilsheim to downtown Frankfurt marked the real beginning of their new life in Germany. Rosa Orlean is still living in Frankfurt today.

Rosa Orlean in the Zeilsheim DP camp, 1945–1946.
Private collection Rosa Orlean, Frankfurt am Main

Rosa Orlean (left) with a friend in the vegetable garden of the Zeilsheim DP camp, 1945–1946. Private collection Rosa Orlean, Frankfurt am Main

Rosa Orlean and her husband Stefan at their wedding on April 10, 1949. Private collection Rosa Orlean, Frankfurt am Main

ABRAHAM ROZENBERG (1928–2013)

Abraham Rozenberg was born in 1928 in the Polish city of Sosnowiec where his parents ran a bakery. The family was torn apart during the German occupation of Poland. His father Shamshe was deported to Buchenwald in 1940. In 1943, Abraham was separated from his mother Leah and his younger brothers Favel (Felek) and Issosre (Jurek) during a "selection" outside the railway station in Sosnowiec. Abraham was initially taken to the camp of Fünfteichen, a subsidiary of the concentration camp in Gross-Rosen. From there, he was deported to Buchenwald where, early in 1945, he encountered his frail father in the camp infirmary. Soon after, Abraham was sent on a death march to Theresienstadt where he was finally liberated by the Red Army.

When Abraham Rozenberg returned to Sosnowiec after the war he found that none of his relatives there had survived. His mother and brothers were presumably murdered in Auschwitz. In August 1945, along with other child and adolescent survivors, he traveled via Prague to Windermere (UK) where he was trained as a mechanic and made preparations to move to Israel. In 1948, he found out that his father had also survived and now lived in the small German town of Friedberg, located north of Frankfurt am Main. Abraham went to live with his father, and he joined the boxing team of Eintracht Frankfurt the following year. He soon became a star, winning the Hessian championships three times. In 1950, he competed in the Maccabiah Games in Israel, officially representing the *She'erit Hapletah Germania* (Surviving Remnant in Germany). In 1951, he also made it to the finals of the German Championship in Hamburg.

In 1955, Rozenberg followed his father to the U.S. He became a professional boxer and trained with world champion Rocky Marciano but decided to return to Frankfurt in 1957. He initially worked as a doorman and later ran a pub that bore his nickname, "Bei Romme." His establishment counted Oskar Schindler among its regular patrons. Rozenberg got married in 1973. He and his wife Esther had two sons, Doron and Yuval.

Abraham Rozenberg wearing boxing shorts adorned with the Star of David, after he became Champion of Hesse, 1950. Private collection Rozenberg family, Frankfurt am Main

K.O. victory for Abraham Rozenberg, around 1950. Abraham Rozenberg, born in Sosnowiec in 1928, was liberated by the Red Army near Theresienstadt, after a death march from Buchenwald. Together with other surviving children and adolescents, he was subsequently sent to Britain for recuperation. His talent for boxing was discovered there. Private collection Rozenberg family, Frankfurt am Main

The title pages of a photo album that Abraham Rozenberg received on the occasion of his long membership from his club, Eintracht Frankfurt, in 1955. Rozenberg became a member of Eintracht in 1949, after he had arrived in Frankfurt in 1948 to be reunited with his father. Nevertheless, the club congratulated him on his ten-year membership. Private collection Rozenberg family, Frankfurt am Main

JEWISH COURTS OF HONOR

IN THE AMERICAN ZONE OF OCCUPIED GERMANY AND THE ALLIED JUDICIARY

KATARZYNA PERSON

In September 1946, at the height of migration of Eastern European Jews to DP camps in Germany, Austria, and Italy, the Jewish attorney, M. Cukerfajn, wrote an article in the popular Jewish daily *Undzer hofenung* (*Our Hope*) published in the Eschwege DP camp in Hesse, Germany. Describing the establishment of a camp court in the newly established displaced persons' camp "Herzog" in Hessisch Lichtenau in eastern Hesse,[1] Cukerfajn wrote:

> the Jewish committee has rightly decided, during one of its meetings, to create a citizen's court here in our camp, assuming that we are building a small society that is bound by common rules that can be broken by one of us, and in the wish that such situations should be handled by us, and not by strangers. It should be clear that this institution is not intended to spread fear, nor will it impose itself on anyone by force. It has merely been called to aid the committee in matters of order and justice in our camp.

Further on, Cukerfajn added:

> Our citizen's court has no desire to punish or, as I have mentioned, spread fear. Its only desire is to resolve genuine conflict and, at the same time, draw attention to bad behavior so that deeds that are deemed harmful should not be repeated. This is the kind of guide that our citizen's court should be, and that was the intention behind organizing this institution in our camp.[2]

The court in Herzog DP camp headed by Cukerfajn was one of hundreds of courts set up in all major displaced persons' camps in postwar Germany.[3] These DP courts, elected by camp residents, also functioning under the names of honor courts, disciplinary committees, or advisory committees,[4] not only served the everyday needs of the community but were also a crucial tool in asserting the agency of displaced persons and in shaping their future as they, and not the Allied occupation authorities, envisaged it.

DP camps were administered by UNRRA (United Nations Relief and Rehabilitation Administration) and later its successor agency, the International Refugee Organization (IRO), together with aid agencies, in particular the JDC. They became centers of grassroots activities, initiated by the survivors themselves, who used this interim time in Germany to work on rebuilding their shattered communal life. As part of that effort, survivors organized political activities and parties, published newspapers, organized Yiddish language cultural life, and above all became involved in various forms of commemoration of both their loved ones and their destroyed communities, using the past as a foundation stone for their new, shared future.

Among the key institutions set up in newly established camps were internal camp courts. As with many survivor initiatives, the specifics of their operations differed substantially in each camp and were to a large degree dependent on the good will of the local Military Government and UNRRA camp authorities.[5] While their existence was often threatened and their enforcement powers were minimal, as Cukerfajn pointed out, setting up such courts was not only a necessary part of the everyday administration of the camp, but also a key element in regaining agency and taking responsibility for internal justice. The courts thus dealt with a plethora of issues that emerged as a result of the formation of small and extremely diverse communities composed of people who came from different localities, spoke different languages, had various religious and political backgrounds, and very different wartime experiences. The issues included conflicts surrounding the distribution of parcels or food in the camps, problems arising from overcrowding and housing allocations, and offenses such as drunkenness, theft, brawls, and slander, including omnipresent accusations of wartime crimes against fellow Jews. In many camps, cases relating to the violation of Jewish religious law were investigated by rabbinical courts.

As Cukerfajn stresses, both types of courts aimed to assure "that such situations should be handled by us, and not by strangers." They were to a large extent influenced by the Talmudic tradition of not turning one's own over to non-Jewish authorities, but their formation was also the consequence of an understandable decision by the DP community to ensure that the unique experiences of Holocaust survivors, in particular the trauma they endured and its effect on their postwar lives, would be adequately addressed. Jewish DPs shared

The honor court in the Leipheim DP camp, 1946–1947.
Yad Vashem, Jerusalem

an underlying belief that only survivors within the community could understand the burden of such experiences. This view of the role of the court meant that handling justice in DP camps had to be restricted to those who understood the experiences of camp and ghetto survivors who had endured the war in occupied Europe. This ruled out non-Jews, but also, in the opinion of many, those Jews who did not have any direct experience of the Holocaust. "Those gentlemen from Russia," as one of the ghetto survivors bitterly wrote in a letter after testifying in a DP camp trial, referring to Jews who survived in the Soviet Union and were generally not seen as authentic survivors of Nazi atrocities, "speak loudly of heroism, but only we know that the true heroes remain silent today."[6] Thus, discussion around the functioning of these courts became an important part of negotiating the hierarchies in the Jewish DP community, and in particular the division among direct survivors, repatriates from the Soviet Union who, from 1946, formed the vast majority of DPs, and Jews who arrived in the camps from Western Europe and America as soldiers or as representatives of Jewish aid organizations.

Fear of a lack of understanding by those outside the survivor community, in particular non-Jews, was grounded in reality. Throughout their stay in postwar Germany, DPs were subject to military government law and directives. From the moment the DP camp system was set up as the war was ending, DPs of all nationalities lived under the threat of Allied court martial.[7] Even after the end of military action in Germany, the Jewish survivor community was repeatedly informed by their press of cases where survivors standing in front of military courts were mistreated,[8] particularly when accused of offenses that violated military government law: illegal possession of arms or illegal crossing of borders and, most frequently, "black-market" trading. Such was the case of 20-year-old Chaim K., a former inmate of Buchenwald, who was sentenced to fifteen years in prison by a British military court for illegal possession of arms. During the trial K., who did not speak English or German, the two languages in which the trial was conducted, did not receive any help from the Polish liaison officer, assistance to which he was entitled.[9] He was acquitted only because his case was reported to London by representatives of Jewish aid organizations, and thus reached the international public. Such instances reinforced the survivors' determination to deal with criminal issues on their own. American military authorities conceded in their internal correspondence that "the Jewish camp offenders will not be turned over to the Military Government Courts [...] and furthermore that [Jewish] witnesses will not appear against a member of the camp in the Military Government Courts."[10]

The honor court cases which represented the essence of restoring agency through judging one's own, and which gripped the survivor community more than any others were those relating to accusations of collaboration, understood as cooperation with the enemy of the Jewish people. Survivors classified former members of the *Judenrat*, the *Jüdischer Ordnungsdienst* (i.e., the Jewish police), or *kapos* (prisoner functionaries) in forced labor and concentration camps under this general rubric of collaboration. Behaviors considered as collaboration ranged from profiting economically from the Germans, bribery, and violence toward fellow camp prisoners or ghetto inhabitants, to handing Jews over to the Germans to be killed. In the Jewish DP communities, as was the case in other communities across Europe struggling with the legacy of the Second World War, the vast majority of these issues were sorted out in an informal, extra-judicial way, outside the formal court system. Even though there is no data on how many suspected collaborators were killed in the camps following liberation, beatings were undoubtedly very widespread.[11] In November 1945, the *Landsberger lager-cajtung* published in the Landsberg DP camp, one of the most important Jewish centers in Bavaria, pointed to "many instances of Center residents attacking people designated as *kapos* by individuals and seriously injuring them" and appealed to the DPs not to engage in this sort of "vigilante justice."[12] The creation of honor courts was in many respects a reaction to this situation. It was an attempt to regulate lynch law in the camps by creating institutions that the survivors could trust and that would still enable them to deal with internal community matters without resorting to outside authorities.

In the case of trials regarding collaboration, the imperative to keep these proceedings within the Jewish community was even more pronounced than in other cases. Survivors were, understandably, worried about reinforcing the antisemitic myth of Jewish complicity in the Holocaust. As Laura Jockusch has noted, many survivors "shared" the feeling "that non-Jewish courts could not be trusted to adjudicate crimes committed by Jews against other Jews" as well as "the strong belief–indeed, the sense of urgency–that Jews not only had the right but also the duty to deal with these internal matters themselves."[13] As the survivors already envisaged building a national homeland in Israel on the basis of the displaced persons' community, their camp justice system was to go far beyond keeping order in the camp and upholding a good image in the eyes of the Allied administration. It was also to be a crucial tool in creating a new future: a healthy community, which would be able to function anew, without any shadow cast by the wartime behavior of its individual members.

Locating those suspected of collaboration proved to be a difficult task. Yet, a surprisingly high number of people were put on trial on the basis of very effective informal networks of information exchange which tracked the postwar migration paths of Holocaust survivors. There was also substantial exchange between Jewish institutions set up in postwar Poland, displaced persons camps, and Jewish organizations in Western Europe, the United States, and South America. They sent information to each other regarding possible places of

Jewish police in the Zeilsheim DP camp detain a
former *kapo* who was recognized on the street,
1945–1948.
United States Holocaust Memorial Museum,
Washington D.C., courtesy of Alice Lev

The honor court in the Hofgeismar DP camp,
1946–1949. Yad Vashem, Jerusalem

residence of putative collaborators and shared documents and testimonies in their possession regarding wartime behavior.[14]

Initially, camp courts handled the trials of people accused of collaboration. For instance, one of the first cases tried in front of the Hessisch Lichtenau court (mentioned at the beginning of this essay), was that of a suspected collaborator. The 23-year-old Jakow Flajszheker was accused of having,

> from the beginning of 1942 to the end of 1943, while working in camp Skarzysko-Kamienna as a disinfector of the bath facilities,[15] tormented the Jewish inmates and women in particular, beating them over the face and body, forcing them to undress in his presence, stealing valuables from newly arrived inmates, and many other brutal acts.[16]

After acknowledging that the accusations were at least in part true, Flajszheker was sentenced to three months' incarceration in the camp's jail (even though the court had no official power to impose imprisonment), and subsequent immediate removal from the vicinity of the camp. The court stressed, however, that a year after his sentencing, Flajszheker "will have the possibility of appealing to any Jewish court to have his crimes pardoned if he can prove that during the year, through his behavior and his work for the good of Jewish society, he has earned recognition as a full-fledged citizen." This possibility of rehabilitation and re-integration, standing in stark contrast to standard judicial procedures, lay at the heart of justice as understood and administered by survivors.

Not all such court decisions were accepted unconditionally. Lenient sentences for serious wartime crimes, such as in Flajszheker's case, often met with vocal protest from members of the DP community, especially those who suffered at the hands of Jewish collaborators. The author of an article published in the summer of 1946 in the Jewish DP newspaper, *A Heim*, lamented the "lack of discipline of our masses, truly laughable actions of our security and legal bodies [...] [and] a cowardly behavior of our judges," and complained about the leniency of the sentences: "according to what codex do those gentlemen work? Maybe according to the Jewish Torah? But there are points there such as 'an eye for an eye' guaranteeing that everyone will get a deserved sentence."[17]

Such sentences were, of course, a direct result of the courts' very limited punitive powers, but they also reflected another, more complex rationale. Despite the mounting pressure of public opinion within an agitated DP community, the final decision of the Jewish DP court system was that neither membership in the Jewish police nor being a *kapo* was reason enough to remove someone from postwar Jewish communal life. Only in cases of particular brutality was an individual suspended from holding a position of leadership in the community.

Such a stance was strongly promoted by one of the most influential members of the Jewish DP community, Samuel Gringauz, a Kovno ghetto survivor,[18] who was twice elected President of the Council of the Liberated Jews in Bavaria. Gringauz, the author of the first articles on the organizational aspects of life in the ghetto, including the sociology of the power structure, was a firm believer in the positive rebuilding of the community, stating that the only way towards "inner purification and moral recovery" was not through blind revenge but through productive work and education.[19]

From the summer of 1946, local camp courts were supervised by the Central Jewish Honor Court in Munich set up by the Central Committee of Liberated Jews, with members of the Central Court elected by the delegates attending the U.S. zone survivor congresses. A year later, the committee set up a new body, the Rehabilitation Commission, which focused solely on cases of alleged collaboration with the Nazis. Starting in 1948, this body took over all cases relating to accusations of collaboration. The rationale was that the commission would be more proficient than local camp courts at locating evidence and providing witnesses. Moreover, because it functioned under the direct supervision of the Central Committee (which held the approval of the U.S. Military Government), it was believed to be more appropriate to carry out these prominent trials. The commission also served as the court of appeal for those who thought they had been wrongly judged by camp courts, and dealt with rehabilitation requests. This was particularly important as denunciations of camp inhabitants accused of collaboration were not always legitimate or filed in good faith. As archival documentation clearly shows, many (and indeed sometimes overdetermined) motivations were at play, including acts of personal revenge or jealousy. Denunciations could be used to address tensions around unsettled pre- or postwar scores, somebody's elevated position in the DP society, or their luck in obtaining emigration visas.

In cases of particular gravity, the commission decided to refer those sentenced to the Allied Military Courts in the British and American zones. To underline the weight of this decision, once in front of this court, the suspected collaborators forfeited all help from the Jewish DP community. One of the most notorious cases was that of Norbert Jolles, originally from Galicia, a former camp elder in the ammunition factory of the Hasag concentration camp in Częstochowa. He was unequivocally described by former camp prisoners as a sadist who singlehandedly ruled the camp and had the right to beat not only the Jewish prisoners, but even some of the German overseers. Testimonies suggested that he had influence on the contents of deportation lists and could thus ensure the death of all those who held incriminating evidence against him. As one person testified: "Jolles was kind of a specter throughout the camps, and everybody was in great fear of him. If anybody wanted to threaten us, menace was clad in the words: Jolles will come to see you."[20] Jolles's culpability was magnified by the fact that he could have used his power in the camp or the ghetto to help other prisoners. Witnesses claimed that, "if only he had been willing to act in our favor, everything would have become easier for us", and that he "could have been able to spare people's lives if only he intended to do so."[21] The Rehabilitation Commission in Munich not only sentenced Jolles as a traitor to the Jewish People (the most severe and damaging charge) and referred him to the American Military Court but also addressed the Polish Military Mission in Berlin, asking that it initiate a motion to extradite him to Poland. According to Jolles's file in the Instytut Pamięci Narodowej in Warsaw, his extradition was discussed by the Polish authorities in 1950, yet was never carried out due to lack of adequate proof of his guilt.[22] Another Jew tried by military courts, Ignatz Schlomowicz, was charged with war crimes which he had allegedly committed as a *kapo* in Bergen-Belsen. He was tried as part of the Belsen trial in the British Zone in Hamburg along with the infamous Stella Goldschlag, a "Jew catcher" who handed over several hundred Jews in hiding in Berlin to the Nazi authorities.[23] However, as Laura Jockusch notes in her study of postwar honor courts in occupied Germany, cases of Jews tried by the Allied courts remained the exception to the rule.[24]

DP honor courts, like other Jewish DP institutions, were only a temporary measure. With the establishment of the State of Israel and introduction of the American Displaced Persons Acts of 1948 and 1950 in the United States, DP camps gradually closed down, and most of their inhabitants left Europe. Yet, for such a short-lived phenomenon, DP honor courts played an astonishingly important role in the reconstruction of a community shattered by the Holocaust. As Rivka Brot writes, by setting up the courts, Jews "fought to be recognized as a distinct national community with political, cultural, and legal autonomy to whatever extent possible under the existing circumstances."[25]

By setting up their own courts, Jews sought to escape imposed, non-Jewish interpretations of their experience of war and persecution. In order to do this without any recourse to serious punishment, and to retain credibility within their communities, courts had to engage in a mature, non-politicized conversation with the past, facing and judging their demons to the best of their abilities. Despite the horrific persecution which it endured, the community almost immediately focused on taking responsibility for its own wartime actions. This proved just as important as getting revenge on those who bore the greatest responsibility for crimes committed against it. Judging one's own was not only a matter of justice but one of survival and reconstruction–in the form of institution building in transit–after extreme trauma and devastation. This significantly contributed to the Jewish collective's ability to at least consider moving on from under the dark shadow of the war.

The honor court in the Föhrenwald DP camp,
Dr. Zygmund Herzig in the middle, 1945–1950.
As in the courtroom in the Hofgeismar DP camp,
a famous image of Theodor Herzl overlooks the
court at work. Courtesy of Dr. Hanna Herzig, Tel Aviv

The office of the Jewisch honor court in the Föhrenwald DP camp, 1945–1950. Courtesy of Dr. Hanna
Herzig, Tel Aviv

[1] Camp Herzog was set up in July 1946 in former factory workers' barracks. Housing approximately 1,200 Jewish DPs, it was dissolved in January 1949.

[2] M. Cukerfajn, "Undzer lager-gericht," *Undzer hofenung* no. 12, September 25, 1946, 7, translation from E*xperiencing History: Holocaust Sources in Context*, https://perspectives.ushmm.org/item/a-verdict-from-our-camp-tribunal (translator not indicated).

[3] These were created not only by Jews but also by other national groups. See, for example, "Sądownictwo i samorząd. Osiągnięcia obozu wysiedleńców w Wentorf," *Defilada* no. 9, May 9, 1946, 6, quoted in Jakub Żak, "Polscy dipisi w zachodnich strefach okupacyjnych Niemiec na łamach polskiej prasy emigracyjnej (1945–47)," *Naukowy Przegląd Dziennikarski* no. 23 (2017), 102; archival documentation relating to Polish courts in the archive of the Piłsudski Institute in New York City, zespół archiwalny nr 024, Uchodźcy Polscy w Niemczech 1939–1952. On the search for justice among survivors of the Holocaust, see *Jewish Honor Courts: Revenge, Retribution, and Reconciliation in Europe and Israel after the Holocaust*, ed. Laura Jockusch and Gabriel N. Finder (Detroit: Wayne State University Press, 2015).

[4] On these terms, see Rivka Brot, "Conflicting Jurisdictions: The Struggle of the Jews in the Displaced Persons Camps for Legal Autonomy," *Dapim: Studies on the Holocaust* 31.3 (2017), 196–197.

[5] Specifically on the legality of the Jews' courts, see Brot, "Conflicting Jurisdictions."

[6] Abraham Steczer to Hermann Altbauer, March 10, 1948, YIVO Archive, RG 294.3, MK 489, Microfilm reel 17, folder 189. Similar doubts regarding the ability of those with no camp experience to judge former functionary prisoners were expressed in other places in postwar Europe. For the Polish case, see Zofia Wóycicka, "U 'kresu pewnej moralności': dyskusje wokół procesów więźniów funkcyjnych w Polsce 1945–1950," *Zagłada Żydów Studia i Materiały* 3 (2007), 363–364.

[7] In May 1945, Polish (at that point that also included Polish Jewish) DPs in Dortmund were threatened with court martial for not submitting to curfew rules, spending nights outside their barracks, or leaving the camp without a permit. See "Przepisy dla uczestników obozu Nr. 2, 2 maja 1945," *Głos Wyzwolenia. Pismo obozowe wyzwolonych z niewoli niemieckiej robotników przymusowych w Dortmundzie* no. 8, May 3, 1945, 4.

[8] As Rivka Brot notes, the military government judiciary in the American zone included three courts: "a general court, the higher instance; an intermediate court; and a summary court, the lower instance by which most of the DPs were tried" (Brot, "Conflicting Jurisdictions," 177, *n*12). See also Oscar A. Mintzer, *In Defense of the Survivors: The Letters and Documents of Oscar A. Mintzer, AJDC Legal Advisor, Germany, 1945–46* (Berkeley: Judah L. Magnes Museum, 1999).

[9] Control Office for Germany and Austria, Letter to Brian Robertson, March 11, 1946, The National Archives (TNA), London, FO 1032/2257, Treatment of Jewish DPs and other irrepatriables: vol II.

[10] Memorandum from Major General H. L. McBride, Headquarters Ninth Inf. Div., to the Commanding General Third US Army, November 21, 1946, UNRRA Archive, New York, S-0425-0018-12, Legal Matters—Courts—Camps.

[11] On "the Poles cleaning out their *capos*" in the Wildflecken DP camp, see the memoir of Kathryn Hulme, deputy director of an UNRRA team: Kathryn Hulme, *The Wild Place* (Boston: Little, Brown, 1953), 14.

[12] "Appeal to Residents of the Landsberg Center," *Landsberger lager-cajtung* no. 5, November 12, 1945, 6.

[13] Laura Jockusch, "Rehabilitating the Past? Jewish Honor Courts in Allied-Occupied Germany," in *Jewish Honor Courts*, ed. Jockusch and Finder, 52.

[14] On this, see Katarzyna Person, "Jews Accusing Jews. Denunciations of Alleged Collaborators in Jewish Honor Courts," in *Jewish Honor Courts*, ed. Jockusch and Finder, 225–246.

[15] The Skarżysko-Kamienna forced labor camp for Jews was located in the Polish town of Skarżysko-Kamienna and belonged to the German Hasag concern. It was in operation from August 1942 to August 1944. Between 18,000 and 23,000 Jews perished in the camp.

[16] "Urteil fun lager-gericht n. 146," *Undzer hofenung* no. 12, September 25, 1946, 7. On postwar Jewish courts dealing with sexual violence, see Ewa Koźmińska-Frejlak, "'I'm Going to the Oven Because I Wouldn't Give Myself to Him': The Role of Gender in the Polish Jewish Civic Court," in *Jewish Honour Courts*, ed. Jockusch and Finder, 247–278.

[17] Ben Ami, "Wi zat ojs bei undz der gerechtikajts-organ?" *A Heim* no. 13, June 4, 1946, 11.

[18] Interview with Samuel Gringauz, Leo Baeck Institute Archives, AR 25385. For a discussion of the role played by Gringauz in the DP camps, see Ze'ev Mankowitz, *Life between Memory and Hope: The Survivors of the Holocaust in Occupied Germany* (Cambridge: Cambridge University Press, 2002), 173–191.

[19] Samuel Gringauz, "In cejchn fun martirertum, hofnung un arbet," *Landsberger lager-cajtung* no. 14, January 18, 1946, 1, quoted in Mankowitz, *Life between Memory and Hope,* 187.

[20] Testimony of Leib Storch, Yad Vashem Archive, M.21.2, folder 4.

[21] Testimonies of Chaim Fisz and Rola Klempner, Yad Vashem Archive, M.21.2, folder 4.

[22] Instytut Pamięci Narodowej Archive, GK 164/1424, Norbert Jolles.

[23] On Stella Kübler-Isaacksohn (*née* Goldschlag), see Peter Wyden, *Stella: One Woman's True Tale of Evil, Betrayal, and Survival in Hitler's Germany* (New York: Simon & Schuster, 1992).

[24] Jockusch, "Rehabilitating the Past," 52.

[25] Brot, "Conflicting Jurisdictions," 193. See also Rivka Brot, Be'eyzor haafor: hakapo hayehudi bemishpat (Tel Aviv: The Open University Publishing House, The David Berg Institute for Law and History, 2019).

BIBLIOGRAPHY

Ami, Ben. "Wi zat ojs bei undz der gerechtikajts-organ?" *A Heim* no. 13, June 4, 1946, 11. / "Appeal to Residents of the Landsberg Center." *Landsberger lager-cajtung* no. 5, November 12, 1945, 6. / **Brot, Rivka.** "Conflicting Jurisdictions: The Struggle of the Jews in the Displaced Persons Camps for Legal Autonomy." *Dapim: Studies on the Holocaust* 31.3 (2017), 171–199. / **Cukerfajn, M.** "Undzer lager-gericht," *Undzer hofenung* no. 12, September 25, 1946, 7. / **Hulme, Kathryn.** *The Wild Place.* Boston: Little, Brown, 1953. / **Jockusch, Laura.** "Rehabilitating the Past? Jewish Honor Courts in Allied-Occupied Germany." In *Jewish Honor Courts: Revenge, Retribution, and Reconciliation in Europe and Israel after the Holocaust,* edited by Laura Jockusch and Gabriel N. Finder, 49–82. Detroit: Wayne State University Press, 2015. / **Jockusch, Laura and Gabriel N. Finder**, eds. *Jewish Honor Courts: Revenge, Retribution, and Reconciliation in Europe and Israel after the Holocaust.* Detroit: Wayne State University Press, 2015. / **Koźmińska-Frejlak, Ewa.** "'I'm Going to the Oven Because I Wouldn't Give Myself to Him': The Role of Gender in the Polish Jewish Civic Court." In *Jewish Honor Courts: Revenge, Retribution, and Reconciliation in Europe and Israel after the Holocaust,* edited by Laura Jockusch and Gabriel N. Finder, 247–278. Detroit: Wayne State University Press, 2015. / **Mankowitz, Ze'ev.** *Life between Memory and Hope: The Survivors of the Holocaust in Occupied Germany.* Cambridge: Cambridge University Press, 2002. / **Mintzer, Oscar A.** *In Defense of the Survivors: The Letters and Documents of Oscar A. Mintzer, AJDC Legal Advisor, Germany, 1945–46.* Berkeley: Judah L. Magnes Museum, 1999. / **Person, Katarzyna.** "Jews Accusing Jews. Denunciations of Alleged Collaborators in Jewish Honor Courts." In *Jewish Honor Courts: Revenge, Retribution, and Reconciliation in Europe and Israel after the Holocaust,* edited by Laura Jockusch and Gabriel N. Finder, 225–246. Detroit: Wayne State University Press, 2015. / "Przepisy dla uczestników obozu Nr. 2, 2 maja 1945." *Głos Wyzwolenia. Pismo obozowe wyzwolonych z niewoli niemieckiej robotników przymusowych w Dortmundzie* no. 8, May 3, 1945, 4. / "Urteil fun lager-gericht n. 146." *Undzer hofenung* no. 12, September 25, 1946, 7. / **Wóycicka, Zofia.** "U 'kresu pewnej moralności': dyskusje wokół procesów więźniów funkcyjnych w Polsce 1945–1950." *Zagłada Żydów Studia i Materiały* 3 (2007), 355–385. / **Wyden, Peter.** *Stella: One Woman's True Tale of Evil, Betrayal, and Survival in Hitler's Germany.* New York: Simon & Schuster, 1992. / **Żak, Jakub.** "Polscy dipisi w zachodnich strefach okupacyjnych Niemiec na łamach polskiej prasy emigracyjnej (1945–47)." *Naukowy Przegląd Dziennikarski* no. 23 (2017), 95–127.

The honor court in Ulm investigates a suspected
former *kapo*, 1947. Yad Vashem, Jerusalem

AMSTERDAM
THE CITY OF CONFLICTS

KATA BOHUS

In Amsterdam, one neighborhood is largely deserted.
The houses are empty and rotting again.
The streets are so quiet, full of gaping holes.
Where are the people?
Will I ever see them again?
Where are the hawkers with fruits and flowers and where is
the rag man who always came?
Where are the tens of thousands who cannot be named here?
Where are the Jews of Amsterdam?

Hans Krieg, 1947[1]

British and Canadian troops liberated Amsterdam in May 1945. Dutch Jews had suffered the most devastating losses of any West European Jewish community during the war: less than 25 percent (some 35,000) of them survived. Of Amsterdam's prewar Jewish population of 77,000, barely 15,000 remained.[2] Most survivors were convinced that the history of Dutch Jewry was over. Yet, paradoxically, the very same people were also working on rebuilding Jewish life.[3] During the postwar years, the debate over how this rebuilding should take place dominated Jewish discourse in the capital.

Although the Jewish Coordination Committee (*Joodse Coördinatie Commissie*, JCC), the main organ of institutionalized Dutch Jewry after the war, established its Amsterdam branch in the summer of 1945, Dutch authorities did not fully acknowledge the legitimacy of the Jewish community. This became clear during the struggle to recover orphaned children. Roughly 3,500 Jewish children survived the war hidden by non-Jewish families in the Netherlands. Of these, 1,300 were under 15 years of age.[4] A governmental committee called the Commission for War Foster Children (*Commissie voor Oorlogspleegkinderen*, OPK) was established in August 1945 to rule on their guardianship. The OPK did not acknowledge the collective right of the Jewish community to have these children returned to its surviving members or have them placed under the care of its institutions. Thus, many children remained with their Christian foster parents and grew up unaware of their Jewish origins. The

Lina Kaufmann and her daughter Marion reunited after
liberation. The mother and daughter hid separately during the war. Marion Kaufmann was in a Catholic convent,
then on a farm just outside Amsterdam. Her mother first
hid in a windowless room in the city, then spent a year
and a half living in a haystack. The photo was taken
upon their return to Amsterdam in 1945.
United States Holocaust Memorial Museum, Washington
D.C., courtesy of Marion I. Cassirer

struggle over the fate of the "hidden children" was perhaps the most dramatic part of Dutch Jewry's efforts to build a future after the catastrophe.

The old Jewish district in Amsterdam was almost entirely dismantled during the so-called Hunger Winter of 1944–45, when the wooden parts of the buildings were used for firewood. The famous Portuguese Synagogue, the Esnoga, survived due to its status as a protected national historic monument. The library attached to the synagogue, Etz Hayyim, reopened in 1947, after most of its manuscripts and collections had been successfully recovered from the notorious former Nazi-run Institute for the Study of the Jewish Question in Frankfurt.[5] On May 9, 1945, Rabbi Justus Tal, who had survived the war in hiding in Amsterdam, addressed the survivors gathered in the Esnoga for the first postwar religious service. Tal was appointed as the Chief Rabbi of Amsterdam in 1951 and he later chaired the Chief Rabbinate of the Netherlands as well. Along with the few surviving rabbis, Tal did everything to maintain "the typical Dutch character of their Judaism."[6] This meant adherence to a "moderate Orthodoxy," in which the rabbi and Jewish religious law (*halakhah*) maintained full authority in the synagogue but community members were integrated into Dutch civil society. It also meant that Dutch Orthodoxy should be protected from "foreign" influences, either from the liberal or the ultra-Orthodox side.[7] One of the consequences of the Holocaust was that postwar Dutch rabbis "were more interested in orthodoxy than worldly interaction."[8] They felt safer in the secluded world of religion and considered themselves the guardians of the species *hollandia judaica*.

Regular religious services began to take place again in the Ashkenazi and Portuguese communities in Amsterdam (both were Orthodox) fairly soon after the end of the war.[9] The rabbinate emerged as the most important ally of the strictly Orthodox *Agudas Jisroel* movement. This organization and its workers' wing, *Poale Agudat Jisrael*, played a decisive role in rebuilding the infrastructure of Jewish life after the war. They established a reception center for survivors in Amsterdam, founded various journals, and organized regional days of Jewish education (*Limmud* days). A separate youth movement, *Hasjalsjelet*, was also launched and managed to reach some of the non-Orthodox youth. Though there was a liberal Jewish community (*Liberaal Joodse Gemeente*) in Amsterdam, it formed a small German Jewish enclave among Dutch Jews until the mid-1950s, when its membership increased considerably.

Secular Zionism also attracted many (mostly young) survivors and emerged as the main alternative to the traditional Orthodox Dutch Jewish identity. Dutch Jews' long-standing weekly, *Nieuw Israëlietisch Weekblad*, reappeared on May 17, 1945, just twelve days after the liberation of Amsterdam. In contrast to its prewar Orthodox orientation, it was now Zionist.[10] The Dutch Zionist Union (*Nederlandse Zionistenbond*) was the first prewar Jewish organization to recover. It

The first postwar service in the Portuguese
Synagogue, May 9, 1945. Photo: Boris Kowadlo,
Nederlands Fotomuseum Rotterdam, Netherlands

counted 706 members in the Dutch capital at the end of 1945, but within a year, this number grew to 1,039.[11] The Zionists enjoyed the support of the Jewish Coordination Committee. They established *hakhsharot* (camps where young Dutch Jews were prepared for emigration to Palestine), and organized a protest in Amsterdam against the British government's policies in the Middle East. The Jewish Agency maintained an office in the city, providing assistance to those who wanted to emigrate to Mandate Palestine.[12] Although many Dutch Jewish survivors did indeed leave the country, only about 1,000 of the estimated 6,000 Jews who left in the immediate postwar years went to Palestine/Israel.[13]

Dutch non-Jews, preoccupied with their own survival, did not treat their returning Jewish compatriots with much compassion, nor were they willing to acknowledge the Jews' greater losses and suffering during the war. The contemporary Dutch attitude towards Jews was aptly summarized in an article in the resistance magazine *De Patriot* in July 1945, which urged Jews to be thankful for what they had and "show their gratitude first of all by making up what has to be made up to those who have become victims on behalf of Jews." They were, after all, "certainly not the only ones who had a bad time and who suffered."[14] In 1951, Amsterdam erected its first Holocaust memorial. The primary aim of "The Gratitude Monument" was to commemorate those who helped hide Jews during the war. The notion of a united Dutch resistance to anti-Jewish actions and the German occupation forces became a founding myth of postwar Dutch society.

As a consequence of this line of thinking, all Dutch war victims were commemorated equally and there was a general reluctance to honor Jewish victimhood in particular. The case of the Hollandsche Schouwburg in Amsterdam showcases this phenomenon. The Schouwburg had been a theater before the war but in 1942 and 1943, it served as a collection point for at least 46,000 Jews awaiting deportation.[15] In November 1945, it reopened as an entertainment venue, which soon evoked Jewish protests. Years of disagreement followed, and the conflict came to involve the building's new owners, the municipality of Amsterdam, and a Jewish foundation set up to fight for ownership of the building. Only in 1958 did the Amsterdam city council finally decide to establish an official commemorative site for Jewish Holocaust victims in the building.

Having lost about 80 percent of their prewar members and surrounded by a mostly callous non-Jewish Dutch majority, the small postwar Jewish community of Amsterdam struggled to define itself in this new reality: many turned to traditional Dutch Jewish Orthodoxy, others to secular Zionism. Though a few thousand Jews continue to live in Amsterdam to this day, most Jewish sites are only mementos of the destroyed community.

Zionist summer camp in which many young Amsterdam
Jews took part, ca. 1946–1947. Jewish Historical
Museum Amsterdam

The ship "Negbah" leaving the port of Amsterdam
for Israel with Dutch Jews on board, 1948.
Jewish Historical Museum Amsterdam

The building of the Hollandsche Schouwburg in
Amsterdam, which had served as a collection point for
Dutch Jews awaiting deportation during the war, 1955.
Jewish Historical Museum Amsterdam

1 See "Hollandsche Schouwburg ontdekt uniek naoorlogs lied. Waar bleven de Joden van ons Amsterdam," accessed July 8, 2019, https://yadvashem.nl/hollandsche-schouwburg-ontdekt-uniek-naoorlogs-lied-waar-bleven-de-joden-van-ons-amsterdam/.
2 Peter Tammes, "Surviving the Holocaust: Socio-demographic Differences among Amsterdam Jews," *European Journal of Population* 33.3 (2017), 293; Edward van Voolen, "Ashkenazi Jews in Amsterdam," Museum of the Jewish People at Beit Hatfutsot, accessed April 16, 2019, https://www.bh.org.il/ashkenazi-jews-amsterdam/.
3 Bart Wallet, "Eine Familie von Gemeinschaften. Die Dynamik des Judentums in den Niederlanden in der Nachkriegszeit" (draft paper, 2018), 2. The author would like to thank Bart Wallet for making the manuscript available.
4 Diane L. Wolf, *Beyond Anne Frank: Hidden Children and Postwar Families in Holland* (Berkeley: University of California Press, 2007), 116.
5 "The Netherlands," *American Jewish Year Book* 50 (1948/49), 332. For more on the systematic theft of Jewish cultural assets during the war and their subsequent recovery, see Elisabeth Gallas's contribution to this volume.
6 Chaya Brasz, "After the Shoah: Continuity and Change in the Postwar Jewish Community of the Netherlands," *Jewish History* 15.2 (2001), 154.
7 Wallet, "Eine Familie von Gemeinschaften," 2–3.
8 Ido de Haan, "Prominent Jews. Absence and Presence of Jews in Postwar Netherlands" (unpublished manuscript, 2019), 2. The author would like to thank Ido de Haan for making the manuscript available.
9 For a detailed history of these communities, see *The History of the Jews in the Netherlands*, ed. Hans Blom, Renate G., Fuks-Mansfeld and Ivo Schöffer, translated by Arnold J. Pomerans (Oxford: Littman Library, 2007).
10 Chaya Brasz, *Removing the Yellow Badge. The Struggle for a Jewish Community in the Postwar Netherlands* (Jerusalem: Institute for Research on Dutch Jewry, 1995), 102.
11 Henriëtte Boas, "De Nederlandse Zionisten Bond na de bevrijding," first published in *Het beloofde land* in 1995, accessed April 23, 2019, https://likoed.nl/1995/06/de-nederlandse-zionisten-bond-na-de-bevrijding/.
12 Wallet, "Eine Familie von Gemeinschaften," 1.
13 Brasz, "After the Shoah," 152.
14 Dienke Hondius, *Return: Holocaust Survivors and Dutch Anti-Semitism* (Westport, CT: Praeger, 2003), 59.
15 David Duindam, *Fragments of the Holocaust: The Amsterdam Hollandsche Schouwburg as a Site of Memory* (Amsterdam: Amsterdam University Press, 2019), 9.

ABEL JACOB HERZBERG
(1893–1989)

Abel Jacob Herzberg was the son of Russian Jewish immigrants. He studied law in Amsterdam and was the chairman of the Dutch Zionist Union for several years prior to the war. During the Second World War, he was interned in Bergen-Belsen and was liberated by the Red Army on a train that had left the camp shortly before its liberation. His wife, Thea, also survived, and so did his three children, Esther, Ab, and Judith, who had been in hiding with non-Jewish foster parents in the Netherlands.

After the war, Herzberg returned to Amsterdam and reunited with his family. In 1946, he published *Amor Fati* (1946), the first of his many publications about Jewish experiences during the war. In 1950, under the title *Tweestromenland* (*Between two Streams*), he also published the diary he had kept in Bergen-Belsen. A prolific writer of magazine articles and books, Herzberg spoke up on all major postwar issues related to the wartime persecution of Jews. He received several prestigious Dutch literary awards, including the Wijnandts Franckenprijs for *Amor Fati* in 1949, and the P.C. Hooft Prijs for his lifetime achievements in the literary field in 1974.

After the war, he also became a partner in Rients Dijkstra's law firm. In this capacity, he gave legal counsel to Abraham Asscher and David Cohen, two wartime Jewish leaders who had been indicted by the Jewish Council of Honor on charges of collaboration. This role did not make Herzberg popular within the Jewish community, but he was convinced that Asscher and Cohen had not coope-rated with the Nazis, and that nobody was entitled to pass judgment on them.

Even though two of his three children moved to Israel, Abel Jacob Herzberg stayed in Amsterdam until the end of his life.

Abel J. Herzberg speaks at the commemoration of the 50th anniversary of Theodor Herzl's death in the Portuguese Synagogue in Amsterdam, 1954. Photo: Boris Kowadlo, Nederlands Fotomuseum Rotterdam, Netherlands

Joint meeting of the Dutch Zionist Union and the
fundraising organization for Israel, United Israel Appeal,
in Amsterdam, 1953. Abel J. Herzberg third from left.
He was a long-time member of the Zionist Union.
Photo: Boris Kowadlo, Nederlands Fotomuseum
Rotterdam, Netherlands

Abel J. Herzberg gives a speech on the Museumplein
in Amsterdam on the occasion of the proclamation of
the State of Israel, May 16, 1948. Photo: Jaap Vaz Dias,
Literatuurmuseum, Den Haag, Netherlands

BLOEME EVERS-EMDEN
(1926–2016)

Bloeme Evers-Emden was born into a poor socialist Jewish family in Amsterdam as Bloeme Emden. During the war, she went into hiding with friends of her parents. Despite moving from place to place frequently, she was discovered and deported to Auschwitz in 1944. She was later transferred to the Liebau concentration camp where she was liberated by the Red Army. She was the only member of her family to survive; her mother, father, and younger sister, Via Roosje, perished in the Sobibor extermination camp.

Together with a small group of friends she walked back to the Netherlands after their liberation, a journey that took six weeks. First, she lived in The Hague with a friend, another survivor. She met Hans Evers, an art appraiser, there, whom she later married. The couple moved to Amsterdam and had six children. Meanwhile, Bloeme Evers-Emden was working as a nurse. She signed up to a *hakhsharah*, but Hans did not want to move to Israel, so the couple stayed in the Netherlands. She later recalled that, at the time, she was unable to talk about her experiences during the war.

She began studying psychology part-time at the University of Amsterdam in 1964 and researched the trauma of Jewish children who had been hidden during the war. Bloeme Evers-Emden completed her doctorate in psychology in 1989 and undertook groundbreaking research on the psychological consequences of hiding during the war, focusing not only on the children, but also on their parents and foster parents. Her autobiography, *Als een pluisje in de wind* (*Like Lint in the Wind*), was published in 2012.

Bloeme Emden, 1948. Jewish
Historical Museum Amsterdam

Bloeme Emden's portrait with her father Emanuel and younger sister Via, ca. 1942. Only Bloeme Emden survived the war. United States Holocaust Memorial Museum, Washington D.C., courtesy of Bloeme Evers-Emden.

Bloeme Emden's registration form for a *hakhsharah* training program of the Association of Palestinian Pioneers in the Netherlands, 1948. The main goal of the program was to prepare young Jews for emigration to, and life in, Palestine. Despite registering, Bloeme Emden did not move to Israel at that time. Jewish Historical Museum Amsterdam

OUR COURAGE
THE MEANING OF ZIONISM FOR SURVIVORS IN THE AFTERMATH OF THE HOLOCAUST

AVINOAM PATT

The Jewish Displaced Persons, or *She'erit Hapletah* (Surviving Remnant), emerged from the catastrophe of the Holocaust to form a vibrant, active, and fiercely independent community that played a prominent role in diplomatic negotiations ultimately leading to the creation of the State of Israel. International observers tasked with finding a solution to the problem of Jewish statelessness among survivors gathered in the DP camps of postwar Europe interpreted their widespread "Palestine passion" as necessitating a diplomatic solution that would result in the creation of a Jewish state in Palestine. For this reason, it is important to understand the sources and significance of Zionism for the *She'erit Hapletah* in postwar Germany. How was a situation so amenable to the Zionist project created in such a short period following the war? Why did so many young Jewish survivors choose such a course so quickly, and why did the course they chose come to characterize the conduct of Jewish Holocaust survivors as a whole? Finally, what was the appeal of Zionism for the Jewish DP population, and what did it mean to them, in practice, on the everyday level, as they awaited a resolution of their stateless condition after the war? These are not idle questions; the answers to them bear heavily upon our understanding of the history of the establishment of the State of Israel in 1948.

Following the Second World War, the seemingly overwhelming Zionist enthusiasm of the Jewish DPs, demonstrated in part by the gravitation of a significant portion of Jewish DP youth to *kibbutzim* and *hakhsharot*, the election of ardently Zionist Jewish DP camp committee leaders, and the creation of educational and cultural networks that envisioned a Jewish future in Israel, were all vital in informing the diplomatic decisions of international observers representing the United States, Britain, and the United Nations (UN) who weighed the desires of the large Jewish refugee population in Europe. Zionism proved appealing and fulfilled a crucial function for survivors, aid agencies, and American occupiers in postwar Germany. It offered meaning to a broad swath of the surviving population, even for those Jewish DPs who eventually journeyed to destinations other than Israel. This support would lead to the creation of a flourishing Zionist network in the American occupation zone that did in fact ultimately aid in the creation of the State of Israel.

THE JEWS IN GERMANY AFTER LIBERATION

Immediately following liberation, the 50,000 or so Jewish DPs faced a difficult decision: should they attempt to return to their home countries or remain in occupied Germany? Unsure of what awaited them at home and often fairly certain that their families had been destroyed during the war, those who decided to stay in a DP camp also had to face the fact that this, initially, meant continuing to live with collaborators, mostly Baltic DPs, who also refused to return home. Jewish survivors who had made the decision to remain in Germany thus faced a choice: they could move to a DP camp or they could settle in German towns and cities, a choice that some 15,000 German Jewish survivors, most of them outside of DP camps in 1945, were more likely to make.[1]

Some of the first foreign Jews to encounter the surviving Jewish population were chaplains serving with the American military. One particularly active chaplain, Abraham Klausner, reported to his superiors in the United States on the conditions faced by Jewish DPs in Germany. One month after liberation, Klausner visited approximately 14,000 Jews living in seventeen DP camps. He found deplorable conditions, poor accommodation, no plumbing, no clothing, rampant disease, continuing malnourishment, and a lack of any plan on the part of the American military. "Liberated but not free, that is the paradox of the Jew," he concluded.[2] And indeed, of the approximately 50,000 to 60,000 Jews liberated on German territory, many thousands perished from complications arising from disease, starvation, and the camp experience.[3]

While organizing amongst themselves, the DPs and chaplains like Klausner continued to describe the poor conditions facing the DPs in letters to military authorities and international Jewish organizations. Jewish DPs pleaded for assistance from the U.S. military government and the United Nations Relief and Rehabilitation Administration (UNRRA) to rectify their miserable situation.[4] Together with other chaplains and scattered soldiers of the British Army's Jewish Brigade, Klausner played an important role in communicating this demand to the outside world–especially at a time when the *Yishuv* was still uncertain as to whether the DPs could aid them in the struggle to create a state.

While demonstrating striking resourcefulness in the wake of tragedy, the survivors in the Munich region (Dachau, Landsberg, St. Otillien, and the

U.S. army chaplain Rabbi Abraham Klausner speaks at the first postwar Zionist conference in Munich, 1945. Photo: George Kadish/Zvi Kadushin, United States Holocaust Memorial Museum, Washington D.C., courtesy of George Kadish/Zvii Kadushin

General Joseph McNarney signs the charter recognizing the Central Committee of Liberated Jews in Bavaria, in which the American Army acknowledged the Central Committee as the official representative body of Jewish DPs in the American zone of Germany, 1946. United States Holocaust Memorial Museum, Washington D.C., courtesy of Herbert Friedman surrounding area) were also disenchanted with the Jewish relief organizations. Their slow arrival gave rise to a sense of abandonment that would remain a central feature of the Surviving Remnant's constant striving for independence.

Discouraged by the delay of aid from world Jewry and the sense that "mankind" would not be capable of understanding what the surviving Jewish population had endured, Zalman Grinberg, a survivor from Kovno liberated from Kaufering who had taken control of the military hospital at the St. Ottilien monastery, worked with Klausner to take matters into their own hands.[5] Assisted by survivors and representatives from the Jewish Brigade, they convened the first meeting of the Central Committee of Liberated Jews in the U.S. zone of Germany (CCLJ) on July 1, 1945, at the Feldafing Displaced Persons camp near Dachau.[6] The Central Committee's mission was to champion the interests of the Jewish DPs and to draw the attention of the U.S. Army and UNRRA to their plight. In September 1946, the CCLJ finally gained official U.S. Army recognition as "the legal and democratic representation of the liberated Jews in the American Zone." The political organization of the *She'erit Hapletah*, and the priorities of its largely Zionist leadership, would greatly influence the options available to the Jewish DP population as a whole. The committee called for unity among the Jews in the effort to build the Jewish State, and demanded that the British open the gates of Palestine.[7] The CCLJ would maintain its passionate Zionist position throughout its existence; the United Zionist Organization (UZO), a group founded by veteran Zionist activist Yitzhak Ratner, aided the CCLJ in its Zionist advocacy.[8]

The newly formed DP leadership, with the support of American Jewish chaplains like Rabbi Klausner and GIs, worked to ameliorate conditions in the DP camps and prevent Jewish DPs from being housed with non-Jewish DPs perceived as former collaborators. In the months after liberation, the Jewish DP population continued to increase as the U.S. Army struggled to cope with the influx of increasing numbers of Eastern European Jews. Reports by survivors and Jewish chaplains about continuing deprivation and poor organization of the relief effort in the liberated camps eventually prompted American officials to take a greater interest in the problem of the displaced persons. President Truman dispatched Earl Harrison to Europe in the summer of 1945 to "determine the extent to which those needs [of the DPs] are being met by military, governmental and private organizations."[9] In his scathing report back to Truman, published in August 1945, Harrison proposed that Jews be separated in their own camps and that 100,000 immigration certificates to Palestine be granted immediately. In response, American authorities moved Jews into separate camps and agreed to the appointment of an Adviser for Jewish Affairs. Harrison's report served to link the resolution of the Jewish DP situation with the situation in Palestine, thereby elevating the diplomatic implications of the Jewish DPs' political stance.

Still, Jewish DPs had the distinct sense that their many calls for assistance continued to fall on deaf ears both in Germany and in the U.S.

The early political leadership of the *She'erit Hapletah*, composed of many former members of Zionist youth groups who had chosen to remain in Germany rather than return to Eastern Europe, was overwhelmingly attuned to the needs of the young survivors in the DP camps.[10] It very quickly became evident that as much as half of the surviving population was under the age of twenty-five, and some 80 percent were younger than forty. These young people, who were more likely to have survived years of persecution because of their hardiness, because they had been selected for work, and because they were less likely to have been responsible for dependent children, were, for the most part, orphaned and alone.[11]

In many cases it was the surviving members of Zionist youth movements and political parties who undertook the self-help work and, in turn, became most active among those seeking to convince survivors not to return to Eastern Europe. For the young Jewish survivors in the DP camps (primarily those under the age of 35), regardless of whether they had experience in a Zionist youth group before the war, *kibbutz* groups emerged as attractive options, providing them with the camaraderie, support, and replacement "family" they so desperately craved. The emerging popularity of the alternative living experiment at Kibbutz Buchenwald demonstrated the value of this option to DP youth and the Jewish DP leadership.[12] Despite reservations about farming the accursed German soil and entering into relationships with German locals, the young farmers believed that the end goal–building of the Land of Israel–justified the temporary transgression of working in Germany. (Eventually, forty such agricultural training farms, or *hakhsharot*, would be established around the American occupation zone of Germany.)

At the first conference of liberated Jews in Germany and Austria, Leib Pinkusewitz, representative of the DPs from Frankfurt, reported on improvements in terms of food and housing. But they desired more than to see their material needs met; they wanted a homeland.

> We have no intentions whatever to remain in Germany. All other nations are removing their sons from Germany, giving them a home in their own fatherland. Whither are we to go? The countries we came from do not spell home to us. There our dearest ones were butchered. Our only way leads to Eretz Israel. Not until we come to Eretz Israel will our life have any meaning.[13]

The July 25, 1945 conference produced fourteen resolutions including a demand for the immediate establishment of a Jewish homeland, its recognition as a

A Jewish farmer works a field in Kibbutz Buchenwald, ca. 1945–1947. The original caption reads: "Kibbutz Buchenwald. Reaping the wheat. The Zionist flag flying proudly over the Jewish Farm. A little piece of Palestine in Germany." Photo: David Marcus, United States Holocaust Memorial Museum, Washington D.C., courtesy of David and Tamara Marcus member of the UN, and unity among survivors. The DP leadership also called upon young survivors to be the revitalizing force in the rebirth of the Jewish people after the catastrophe.

THE ZEILSHEIM DP CAMP AND THE IMPORTANCE OF ZIONISM FOR THE DPS' IDENTITY

In the Zeilsheim DP camp near Frankfurt, the impact of Zionism was central to the creation of a common identity. East European Zionist survivors took the lead in organizing Jewish life.[14] They established two *kibbutzim* dedicated to training for life in the homeland; a smaller *kibbutz*, with 75 members, focused on agricultural training, while the larger, with 250 members, focused on vocational training. JDC worker Sadie Sender, who arrived in Zeilsheim in late September 1945, summarized the situation for JDC leaders in New York some three months after her arrival at the newly established camp: "The Zionist group, being the only body which is organized, is assuming the leadership of the people. Since the majority of these people want to go to Palestine, they can rally around the Zionist banner."[15] She interpreted support for the Zionist leadership among the non-Zionists as a fervent belief that a homeland was necessary even if they had alternative immigration plans. For the Surviving Remnant gathered in Zeilsheim, shared wartime experiences, statelessness, the loss of family and prewar communities, and the intense need to build a new life in the aftermath of catastrophe, created a strong connection to their group in Zeilsheim and to the larger European Jewish community. As a JDC survey revealed, this sense of shared national identity born out of prewar and wartime experiences was not necessarily Zionist; the intense sense of common struggle, common hope for the future, and common sense of abandonment might have been projected onto a Zionist future, but was also unique and distinct from a Palestinocentric form of Jewish national identity.

Another illustration of this shared unity can be seen in a list of Yiddish-language camp newspapers: "Our World, Our Goal, Our Word, Our Hope, Our Front, Our Courage, Our Voice, Our Struggle, and of course, Our Way. As the names indicate," these newspapers were "written by Jews for one another" as a "forum" for "Jews who were bound together by their wartime sufferings."[16]

An early edition of the Zeilsheim DP camp newspaper *Undzer Mut* (*Our Courage*) published in December 1945 captured the longing of the DP population in Zeilsheim for a solution to their stateless condition after years of suffering and wandering: "we hope that on(e) day our wishes will be fulfilled and we shall be free citizens in the land of our forefathers in PALESTINE!" In May 1946, the newspaper's new name expressed the same feeling: *UNTERVEGS* (*En Route*).

After the Harrison report, the JDC joined four other Jewish organizations (the American Jewish Conference, the Jewish Agency for Palestine, the World Jewish Congress, and the American Jewish Committee) to present DP concerns to the United States government.[17] Debates over what might be best for the Jewish DP population as a whole–Zionist education and planning for a future in Palestine vs. preparing for emigration anywhere–represented a tremendous challenge for the JDC, which identified itself as an apolitical organization representing all Jews, giving no preference to one political view over another. Even so, the educational framework that the JDC, working together with the Jewish Agency, ultimately developed, was very much focused on preparing for a future life in Palestine, reflecting what Yehuda Bauer described as "the will of the people."[18]

THE *YISHUV* AND DP ZIONISM

While the youth movement leaders and the DP leadership viewed Zionist educational projects and the creation of *kibbutz* groups as therapeutic activities for survivor youth which also highlighted a future in Palestine, others in the Zionist movement (and in the administration of the American occupation zone) viewed the *She'erit Hapletah* in far more instrumental terms. Both during and after the war, the *Yishuv* continued to question whether traumatized survivors could really be counted on to aid in the creation of the state.[19] Nonetheless, David Ben-Gurion's October 1945 tour of DP camps, the *kibbutzim* and training camps convinced the head of the Jewish Agency of the Zionist enthusiasm and initiative of the *She'erit Hapletah*.

In the wake of the Harrison report, Ben-Gurion submitted a number of suggestions to Eisenhower on how to improve the morale of the Jewish DPs, which included allowing the Jewish DPs to govern themselves, subject to the ultimate authority of the U.S. Army, and providing agricultural and vocational training on confiscated Nazi farms.[20] Other American officials were impressed by the early success of Kibbutz Buchenwald, Kibbutz Nili (located on the former property of Nazi Gauleiter Julius Streicher near Nuremberg), and other *hakhsharot* in not only improving DP morale and spiritual rehabilitation, but in also providing for many of their own food needs and conveniently preparing for their future in Palestine (and not in the United States). Moreover, they served as a possible form of punishment for former Nazis. UNRRA' s support for training farms dovetailed nicely with the Jewish Agency for Palestine's diplomatic goals. UNRRA would be assisted in its efforts to secure land and instructors for farming projects by representatives of the Jewish Agency operating in Germany. The first delegation of twenty Jewish Agency emissaries (so-called *shlichim*), technically working under the auspices of UNRRA, had arrived in Germany in the

A later edition of the Zeilsheim DP camp newspaper
Undzer Mut, February 1946. Ghetto Fighters' House
Kibbutz Photo Archive, Western Galilee, Israel

אויפקלערוננ:

אין איצטיקן, ערשטן נומער אין נארמאלן דרוק, ארויסגע־
געבענעם „אונדזער מוט". אונדזער מוט־האבן מיר גע־
האלמן פאר נויטיק, איבערצודרוקן א טייל ארטיקלען, וועלכע
זענען שוין ווינער צייט פארעפנטלעכט געווארן אין אונדזערע
פאריקע 3 נומערן, וואס זענען אבער ליידער, נישט געווען
גענוג לעזבאר פאר די ברייטע מאסן און דאס צוליב
אומגעהיערע, מעכנישע שוועריקייטן, אין וועלכן מיר זענען
געווען געצוואונגען ארויסצוגעבן די ערשטע 3 נומערן.

די פארדינסטן שרייבן מיר צו אויף דער קאנטא פון
די ס א ו ק א.
און חנם, די ארטיקלען האבן טיילווייז פארלוירן
זייער אקטואליטעט, זענען זיי אבער דאך פון גע־
שיכטלעכן שטאנדפונקט כדאי אפגעדרוקט צו ווערן,־אום
אויסצודריקן די אמת־דיקע אפשפיגלונג פון אונדזער לעבן דא־
רעדאקציע־קאלעגיום.

אינהאלט:

An early edition of the Zeilsheim DP camp newspaper
Undzer Mut, December 1945. Ghetto Fighters' House
Kibbutz Photo Archive, Western Galilee, Israel

middle of December 1945 and worked to a) organize *aliyah*, b) assist the *Bricha* to accommodate "infiltrees" from Eastern Europe who had either remained in Poland after liberation or in most cases first been repatriated from the Soviet Union, c) facilitate agricultural and vocational training, d) offer political instruction, and e) provide Zionist education.[21] With the arrival of more *shlichim* over the course of 1946, the Jewish Agency team expanded its efforts to assist in the opening of *hakhsharot*. For political reasons, the Jewish Agency believed that such agricultural training farms, while preparing youth for life in Palestine, could also increase the visibility of DP Zionism and strengthen the pioneering avant-garde by isolating them from the rest of the DP camp. For the most part, however, Jewish Agency workers adopted a largely instrumental view of young DPs based on a continuing belief that survivor youth were unsuitable for agricultural labor. Haim Hoffman, head of the Jewish Agency delegation from the *Yishuv*, agreed that survivor youth were less than ideal for the type of labor required of agricultural workers, but he also believed that the farms could successfully transform their residents into suitable Zionist material: "after a short time, a different type of person was created from the residents of the camps who was even closer to the Eretz Yisrael type of person."[22]

Through the support of these various groups, the number of farms in the American occupation zone of Germany grew steadily. By June 1946, before the large infiltration of East European Jewish refugees with the *Bricha*, 35 farms with over 3,600 inhabitants had been established, suggesting that, while the stated rationale was to alleviate overcrowding in the DP camps, political concerns may have been as significant as demographic ones. Just as importantly, on the diplomatic level, the high visibility of the *kibbutzim* and *hakhsharot* and the Zionist enthusiasm in evidence there demonstrated to outside observers a perceived state of "Palestine passion" among Jewish DPs. The apparent importance of Zionism for the increasing numbers of arriving DPs confirmed the necessity of the Zionist solution for representatives of the Anglo-American Committee of Inquiry, appointed by the governments of England and the United States after the Harrison report. After beginning their work in London and Washington in January 1946, members of the committee visited the DP camps and Poland to assess the Jewish situation beginning in February.[23] Notwithstanding some concerns over Zionist propaganda and manipulation, on April 20, 1946, the AACI recommended "(A) that 100,000 certificates be authorized immediately for the admission into Palestine of Jews who have been the victims of Nazi and Fascist persecution; (B) that these certificates be awarded as far as possible in 1946 and that actual immigration be pushed forward as rapidly as conditions will permit." The committee came to this conclusion not only because of a lack of any other options but also because the members genuinely believed that this was the truest expression of the Jewish DPs' desires: "[Palestine] is where almost all of them want to go. There they are sure that they will receive a welcome denied them elsewhere. There they hope to enjoy peace and rebuild their lives." The committee based these findings in part on surveys conducted among the Jewish DPs but also on their own observations among them. While many DPs were seen as being reluctant to work, "wherever facilities are provided for practical training for life in Palestine they eagerly take advantage of them."[24]

Survivors in the DP camps also worked to create a collective memory of wartime survival. Survival in ghettos, camps, hiding, and partisan units (with a disproportionate focus on resistance activities) appeared as the quintessential experiences under the Nazis, although a large portion of Jewish DPs had escaped Nazi occupation into the Soviet Union. The first anniversary of the Warsaw revolt marked in the DP camps (on April 19, 1946), for example, highligh-ted the ways in which a specific Zionist memorialization of the Warsaw Ghetto Uprising became a central focal point for remembrance among the diverse population of survivors. Speaking at the commemoration of the revolt, Abraham Klausner linked the battle that had begun in Warsaw with the continued struggle for the creation of a Jewish state in the Land of Israel. The President of the Central Committee, Dr. Zalman Grinberg, spoke about the spiritual and physical resistance in the ghettos and camps, describing the uprising in Warsaw as "the expression of the resistance will of the 6 million killed Jews in Europe."[25] Despite the presence of fighters from other movements in the DP camps, the lessons of the revolt were understood to support the Zionist position, encoura-ging the *She'erit Hapletah* "to turn all their energies to the creation of a sovereign Jewish state in the land of their forefathers."[26] According to this viewpoint, the surviving members of the Zionist elite finally managed to pull off the revolt in Warsaw once they had risen to the dominant position of the surviving Jewish population, demonstrating that only a Jewish people concentrated in their state would be able to realize its full historical strength.

Even so, dissenting voices could be heard in the DP camps, from Jewish Socialist Bundists or the large percentage of Jews who had no interest in resett-ling in the Land of Israel. The satirical DP camp publication, *Afn Tsimbl (On the Cimbalom)*, lampooned the choices of many Zionist DP leaders who worked so hard to convince Jewish DPs to make *aliyah*, even though they wound up in America themselves. One target was the fictional "Moshe Zilberberg, Zionist activist, fighter in the Warsaw ghetto, and presidium member of the Z.K. [Central Committee] of the Liberated Jews in Germany, leader of Feldafing, editor of *Dos Fraye Wort*, etc.," who made the decision to relocate to Lynn, Massachusetts.[27] In similar fashion, a satirical letter purportedly from a mother in Munich to her daughter in New York informed the daughter that her father had become a leftist Zionist, which, the article joked, meant that after sending everyone else to the Jewish state, he and her mother planned to come and live with her in New York.[28]

Such pointed jabs at leaders of the DP camps signaled an underlying truth about the nature of Zionism in the DP camps: while the *She'erit Hapletah* manifested an overwhelming belief in the need for a Zionist solution to the collective problem of Jewish statelessness, individual survivors who tired of the long wait in the DP camps were eager to settle in new home countries and in America in particular. The United States was slow to change immigration policies after the war and, as the months dragged into years, Jewish DPs would become more and more open to alternative migration possibilities. Despite the recommendations of the Anglo-American Committee in April 1946, over the course of 1946 and into 1947, diplomatic efforts stalled and it became clear that for the majority of the Jewish DPs, life would continue at least temporarily in Germany and not on the path to Palestine. The massive influx of Jews from Eastern Europe also led to a major demographic shift in the DP camps; among the Jews who had survived in the far reaches of the Soviet Union were many more families. Over the course of 1946, approximately 100,000 Jews from Eastern Europe were brought to the American zone of Germany by the *Bricha*, some one-third of them organized within the framework of *kibbutzim* run by the pioneering Zionist youth movements.[29] By 1947, 250,000 Jews were gathered in the DP camps of Germany, Austria, and Italy. They were in desperate need of a solution to their stateless condition. On November 29, 1947, when the United Nations voted for the partition of Palestine, they greeted the announcement with great enthusiasm.

CONCLUSION: THE FUNCTIONS OF ZIONISM IN POSTWAR GERMANY

For orphaned young survivors in search of surrogate families in *kibbutz* groups after the war, the ideological pronouncements of Central Committee leaders that surviving youth had an obligation to serve as the vital force in the rebirth of the Jewish people mattered little. Nonetheless, ideology provided a significant foundation for a distinctive form of DP Zionism which supported the postwar political desires of the DPs on the diplomatic level. On the ground, DP Zionism could succeed because it made sense both on the ideological and practical level; without offering pragmatic solutions to the most pressing needs of the young survivors, it could not have attracted and maintained the following that it did.

It is clear that in the wake of the war the DPs played an important role in the creation of the State of Israel. However, even without the retro-active knowledge that Israel would ultimately be created, Zionism was highly successful in fulfilling a positive function for DP youth in the aftermath of the Holocaust by providing a secure environment for vocational training, educa-tion, rehabilitation, and a surrogate family that could ultimately restore their belief in humanity and the future of the Jewish people. For the wider Jewish DP population, Zionism met a symbolic need that had arisen for the Jewish people in the wake of tragedy even if not all would make the Zionist dream their personal reality. In the words of one survivor who intended to live in Montevideo but responded to a survey by indicating that he would make *aliyah* to Palestine, "I may be able to live in Uruguay, but the Jews … the Jews must live in Israel." The Zionism in the DP camps, then, was not monolithic, geared solely to the requirements of the *Yishuv*; it satisfied the needs, economic, therapeutic, and diplomatic, of many different groups in the postwar DP communities.

1 See Atina Grossmann, *Jews, Germans, and Allies: Close Encounters in Occupied Germany* (Princeton: Princeton University Press, 2007), 303, *n*4.

2 On Klausner's report of June 24, 1945, see Alex Grobman, *Rekindling the Flame. American Jewish Chaplains and the Survivors of European Jewry, 1944–1948* (Detroit: Wayne State University Press, 1993), 42–43.

3 See Leonard Dinnerstein, *America and the Survivors of the Holocaust* (New York: Columbia University Press, 1982), 28.

4 See Zalman Grinberg and Marian Puczyc, memorandum for OMGUS and UNRRA, July 10, 1945, YIVO Archive, DP Germany, MK 483, #340.

5 Dr. Zalman Grinberg, Report to the Jewish World Congress, May 31, 1945, YIVO Archive, DP Germany, MK (microfilm group) 483, reel 21.

6 For more on the early and extensive involvement of American Jewish chaplains in the relief efforts and organization of DP institutions, see Grobman, *Rekindling the Flame*. On the Jewish Brigade, see Yoav Gelber, "The Meeting Between the Jewish Soldiers from Palestine Serving in the British Army and *She'erit Hapletah*," in *She'erit Hapletah, 1944–1948. Rehabilitation and Political Struggle*, ed. Yisrael Gutman and Avital Saf (Jerusalem: Yad Vashem, 1990), 60–79.

7 Minutes, Conference of Liberated Jews, July 25, 1945, YIVO, MK 483, reel 61, 721–727.

8 Klausner helped the UZO acquire office space adjacent to the CCLJ in Munich. See Abraham Klausner, *A Letter to My Children. From the Edge of the Holocaust* (San Francisco: Holocaust Center of Northern California, 2002), 41–42; Yehuda Bauer, *Flight and Rescue. Brichah* (New York: Random House, 1970), 61.

9 Arieh J. Kochavi, *Post-Holocaust Politics. Britain, the United States & Jewish Refugees, 1945–1948* (Chapel Hill: University of North Carolina Press, 2001), 89; Dinnerstein, *America and the Survivors*, chapter two.

10 See Zeev W. Mankowitz, *Life between Memory and Hope. Survivors of the Holocaust in Occupied Germany* (New York: Cambridge University Press, 2002), 36; Zeev W. Mankowitz, "The Formation of She'erit Hapletah: November 1944–July 1945," *Yad Vashem Studies* 20 (1990), 337–370. As well as a number of early leaders of the Jewish DPs in Germany–including Samuel Gringauz and Zalman Grinberg–Leib Garfunkel (the head of the organization of Holocaust Survivors in Italy) and the founders of the DP Zionist youth group, Nocham, the United Pioneer Youth Movement, emerged from an early group of survivors from Kovno concentrated in camps connected to Dachau.

11 A June 1945 survey by two Jewish Agency representatives found that 95 percent of the survivors were younger than 35. Ruth Kliger and David Shaltiel, letter to Moshe Shertok and Eliyahu Dobkin, June 11, 1945, Central Zionist Archives (CZA), S6/3659. A survey of Jewish DPs undertaken in Bavaria in February 1946 found that 83.1 percent of their number were between the ages of fifteen and 40, more than 40 percent were aged between fifteen and 24 and 61.3 percent between nineteen and 34. Jewish Population in Bavaria, February 1946, YIVO Archive, MK 488, Leo Schwartz Papers, Roll 9, Folder 57, #581. A study by the AJC in

the U.S. occupation zone over one year after liberation found that 83.1 percent of the Jewish DPs were between the ages of six and 44. YIVO, MK 488, LS 9, 57, #682; Jewish Population, US Zone Germany, November 30, 1946.

12   See Judith Tydor Baumel, *Kibbutz Buchenwald: Survivors and Pioneers* (New Brunswick: Rutgers University Press, 1997).

13   See YIVO Archive, DP Germany, MK 483, Reel 61, #721–727; Laura J. Hilton, "The Reshaping of Jewish Communities and Identities in Frankfurt and Zeilsheim in 1945," in *"We are Here". New Approaches to Jewish Displaced Persons in Postwar Germany*, ed. Avinoam J. Patt and Michael Berkowitz (Detroit: Wayne State University Press, 2010), 199.

14   Hilton, "The Reshaping of Jewish Communities," 214. See also the city text on Frankfurt/Zeilsheim in this volume.

15   Sadie Sender, "Report on Displaced Persons at Zeilsheim," December 25, 1946, accessed January 1, 2019. http://search.archives.jdc.org/multimedia/Documents/Geneva45-54/G45-54_Count/USHMM-GENEVA_00032/USHMM-GENEVA_00032_00330.pdf#search.

16   Ruth Gay, *Safe among the Germans: Liberated Jews after World War II* (New Haven: Yale University Press, 2002), 62–63.

17   The American Jewish Conference was created in August 1943 to unify American Jewish organizations in order to better plan postwar policy. It disbanded in 1949.

18   Yehuda Bauer, *Out of the Ashes. The Impact of American Jewry on Post-Holocaust Jewish Europe* (Oxford: Pergamon, 1988), 211.

19   See for example, Dina Porat, "The Role of European Jewry in the Plans of the Zionist Movement During World War II and Its Aftermath," in *She'erit Hapletah, 1944–1948. Rehabilitation and Political Struggle*, ed. Yisrael Gutman and Avital Saf (Jerusalem: Yad Vashem, 1990), 286–303.

20   See Meir Avizohar, "Bikur Ben-Gurion be-makhanot ha-akurim ve-tefisato ha-leumit be-tom milhemet ha-olam ha-shniah," in *Yahadut mizrah Eiropah bein Shoah le-tekuma 1944–1948*, ed. Benjamin Pinkus (Sde Boker: Ben Gurion University, 1987), 260; Kochavi, *Post-Holocaust Politics*, 94; Judah Nadich, *Eisenhower and the Jews* (New York: Twayne, 1953), 238. Kochavi and Avizohar draw on Ben-Gurion's own report of his visit to the DP camps, June 11, 1945, which is held by the Ben-Gurion Archive. The Jewish DPs were granted the right to self-governance by the U.S. Army in September 1946.

21   Haim Hoffman (Yachil), "Ha-mishlekhet ha-eretz yisraelit le-She'erit Hapletah," *Yalkut Moreshet* 30 (1980), 19.

22   Hoffman, "Ha-mishlekhet ha-eretz yisraelit," 29.

23   "Visit of the sub-committee to the American zone of Austria," Vienna, February 25, 1946, USNA, RG 43 AACI Box 12, 4–5.

24   *Report of the Anglo-American Commission of Enquiry Regarding the Problems of European Jewry and Palestine, Lausanne, 20 April 1946* (London: The Majesty's Stationery Office, 1946), 14.

25   *Unzer veg* no. 29, April 19, 1946, 1.

26   Zeev W. Mankowitz, "Zionism and She'erit Hapletah," in *She'erit Hapletah, 1944–1948. Rehabilitation and Political Struggle*, ed. Yisrael Gutman and Avital Saf (Jerusalem: Yad Vashem, 1990), 220.

27   Moshe Zilberberg was indeed a Zionist leader in Feldafing—in all likelihood, he actually did end up in Massachusetts, where a relative of his was living. See Mankowitz, *Life Between Memory and Hope*, 82; YIVO Archive, Leo Schwarz papers, reel 46/1246.

28   "Letter from Munich to New York," Leo Schwarz papers, reel 46/1251, YIVO Archive.

29   See table: *Bricha* summary of Jewish migration from Poland in 1945 (from July onwards) and 1946 in Yochanan Cohen, *Overim kol gevul. Ha-Brihah—Polin 1945–1946* (Tel Aviv: Zemorah-Bitan, Masu'ah, 1995), 469. Cohen draws on sources in the *Brihah* Archive, Efal, Hativah Z. Netzer, Box 3, Folder 4.

BIBLIOGRAPHY

Avizohar, Meir. "Bikur Ben-Gurion be-makhanot ha-akurim ve-tefisato ha-leumit be-tom milhe-met ha-olam ha-shniah." In *Yahadut mizrah Eiropah bein Shoah le-tekuma 1944–1948*, edited by Benjamin Pinkus, 253–270. Sde Boker: Ben Gurion University, 1987. **/ Bauer, Yehuda.** *Flight and Rescue. Brichah.* New York: Random House, 1970. **/ Bauer, Yehuda.** *Out of the Ashes. The Impact of American Jewry on Post-Holocaust Jewish Europe.* Oxford: Pergamon, 1988. **/ Baumel, Judith Tydor.** *Kibbutz Buchenwald: Survivors and Pioneers.* New Brunswick: Rutgers University Press, 1997. **/ Cohen, Yochanan.** *Overim kol gevul. Ha-Brihah–Polin 1945–1946.* Tel Aviv: Zemorah-Bitan, Masu'ah, 1995. **/ Dinnerstein, Leonard.** *America and the Survivors of the Holocaust.* New York: Columbia University Press, 1982. **/ Gay, Ruth.** *Safe among the Germans: Liberated Jews after World War II.* New Haven: Yale University Press, 2002. **/ Gelber, Yoav.** "The Meeting Between the Jewish Soldiers from Palestine Serving in the British Army and She'erit Hapletah." In *She'erit Hapletah, 1944–1948. Rehabilitation and Political Struggle*, edited by Yisrael Gutman and Avital Saf, 60–79. Jerusalem: Yad Vashem, 1990. **/ Grobman, Alex.** *Rekindling the Flame. American Jewish Chaplains and the Survivors of European Jewry, 1944–1948.* Detroit: Wayne State University Press, 1993. **/ Grossmann, Atina.** *Jews, Germans, and Allies: Close Encounters in Occupied Germany.* Princeton: Princeton University Press, 2007. **/ Hilton, Laura J.** "The Reshaping of Jewish Communities and Identities in Frankfurt and Zeilsheim in 1945." In *"We are Here". New Approaches to Jewish Displaced Persons in Postwar Germany*, edited by Avinoam J. Patt and Michael Berkowitz, 194–226. Detroit: Wayne State University Press, 2010. **/ Hoffman (Yachil), Haim.** "Ha-mishlekhet ha-eretz yisraelit le-She'erit Hapletah." *Yalkut Moreshet* 30 (1980), 7–40. **/ Klausner, Abraham.** *A Letter to My Children. From the Edge of the Holocaust.* San Francisco: Holocaust Center of Northern California, 2002. **/ Kochavi, Arieh J.** *Post-Holocaust Politics. Britain, the United States & Jewish Refugees, 1945–1948.* Chapel Hill: University of North Carolina Press, 2001. **/ Mankowitz, Zeev W.** "The Formation of She'erit Hapletah: November 1944–July 1945." *Yad Vashem Studies* 20 (1990), 337–370. **/ Mankowitz, Zeev W.** "Zionism and She'erit Hapletah." In *She'erit Hapletah, 1944–1948. Rehabilitation and Political Struggle*, edited by Yisrael Gutman and Avital Saf, 211–230. Jerusalem: Yad Vashem, 1990. **/ Mankowitz, Zeev W.** *Life between Memory and Hope. Survivors of the Holocaust in Occupied Germany.* New York: Cambridge University Press, 2002. **/ Nadich, Judah.** *Eisenhower and the Jews.* New York: Twayne, 1953. **/ Porat, Dina.** "The Role of European Jewry in the Plans of the Zionist Movement During World War II and Its Aftermath." In *She'erit Hapletah, 1944–1948. Rehabilitation and Political Struggle*, edited by Yisrael Gutman and Avital Saf, 286–303. Jerusalem: Yad Vashem, 1990. **/** *Report of the Anglo-American Commission of Enquiry Regarding the Problems of European Jewry and Palestine, Lausanne, 20 April 1946.* London: The Majesty's Stationery Office, 1946. **/** *Unzer veg* no. 29, April 19, 1946.

BARI

THE CITY OF TRANSIT

MORITZ BAUERFEIND

> Emigration is the only path for Jewish refugees and for the remnants of
> Jewry who are living today in various European countries … Palestine
> is concretely the only country in the world which can be the aim of this
> large-scale immigration … The refugees who came to Italy drifted here
> because it is the shortest route to Palestine.
>
> Leon Garfunkel
> February 1946[1]

For many Jewish refugees, the city of Bari on the heel of Italy's "boot" became
an important initial stop on their illegal route to Palestine. The Allies had already
conquered southern Italy in September 1943, setting up refugee camps for
Jewish survivors at a time when the war still raged elsewhere in Europe, and the
systematic annihilation of Jews would continue for another eighteen months. The
Jews who were liberated in southern Italy immediately after the Allied landing
were so-called "old refugees"[2] who had fled the areas conquered by the Nazis
in the late 1930s but who had been interned by the Italian Fascists in camps such
as Ferramonti di Tarsia in Calabria. After the war ended in northern Europe,
some 50,000 "new refugees" arrived in Italy in a more or less organized fashion.[3]
Between 1945 and 1948, roughly 15,000 of them were in Italy at any one time.[4]
From 1945 to 1951, there were 97 DP camps of varying sizes in Italy, of which
60 were located to the south and 37 to the north of Florence.[5]

In the region around the Apulian city of Bari, the Jewish DPs soon began
to plan their new lives. As they saw it, once they had arrived in Italy, they were
practically in Eretz Yisrael.[6] In any event, many of them would have to wait
for years until they could move on to Palestine—and, from 1948 onwards, to
Israel—yet they were determined to take control of their fate even now. They
governed themselves, created agricultural collectives (hakhsharot), completed their
education; they also studied, worked, married, and started families. And they
created a Jewish community in Bari where, as in other parts of southern Italy,
there had been none since the mid-sixteenth century as a result of Spanish rule

New Year's card with a wish to leave for Palestine, inscription in Hebrew: "Happy New Year—year of the redemption of our people and the liberation of our homeland—Italia, Bari 1947." Private collection, Efi Lifnat, Timrat, Israel

New Year's card from the Bari DP camp. United States Holocaust Memorial Museum, Washington D.C., courtesy of Rachel Mutterperl Goldfarb and the Inquisition. All this was made possible by a multifaceted network of international refugee and Jewish aid organizations.[7]

The Union of Italian Jewish Communities (*Unione delle Comunità Israelitiche Italiane*, UCII), which was preoccupied with the reestablishment of its own communities, maintained few official contacts with its stranded brethren. While the census of August 1938 registered 46,656 Jews affiliated with the official Jewish community in Italy, barely 30,000 of them remained after 1945. Of the more than 7,000 Italian Jews whom the German occupiers and their allies had deported, a mere 831 returned home.[8]

Between August 1945 and January 1948, more than 16,000 Jewish passengers left Italy's ports towards Palestine through "La Porta di Sion" (the "Gate to Zion"). At least twelve of the 25 documented passages began in Bari or its immediate environs.[9] However, for many of the passengers, their journey through the bottleneck of the British blockade initially ended in an internment camp on Cyprus. The port of Bari was the crucial Apulian point of departure.

In April 1945, there were 1,400 DPs in the city, 500 of them in the camp and the *hakhsharot*. The other 900 were housed in various locations across the city. However, the bulk of the refugees were based in various localities along or near the coast. The four largest camps in Italy were located on the coast of the Southern Apulian province of Lecce: Santa Maria al Bagno, Santa Maria di Leuca, Santa Cesarea Terme, and Tricase Porto. In April 1945, 7,000 survivors lived there.[10] As these numbers continuously decreased, the four camps in Lecce were closed in February 1947, and the influx now concentrated on Bari.

Here, with the help of Jewish soldiers from the Allied troops, the *Merkaz ha-Plitim* (center for refugees) had already been established in September 1943 as a central port of call for all DPs in the region.[11] It operated a dining hall, a clinic, a synagogue, a school, and dormitories, while also serving as a meeting venue. Under the auspices of the Joint Palestine Emigration Committee (JPEC), established in December 1943, the first passages to Palestine were led by Zionist DPs from Ferramonti and Bari, departing from the port of Tarent as early as February 1945.

In the camps run by the UNRRA (United Nations Relief and Rehabilitation Administration), DPs mostly lived together in groups of 200.[12] The *hakhsharot* comprised smaller groups of 40 to 120 DPs.[13] These institutions were rarely based in large farms or agricultural training communes as they were in other countries such as Poland and Germany. Instead, they were mostly located in villas that had previously been privately owned and were now becoming rapidly overcrowded. Although their training, cultural, and leisure programs were not particularly sophisticated, the DPs generally preferred life in the *hakhsharot*. In particular, they valued their partial autonomy and the absence of fences. These small camps were supported especially by the JDC and members of the Jewish Brigade. As

A train arrives from Munich to Bari, with Jewish DPs
on their way to Israel, ca. 1949. The DPs are waiting for
trucks to take them to transit camps. Photo: Herbert
Steinhouse, JDC Archives, New York

Julius Levine, JDC representative for southern Italy,
inspects the supply of *matzot* destined for
the camps and settlements in the Bari area for Passover
celebrations, 1947. JDC Archives, New York

Zeev Abrahami Gottlib and his twin brother were born in Santa Maria di Leuca in Apulia. In this photo, they are sitting in front of a map of Palestine in 1947. With this photo, their parents wanted to express the desire and hope to be able to emigrate to Palestine soon. Private collection, Zeev Abrahami Gottlib, Israel

Tailor's workshop in the Santa Cesarea Terme DP camp (Lecce province), 1946. Sara Pollak did sewing for a living in the courtyard of the house where she lived with her husband and son, along with her two sisters and their families. Private collection Shmuel (Pollak) Pelleg, Kfar Saba, Israel a result, each inhabitant received fresh meat three times a week, and half a kilogram of fruit and 400 grams of bread each day.[14] The accommodation of Jewish refugees in expropriated villas (that were often not suited to the task) was repeatedly opposed by non-Jewish Italians; the refugees were accused of failing to take care of the properties placed at their disposal. This local opposition did not, however, precipitate any major demonstrations or confrontations.

Surviving Jewish members of Italian civil society assisted the refugees on an individual basis. For instance, they trained the DPs as fishermen or helped them charter boats for their further travels. But such contacts were the exception, not least due to the lack of a shared language. In the long run, the DPs–who predominantly came from Yugoslavia or Central and Eastern Europe–left few traces in southern Italy. Until they disbanded, many of these DP communities remained entirely dependent on external aid.

When the large camps in Lecce were closed in the spring of 1947, most of the remaining DPs were transferred to the north of the country. For this heterogeneous group, Italy was only ever an interim stop. Nonetheless, it presented these refugees an opportunity to renew their sense of Jewish identity and turn to Zionist ideals, something reinforced not least by the proximity to the Mediterranean and the direct perspective it offered on Eretz Yisrael.

Regardless of whether they initially came from Italy or were trying to establish themselves there as refugees, the Jews' presence was questioned by the attitudes of the non-Jewish majority. In the country in which fascism had originated, a critical scholarly or psychological engagement with the past was systematically avoided. Rather, as far as the period prior to the fall of fascism in particular was concerned, a feigned amnesia prevailed, one designed to facilitate the peaceful coexistence of all parties involved.[15]

---

[1] OJRI was the acronym of the Organization of Jewish Refugees in Italy. The quotation is from Arturo Marzano, "Jewish DPs in Post-War Italy. The Role of Italian Jewry in a Multilateral Encounter (1945–1948)," in *Italian Jewish Networks from the Seventeenth to the Twentieth Century. Bridging Europe and the Mediterranean*, ed. Francesca Bregoli, Carlotta Ferrara degli Uberti, and Guri Schwarz (Cham: Springer, 2018), 160.

[2] Chiara Renzo coined the terms "old" and "new" refugees to distinguish between those who had already arrived in the 1930s and those who arrived after the war. Chiara Renzo, "'Our Hopes Are Not Lost Yet.' The Jewish Displaced Persons in Italy. Relief, rehabilitation and self-understanding (1943–1948)," *Quest. Issues in Contemporary Jewish History* no. 12 (2017), 90–111, esp. 94–96. Accessed September 5, 2019, http://www.quest-cdecjournal.it/focus.php?id=396.

[3] Francesca Bregoli, Carlotta Ferrara degli Uberti, and Guri Schwarz, "Introduction," in *Italian Jewish Networks from the Seventeenth to the Twentieth Century. Bridging Europe and the Mediterranean*, ed. Francesca Bregoli, Carlotta Ferrara degli Uberti, and Guri Schwarz (Cham: Springer, 2018), 16.

[4] Renzo, "Our Hopes," 102. An UNRRA report from Mai 1946 noted that the organization was supporting 17,095 Jewish DPs, 7, 152 of them in camps, 5,943 in *hakhsharot*, and 4,000 in various towns. This was the highest number of Jewish DPs that the UNRRA, having taken up

its work in Italy soon after the liberation of Rome in the summer of 1944, supported at any one point in time.

5   Marzano, "Jewish DPs in Post-War Italy," 161.

6   Shmoel Mordekai Rubinstein, *Memories*, available in Hebrew online http://srmemo.blogspot.it/2008/08/blog-post_185.html, quoted in Renzo, "'Our Hopes,'" 96.

7   These included the UNRRA (later IRO) and the following Jewish organizations: JDC, ORT, and HIAS. At the national level, alongside the OJRI, the Italian Zionist Federation also supported the DPs. While the UNRRA played a crucial role in providing food aid for the DPs, the JDC mainly funded their accommodation, and HIAS bore principal responsibility for the organization of specific activities.

8   Guri Schwarz, *After Mussolini. Jewish Life and Jewish Memories in Post-Fascist Italy* (Edgware: Vallentine Mitchell, 2012), 5.

9   Here, too, reliable figures are hard to come by, given the prevalence of faulty or forged documents. For estimates, see Idith Zertal, *From Catastrophe to Power. Holocaust Survivors and the Emergence of Israel* (Berkeley: University of California Press, 1998), 17; Marzano, "Jewish DPs in Post-War Italy," 154–155; Chiara Renzo, "The Organization of the Jewish Refugees in Italy. Cultural Activities and Zionist Propaganda inside the Displaced Persons Camps (1943–48)," *Remembrance and Solidarity. Studies in 20th Century European History* no. 5 (2016), 65.

10 I owe these figures to Chiara Renzo's examination of the holdings of the Allied Control Commission.

11 From October 1944: *Merkaz la-Golah be-Italia*–Center for the Diaspora in Italy.

12 Arturo Marzano, "Relief and Rehabilitation of Jewish DPs after the Shoah. The *Hachsharot* in Italy (1945–48)," *Journal of Modern Jewish Studies* 18.3 (2019), 8.

13 Marzano, "Jewish DPs in Post-War Italy," 158.

14 Marzano, "Jewish DPs in Post-War Italy," 159.

15 See Schwarz, *After Mussolini*, 174–175; Arturo Marzano, "'Prisoners of Hope' or 'Amnesia'? The Italian Holocaust Survivors and their Aliyah to Israel," *Quest. Issues in Contemporary Jewish History* no. 1 (2010), 92–107.

RIVKA COHEN
(BORN 1946)

Cohen was born in 1946 in the small Apulian town of Santa Maria di Leuca. Her parents were Jewish survivors from Hungary. Having made their way from Budapest via Trieste, Milan, and Rome, they arrived in February 1946 at the DP camp in Santa Maria al Bagno, which was located in the province of Lecce. They were accompanied by the mother's twin sister and her husband as well as the father's sister. They had learned of a training facility sponsored by the *Torah ve-Avodah* movement in Santa Maria al Bagno when they attended an information bureau run by the Jewish Brigade in Milan. In Santa Maria al Bagno, the two young couples were given a small house with two bedrooms and a kitchen. The two twin sisters were pregnant, and each gave birth to a girl in the maternity hospital in Santa Maria di Leuca in August 1946. They named them after the girls' grandmothers who had been murdered in the Shoah: Hannah-Rivka (Friedman-Cohen) and Sara-Rivka (Rosenfeld-Nevo).

When the refugee camps in the province of Lecce were closed down in April 1947, Rivka and her parents, along with her aunt, uncle and her cousin, moved to the transit camp Bari-Palese, where they lived in large asbestos huts. On December 24, 1947, following a detour via the northern Italian town of Abbiate, they left Italy, departing from the port of Civitavecchia (near Rome) for Palestine.

In 2014, Rivka Cohen returned to Santa Maria di Leuca, her place of birth, to participate in Yael Katzir's documentary, *Shores of Light*.

Rivka Cohen's parents, aunt and uncle with Rivka (left) and her cousin as babies in Santa Maria al Bagno, 1946. Private collection Rivka Cohen, Israel

Kindergarten in Bari. Rivka Cohen on the far left,
her cousin Rivka Rosen with ribbon in her hair, 1947.
Private collection Rivka Cohen, Israel

Fathers and daughters on the beach in Bari, 1947.
Rivka Cohen and her father are on the left. Private
collection Rivka Cohen, Israel

FERENCZ GOLDSTEIN (FRANCESO GODELLI) (1914–1978)

Goldstein was born into a Hungarian-speaking family in the Transylvanian (and now Romanian) town of Bistriţa in 1914. At the time, the town was part of Austria-Hungary. When Transylvania became part of Romania after the First World War, the family moved to the Italian city of Fiume (now the Croatian city of Rijeka). Ferencz (whom his friends and relatives called Feri) later studied lite-rature in Padua. Following his graduation in 1938, he returned to Fiume where he supported his family financially by offering private instruction.

In 1940, as a result of the new "Racial Laws," the Goldsteins not only lost their Italian citizenship but were also dispersed. Ferencz, his father and one of his brothers were interned in the Notaresco concentration camp, located in the central Italian region of Abruzzo. Given his weak health, Goldstein's father was subsequently allowed to return to Fiume where, with the assistance of a number of doctors, he was able to hide in a hospital. With the help of Yugoslav partisans, Ferencz's mother and sister were able to survive underground, yet his youngest brother was deported to Auschwitz. Having eventually managed to escape, with this other brother, from the Notaresco concentration camp in 1944, Ferencz was arrested by the Germans. He then escaped again and, despite difficulties, eventually made his way to Bari, which by that time had already been liberated by the Allies.

Given his language skills, the Allies employed Ferencz to translate radio broadcasts. He found private lodgings and decided to stay in Bari. He chan-ged his name to Francesco Godelli and applied for a teaching position that he secured despite lacking the requisite training and relevant documents. He married one of his (Catholic) colleagues and joined the Jewish community in Bari, which was disbanded in the early 1950s after the DPs had departed. Francesco Godelli died of a heart attack in 1978 at the age of 64. He is buried in the Jewish cemetery in Bari.

Ferencz Goldstein (Godelli), ca. 1946–1947.
Private collection Silvia Godelli, Bari, Italy

Ferencz Goldstein (Godelli), standing on the far right, with his teaching colleagues, 1950s. Private collection Silvia Godelli, Bari

Ferencz Goldstein (Godelli) with his wife Elisa, ca. 1945–46. Private collection Silvia Godelli, Bari, Italy

STRENGTHENING THE ORTHODOX TRADITION IN JEWISH DP FAMILIES
INTERGENERATIONAL PROCESSES[1]

LENA INOWLOCKI

If one visits the Jewish Community Center in Frankfurt am Main today, one can expect to see young women wearing *sheitels* and men in *tzitzit*. They may be employed by the Jewish community or picking up their children from the kindergarten: girls in long skirts and boys wearing *kippah* and *tzitzit*, some even with *peyes*. It seems as though it had always been like this. After all, Orthodox observance has a long tradition and where would one expect to see it if not in the context of a Jewish institution that supports Orthodox families in their observance? Yet in fact, all this bears witness to a relatively recent development that has resulted from migration, transmigration, and the global trend towards renewed religious observance, and marks one of the changes in the life of the community in recent decades. In the years after 1945, when DPs and the families they created formed the majority of the reestablished Jewish community, these developments could not have been foreseen. Looking back at this time and the decades that have since passed, I want to focus on how (former) DPs, their children, and grandchildren have experienced the period since 1945 and how they have responded to, and influenced, processes of social and political change.

My discussion draws upon the research I have undertaken on three generations of women and girls from Jewish DP families. In the late 1980s and early 1990s, I explored how it had at all been possible, given the persecution during the Shoah, the destruction of the Jewish lifeworlds in Poland, and the often long years of temporary arrangements, to convey a sense of continuity.[2] My research focused specifically on the female members of the families in question since the transmission of tradition in the sphere of the home is generally considered their responsibility.[3] It turned out that the emphasis on tradition had not been maintained by the older generation but initiated and intensified by the daughters and granddaughters. This trend also reflected the desire to juxtapose a constructive family atmosphere to the impact of the persecution endured during the Shoah. Moreover, particularly in Germany, never realized emigration plans were frequently adopted by the younger generations. In what follows, I will draw on the accounts of the three generations of women I was able to interview in the years around 1990 to reconstruct the transformation processes engendered in the postwar communities in the first decades after the war.

Some of the older women I interviewed in Antwerp, Amsterdam, and Frankfurt had given up on religious observance after the Shoah because they had lost, or had abandoned, their belief in Judaism. Others maintained, to the extent that circumstances allowed, the level of observance they knew from their parental homes. Up until the 1970s, the daughters born in the postwar years went even further in abandoning traditional practices. Yet in the 1980s, when it came to their own children, they became increasingly interested in ensuring that the children would maintain their sense of Jewishness despite living in a non-Jewish environment. In Antwerp and Amsterdam, Jewish schools that were more Orthodox in their orientation than their predecessors were meant to facilitate this renewed focus on religious literacy. At the time, Frankfurt did not yet have a Jewish school but, as one example will demonstrate, comparable efforts were also undertaken there.

In the late 1980s, a process of increasing retraditionalization began to un-fold, in the first instance primarily in Antwerp. In Amsterdam and Frankfurt, too, it led to intergenerational debates and negotiation processes in the families of former Jewish DPs. The status of religion, both as a form of knowledge and of practice, was changed by the way it was taught in the schools. The focus was no longer on the parent generation and their personal recollections of persecution during the Shoah but rather on the creation of a constructive and future-oriented vision of family life. The women in the middle and younger generations, i.e., the daughters and granddaughters of the survivors, referred to this intensification of religious learning in a rather dramatic and paradoxical manner as a form of "brainwashing." How are we to interpret this?

Let us begin with the postwar years. In 1945, no more than a few hund-red members of Frankfurt's once substantial Jewish community, having mana-ged to evade their deportation and murder, still lived in the city. Beginning later that year, large numbers of survivors from Poland came to Frankfurt, the center of the American occupation zone in Germany, hoping (though sometimes in vain) to emigrate from there.[4] Many of them had previously been repatriated to Poland after surviving the Shoah in the Soviet Union. In the 1950s, Jewish families from Hungary and Romania came to Frankfurt, as well as families from Israel whose older generation had moved to Eretz Yisrael either in the 1930s or immediately after their liberation.

Opening of the Jewish community kindergarten
in Gagernstrasse in Frankfurt am Main, 1950. Institute
for the History of Frankfurt

The survivors thought of Frankfurt and the DP camp in Zeilsheim as a temporary abode from which they hoped to make their way to the Americas, Palestine, Australia or some other country that might take them in. For those whose emigration plans failed, life in Germany remained an ambivalent affair: "Those who stayed in Germany–be it for health reasons, because they could not secure a visa or because they had already carved out a modest existence for themselves–were confronted with overt disdain."[5] This held true especially for those German Jews who returned from Israel in the late 1940s and 1950s, and for returning former DPs.[6] Following the disbanding of the final Jewish DP camp in Föhrenwald, Bavaria, a large number of families also came to Frankfurt from there. In these families, even the children spoke Yiddish. Initially housed in the building of a former school run by the Jewish community prior to the war on Röderbergweg 29, they gradually moved into their own homes in the area and attended the synagogue located on the ground floor of the former school building.[7]

Where the survivors' emigration plans did not come to fruition, emigration often became an integenerational family project. The Zionist youth movement in Germany, established in Frankfurt in 1959, encouraged numerous members of the younger generation to move to Israel after their school-leaving exams. Even children of former German Jews who had fled to Palestine in the 1930s but returned from there in the 1950s now saw their future in Israel. The presence of numerous U.S. military personnel in Frankfurt with their headquarters in the former I.G. Farben building created an extraterritorial connection between the former persecutees and their liberators, and a sense of proximity, however illusory, to the dream destination of the U.S. In the postwar years, a number of *bar mitzvot* were celebrated in the casino annex of the I.G. Farben building. In the event, many younger members of the former DP families did emigrate, mainly to Israel and the U.S. Having formed the majority of the community from the 1950s until well into the 1970s, these families now found themselves in the minority.

Initially, only a small number of families in postwar Frankfurt maintained an Orthodox lifestyle. Families who valued Orthodox observance highly, moved to Antwerp or sent their children to boarding schools. Kosher meat was not available in Frankfurt on a regular basis until the mid-1950s. Given the significance of the Sabbath and the Jewish holidays, the Jewish calendar nevertheless continued to structure the year in many of the Jewish families who had come from Poland. For many years after the war, the significance and practice of religion were inextricable from the unbounded sorrow of the parents. Every ritual, every religious holiday reminded them of the homes they had been robbed of and their many murdered relatives. However unspoken the persecution endured by oneself or one's relatives may have been, the despair and sorrow was eloquently conveyed in every gesture: when lighting the candles, when gathering to pray in the synagogue, when commemorating the November Pogrom of 1938 in front of the former synagogue on Friedberger Anlage, or at social gatherings, such as a Yiddish film screening at the former MGM Cinema on Schäfergasse.

To be sure, the children were sent to weekly religious instruction and *kabbalat shabbat* (Friday night prayer service) in the fomer community center on Baumweg, so as to strengthen their theoretical and practical knowledge of Judaism. However, until the 1970s, religious observance was largely the preserve of the older generation. For the children of the DPs, the experience of the religious rituals that were practiced but not explained was connected in a vague but emphatic way to the ever-present (but rarely discussed) persecution of their parents. In an intergenerational conversation between a mother who had survived the Shoah in Poland and was only able to rescue individual members of her family, and her daughter who was born in Frankfurt around 1950, the mother explained that she and her husband had never spoken about the persecution in order to protect the children. To this her daughter responded by saying: "You were *always* talking about it."[8]

The mother was not unlike many other women in her generation who came from Orthodox families and who had already pursued a secular course in their youth in Poland and expressed their Jewishness by engaging in cultural activities and joining socialist and/or Zionist organizations.[9] While some of the survivors despaired of humanity and of God and abandoned Judaism, others were keen to start celebrating the Sabbath and the Jewish holidays as soon as they arrived in the DP camps. For many of the non-religious survivors, the religious holidays took on an increased significance after the Shoah as an expression of their Jewishness, and their support for a Jewish state in which Jews would be able to live without fear of persecution.[10]

In the 1960s, as adolescents, many members of the DP families' younger generation became increasingly involved in the Jewish youth movement and the emerging critical counterculture and protest movement in the schools and universities, and thus moved away from religious observance.[11] For them, these political and cultural activities, as well as their struggle against authoritarianism and oppression were closely connected to the Shoah. Among the developments of considerable significance to them in the 1970s and 1980s were the creation of the "Jewish Group" in Frankfurt; the publication of the journal *Babylon – Beiträge zur jüdischen Gegenwart*; the protests against the joint visit by Reagan and Kohl to the military cemetery in Bitburg on 5 May 1985; the protests against the performance of Rainer Werner Fassbinder's play, *Garbage, the City and Death*, also in 1985; and the conflict regarding the plans of the municipal authority to erect an administrative building on the ruins of the former Jewish quarter in Frankfurt.[12]

Here as elsewhere in the world, in the 1970s and 1980s, the process of secularization seemed irreversible. Against this backdrop, developments transpiring

People, including a Zionist youth group, in front of the Memorial Monument to Murdered Jews in the Frankfurt am Main-Zeilsheim DP camp, 1946. Jewish Museum Frankfurt, courtesy of Andrea Szapiro

Living room in the apartment of Jewish survivors in Frankfurt, 1948. Jewish Museum Frankfurt

in the Jewish community in Antwerp in the mid-1980s were all the more impressive. My nostalgic and romanticizing gaze as an outsider saw a *shtetl* and was
taken in by the optical illusion of what seemed to resemble the Polish Jewish
lifeworld prior to the Shoah, as though nothing had changed for generations.

In fact, though, the reestablished community in Antwerp differed in many
respects from its prewar predecessor.[13] Since the poorer members of the community had been murdered in disproportionate numbers during the Shoah, the
once formative socialist and communist Jewish organizations no longer existed.
Instead of the socialist Poale Zion, the religious Mizrachi movement now
dominated Zionist activism in the city. While some Hasidic groups had been
part of the community prior to the war, from the late 1940s onwards and in the
course of the 1950s, increasing numbers of strictly observant and Hasidic Jews
settled in Antwerp.[14] The Orthodox currents had in fact only gradually become
such an important factor, and during my visits in the late 1980s I could observe
how this process continued to unfold. I was able to trace the biographical and
intergenerational discussions that took place in the families I interviewed in
connection with the new significance of, and orientation towards, Orthodox
traditions within the community. The intensification of Orthodox observance
originated with the younger generation, with young Jews who were still at
school. As a result, their mothers too, who had previously shown little interest
in traditional practices, were increasingly compelled to observe the new rules.
They started wearing longer skirts instead of jeans and began to cover their hair,
first with a hairband, then with a headscarf which they could put on or take off,
depending on the occasion. And they changed their patterns of consumption as
they moved towards running kosher households, for example, by buying newly
marketed kosher milk which then, for a time, still found itself next to the conventional milk in the fridge. Both the mothers and the daughters commented on the
impact of these changes on their measure of religious observance, which they
had experienced as conflicted. At the same time, the lifestyle changed, even of
those who were critical of the social pressure that was being created. In the
1970s, Jews had commonly met their future spouses through their siblings,
friends, when going to cafés or the pictures. But in the 1980s, the younger siblings
in those same families expected their marriages to be arranged, reviving a
practice that had largely gone out of fashion even in the generation of the older
Jewish women from Poland.

The girls and women confronted the retraditionalization of their lifestyle both individually and in their relationships as mothers and daughters. The
women of the middle and older generations were ambivalent in their attitude
towards new Orthodoxy. To be sure, it guaranteed the continuity of a long-
standing line of tradition, but it did so in a form that was very different from the
ways in which religion had hitherto been practiced and tradition transmitted

in their families.[15] The granddaughters of the survivors offered vivid accounts of the ways in which Orthodox observance had asserted itself and what that process had meant to them. Girls and women who opted for a more strictly Orthodox tradition had to ask themselves why, by observing the religious laws and accepting the concomitant gender inequality, they were effectively entering into a new form of dependence of their own free will. The religious instruction for girls notwithstanding, reflection upon their personal religious convictions also contributed to the retraditionalization process. The sense of "having the choice" was crucial to this process.[16]

The religious instruction of the daughters instilled in them a new aware-ness of the rules involved in maintaining tradition. This found its expression, for example, in the pressure they exerted on their parents to take a more observant approach to all aspects of family life. The women of the middle generation who were most directly confronted with this transformation were rather ambivalent about the traditional rule-oriented education of their daughters, describing it as a form of "brainwashing" or "indoctrination." This hyperbole reflects the assumption that, in a mainly non-Jewish environment and given the rupture in the transmission of tradition and the destruction of the old Jewish lifeworld, other forms of religious instruction were simply no longer possible.

I want to elucidate the impact of these changes with three vignettes.[17] They relate to the intensification of the Jewish learning of a young woman in Antwerp called Diana;[18] to a disagreement between two Amsterdam-based young women, Daphne and Nurith, and their mother, Mrs. Neumann, about the religious concept of modesty called *tzniut*; and the reflections of Mrs. Wieder, born in the 1950s, upon the religious instruction of her children in Frankfurt in the late 1980s and early 1990s.

ANTWERP

Diana, who grew up in Antwerp, was in her early 20s when I interviewed her. Her parents were involved in the community's welfare organizations but not religious. Diana's grandparents were survivors and former DPs. As Diana's grandmother told me, they had abandoned all religious observance after the Shoah. Diana initially attended the secular Jewish school in Antwerp. Yet in the mid-1980s, she asked her parents to send her to a religous boarding school. There, one of her teachers had "brainwashed" her:

> He began, he tried everything to convince and convince and convince me, for a whole year. Every time, for a whole year, I attended *shiurim* virtually every day, *shiurim*, *shiurim*, *shiurim*.[19] One weekend

> I went to London, I spent a weekend with the Chabad people in
> London. One of these weekends. And that, it really made an enormous
> impression on me. It made an enormous impression on me.

Diana emphasized how important it had been for her to "have the choice" of going to the religious boarding school. She added that the whole process had been triggered by a painful experience. A more observant young relative had refused to respond to her "Shabbat shalom" greeting and accused her of not being Jewish enough because she wore jeans and drove on the Sabbath. She was forced to recognize that she had become an outsider in the increasingly religious community in Antwerp and that even a boy who had only just become a bar mitzvah now represented the mainstream and had the authority to question her Jewishness. Her "choice" reflected the pressure to lead a more observant life than before. Not that she had been able to persuade her parents to run a kosher household when she returned from the boarding school, but she was determined to marry a man more observant than herself.

As was so often the case in DP families, Diana's grandparents, to whom she was very close, had not wanted to talk to her about the suffering they had endured. In order to develop some grasp of what had happened, Diana attended a meeting during a trip to Israel where survivors described their experiences during the Shoah. We might, then, speak of corrective interventions when Diana subjected herself to "brainwashing" to maintain her sense of belonging in an increasingly religious community, on the one hand, and sought to find out about the experience of persecution during the Shoah that her own family could not communicate by meeting with other survivors, on the other. Diana felt compelled to rely on forms of transmission that deviated from the way in which tradition is "normally" passed on from generation to generation.

AMSTERDAM

In the Neumann family, it was not only the grandparents who had been persecuted during the Shoah. Rather, Mr. Neumann had been in a concentration camp as a child. It was his wife who told me this, instantly adding that they did not, "thank God," speak about this in the family. They wanted their children to know that the Shoah had happened, but only on the level of general historical knowledge, not in relation to the suffering their father and grandparents had endured.[20]

Mrs. Neumann and her husband supported an Orthodox Jewish school attended by their sixteen- and fifteen-year-old daughters, Daphne and Nurith. When I interviewed the daughters, they called in their mother to explain why male teachers were allowed to teach them while the boys could not be taught by female teachers. Mrs. Neumann took a pragmatic approach, drawing on gender distinctions and arguing that girls should not make a spectacle of themselves and refrain from behaving "like street urchins." However, the girls themselves explained the differing expectations regarding their conduct with the religious concept of *tzniut*,[21] which led Mrs. Neumann to comment without hesitation that "the children are subjected to a lot of brainwashing there."

The formal instruction the girls received at the Orthodox school differed from the sort of passive transmission of tradition that Mrs. Neumann had encountered in her parental home, one that had not relied on explanations. Her ambivalence towards her daughters' religious instruction resulted from the fact that she considered it desirable and necessary, given that the destruction of the East European Jewish lifeworlds had ruptured the intergenerational transmission that might otherwise have facilitated the continuity of traditional practice and knowledge. It was the task of the Orthodox school to counteract that loss and reinforce religiosity in order to guarantee a continuity that constructively de-centered the memories of the Shoah and the older generation's experience of suffering. As in other families I interviewed, here too, emigration was still on the younger generation's horizon.

FRANKFURT AM MAIN

In Frankfurt, we can interpret the reconnection with Orthodox observance as a paradoxical response to a particularly complex situation. How could one even continue to live? How could one establish a new family and have children after the murder of one's previous family? And how could one live in a place like Germany where the Nazis had reigned only a few years before? Even in the 1950s, a heavy burden of desperate sadness still prevailed among the few survivors and their families. When they assembled at the location of the former synagogue on Friedberger Anlage on November 9 to recall its destruction in the pogrom of 1938, or attended screenings of films their children could not understand, although they evidently had something to do with the oppressive atmosphere they knew from home. For that was somehow connected to the photos on the sideboard which one could not ask the parents about without provoking expressions of despair from them. Nor could one ask them about their previous families, the children who would now be in one's place had they not been murdered. For there would have been no way of knowing each other; rather, one's own life had taken the place of theirs.[22]

That time now seems rather distant. In novels and films about Frankfurt in the late 1940s and 1950s, it is often presented in a manner that makes for humorous anecdotes, for instance, about achieving prosperity with a sizeable dose of *chutzpah* (audacity). Yet this retrospective image has more to do with the current majority perspective than the reality at the time, thereby eliding the prevailing sadness and despair.

When I interviewed her in the early 1990s, Mrs. Wieder recalled her depressing childhood in the late 1950s. She said she had grown up in a "ghetto" into which her parents and their peers, all of whom were survivors, had withdrawn to protect themselves from their German environment. Emigration plans had faltered, and the children of families that had returned from Israel in particular found life in Germany unacceptable. Mrs. Wieder thought it was regrettable that the transmission of religious knowledge and practices had been impossible in her childhood and youth. So now, "of course," she "indoctrinated" her children: once a week, after school, she sent them to an old couple, both of whom were Jewish teachers, so they could familiarize themselves with the lived experience of Judaism as it "used to be in Poland," i.e., in the form she knew from the novels of Isaac Bashevis Singer, as she added with a mixture of irony and longing.

Mrs. Wieder was keen to ensure that her children had a connection with tradition and that they, in marked contrast to the experiences of her own childhood and youth, could develop a positive sense of Jewishness. Her corrective measures in response to the loss of meaning she had experienced amounted to a sort of tightrope act. On the one hand, she insisted that her children attend the lessons with the old Jewish couple, on the other hand, she sought to contain the couple's expectations. They wanted to turn her children into "pious Jews" and urged her to run a kosher household.

There were few structures and institutions in Frankfurt in the late 1980s that could have supported an Orthodox lifestyle. Nor was there any great interest in stricter observance. Yet Mrs. Wieder's generation, i.e., the postwar generation, did have a strong interest in ensuring that their children, whether of school age or older, did not move away from Judaism any further than their own generation had already done. Their fear that all sense of belonging might be lost was linked to the recollection of the Shoah and to emigration plans which, even though they had failed, the younger generation continued to nurture. Like others in her generation, Mrs. Wieder recognized the dilemma that resulted from the fact that there was virtually no conventional way in which the older generation could pass on the tradition and the sense that it was somehow not right to live in Germany after the Shoah. In this respect, the situation in Frankfurt in the early 1990s was not dissimilar to the context in which the Jews in the DP camps debated in 1948 how best to educate their children, even if the issue at stake then was Zionism rather than Judaism. When she visited the camps, the U.S. educator Marie Syrkin criticized the one-sided orientation of the instruction there towards Palestine, complaining of "Zionist indoctrination." According to her account, the teachers responded as follows:

> Maybe it's not good pedagogy to present only one side of a case. But we can't afford such luxuries. The children have nothing, nothing. What should we talk about–the blessings of Poland? They know them. Or the visas for America? They can't get them. The map of Eretz is their salvation. [...] Indoctrination may not be good for normal children in normal surroundings. But what is normal here? ...*Oyf a krume fus past a krume shu.*[23]

EPILOGUE

In contrast to the early years following the establishment of the postwar community, the descendants of the DPs now form a minority among the Jews of Frankfurt. In the years since 1990, migration, transnational lifestyles, and globalization processes have led to the internationalization and diversification of the Jewish community in Frankfurt, and the city itself.[22] The transmigration within Europe, as well as between Israel, the U.S. and Frankfurt, has changed the community whose membership has doubled, especially due to the immigration of Jews from the former member countries of the post-Soviet Commonwealth of Independent States. Half of the roughly 6,000 current members of the community speak Russian. Due to the denial of religious freedom and antisemitic repression they previously experienced, these families were often unable to maintain any form of religious knowledge and practice. Some members of the younger generation have veered towards neo-Orthodoxy. Various religious options have been available since the 1990s, including Chabad[24] and a number of initiatives run by members of the community, such as "Jewish Experience." The overwhelming majority of the community is not religiously observant or continues to engage in the religious practices they have been accustomed to since their childhood. This does not rule out, however, that they are attracted, and respond positively, to neo-Orthodox initiatives.

The structures and institutions of the Jewish community in Frankfurt have changed in remarkable ways. Its educational activities at the preschool and school level have increasingly been extended and now range from early childhood to the school-leaving exam required for university entry. The number of well-attended events and celebrations is considerable. Looking back to the time of the controversial reestablishment of the community at a time when the notion of Jewish life in Germany after the Shoah seemed highly questionable, the community's continued existence and its many activities cannot but impress.

Women dancing together at Renia Lustman's (née
Szuibas) religious wedding, Frankfurt am Main-
Zeilsheim 1946. Jewish Museum Frankfurt, courtesy
of Ruth Himmelfarb, Neuilly

Purim celebration in the Jewish community of
Frankfurt am Main, 1956. Jewish Museum Frankfurt,
courtesy of Karla Ihlder

[1] I am grateful to Atina Grossmann and Kata Bohus, as well as Ina Marie Schaum and Nathan Lee Kaplan for their helpful comments, and to Rachel Heuberger and Susanna Keval for our inspiring discussions on the topic.

[2] I asked the women of the older, middle, and younger generations to tell me their life story with special reference to intergenerational continuities and discontinuities. See Lena Inowlocki, "Normalität als Kunstgriff. Zur Traditionsvermittlung jüdischer DP-Familien in Deutschland," in *Überlebt und unterwegs. Jüdische Displaced Persons im Nachkriegsdeutschland. Jahrbuch zur Geschichte und Wirkung des Holocaust*, ed. Fritz Bauer Institut (Frankfurt a. M.: Campus, 1997), 267–288; Lena Inowlocki, "Wenn Tradition auf einmal mehr bedeutet: Einige Beobachtungen zu biographischen Prozessen der Auseinandersetzung mit Religion," in *Migration und Traditionsbildung*, ed. Ursula Apitzsch (Opladen: Westdeutscher Verlag, 1999), 76–89; Lena Inowlocki, "Doing 'Being Jewish'. Constitution of 'Normality' in Families of Jewish Displaced Persons in Germany," in *Biographies and the Division of Europe. Experience, Action, and Change on the 'Eastern Side'*, ed. Roswitha Breckner, Devorah Kalekin-Fishman, and Ingrid Miethe (Opladen: Leske + Budrich, 2000), 159–178. The accounts of the older women harked back to their childhood and youth in various Jewish contexts in Poland in the 1920s and 1930s, as well as their persecution during the Shoah. They recalled their early years as Jewish DPs in the West European communities of Antwerp, Amsterdam, and Frankfurt. This is where the women of the middle generation were born in the late 1940s and 1950s, and their daughters in the 1970s and 1980s.

[3] The historical perspective on modernity reveals how this task was initially established in relatively privileged Jewish families in the context of their bourgeois emancipation. See Marion A. Kaplan, "Women and the Shaping of Modern Jewish Identity in Imperial Germany," in *Deutsche Juden und die Moderne*, ed. Shulamit Volkov (Munich: Oldenbourg, 1994), 57–74; Paula E. Hyman, *Gender and Assimilation in Modern Jewish History. The Roles and Representations of Women* (Seattle: University of Washington Press, 1995); Shulamit Volkov, "Jüdische Assimilation und Eigenart im Kaiserreich," in *Antisemitismus als kultureller Code* (Munich: Beck, 2000), 257–270.

[4] In 1933, the Jewish community in Frankfurt had close to 30,000 members. In late 1945, somewhere between 450 and 600 Jews lived in Frankfurt (again). Beginning in 1946, Jewish DPs who mainly came from Poland formed the Committee of Liberated Jews which, in late 1948, had 1,200 members. Following the community's merger with the committee in April 1949, it had 1,900 members. Up to the mid-1950s, this number steadily decreased but it then gradually began to rise again. In the course of the 1960s, it increased from 2,700 to 4,300. The share of children and young adults among the members decreased continuously until the 1980s. See Helga Krohn, *"Es war richtig, wieder anzufangen": Juden in Frankfurt am Main seit 1945* (Frankfurt a. M.: Brandes und Apsel, 2011), 25. However, at the end of 2018, the share of children and young adults among the 6,428 members of the Jewish community in Frankfurt stood at twice the average of the Jewish communities in Germany. Since 40 percent of the community are 61 or older, this points to a large number of children in young families, which may also be connected to stronger religious observance. See Andrei Mares and Cornelia Maimon-Levi, "Bericht des Gemeinderats," *Jüdische Gemeindezeitung Frankfurt* 52.2 (2019), 13.

[5] Tobias Freimüller, "Mehr als eine Religionsgemeinschaft. Jüdisches Leben in Frankfurt am Main nach 1945," *Zeithistorische Forschungen/Studies in Contemporary History* 7.3 (2010), 393.

[6] On the postwar years in Frankfurt and the relationship between the German Jews who had returned and the DPs in particular, see the synthetic account by Freimüller, "Mehr als eine Religionsgemeinschaft" (with numerous references); Diner, Dan. "Banished: Jews in Germany after the Holocaust," in *A History of Jews in Germany since 1945. Politics, Culture, and Society*, ed. Michael Brenner (Bloomington: Indiana University Press, 2019), 37–38. For the vantage point of the subsequent generation, born in the 1980s, see Channah Trzebiner, *Die Enkelin oder wie ich zu Pessach die vier Fragen nicht wusste* (Frankfurt a. M.: Weissbooks, 2013).

[7] Edgar Bönisch, "Das jüdisch geprägte Ostend und die jüdischen Institutionen im Röderbergweg," in *Das Gumpertz'sche Siechenhaus – ein „Jewish Place" in Frankfurt am Main. Geschichte und Geschichten einer jüdischen Wohlfahrtseinrichtung*, ed. Birgit Seemann and Edgar Bönisch (Frankfurt a. M.: Brandes und Apsel, 2019), 52–54.

[8] Lena Inowlocki, "Collective Trajectory and Generational Work in Families of Jewish Displaced Persons: Epistemological Processes in the Research Situation," in *Holocaust as Active Memory. The Past in the Present*, ed. Marie Louise Seeberg, Irene Levin, and Claudia Lenz (Farnham: Ashgate, 2013), 38.

[9] Margarete Myers Feinstein, *Holocaust Survivors in Postwar Germany, 1945–1957* (New York: Cambridge University Press, 2010), 205–207.

[10] On the role of religion and religious practice in the DP camps, see Feinstein, *Holocaust Survivors*, 207–214.

[11] See also Freimüller, "Mehr als eine Religionsgemeinschaft," 399.

[12] See Micha Brumlik, *Kein Weg als Deutscher und Jude. Eine bundesrepublikanische Erfahrung* (Munich: Luchterhand, 1996); Krohn, *"Es war richtig, wieder anzufangen,"* 168–174; *Ästhetik und Kommunikation* 14.51 (1983): *Deutsche, Linke, Juden*.

[13] In the interwar period, the Jewish community in Antwerp grew to be the largest in Belgium. Of the almost 14,000 Jews registered in 1942, only a few hundred were able to survive in hiding. Together with those who survived the camps and returnees from the U.S., Cuba, England, and Switzerland, they reestablished the Jewish community in 1945. See Veerle Vanden Daelen, "Returning: Jewish Life in Antwerp in the Aftermath of the Second World War (1944–45)," *European Judaism* 38.2 (2005), 35.

[14] Daelen, "Returning," 38. The rise of Orthodoxy also precipitated working conditions in the diamond industry and diamond trade that were attuned to the Orthodox lifestyle and the establishment of Orthodox Jewish schools. See also Ludo Abicht, *De Joden van Antwerpen* (Antwerpen-Baarn: Hadewijch, 1993).

[15] A transgenerational analysis of the interviews with the grandmothers, mothers, and daughters revealed a change in the relationship between the orientation towards tradition and religiosity. This transformation is reflected, for example, in the fact that some of the interviewed women consciously described themselves as "traditional" as opposed to *"frum"* (pious). They thereby distinguished between a more or less religiously inspired traditional lifestyle and the strict observance of the *mitzvot* (*"frumkayt"*) that was fairly rare among the women. The alternatives "traditional" and *"frum"* did not exist in equal measure for the younger generation, given that, as a result of the destruction of Polish Jewry, they could not draw on a traditional form of life passed down to them; instead, needed to create or adopt new forms of religiosity and tradition.

[16] Lynn R. Davidman has charted this very process for women and girls who strengthened their adherence to Judaism in a Manhattan synagogue and at a Chabad summer camp, respectively. Lynn R. Davidman, *Tradition in a Rootless World: Women Turn to Orthodox Judaism* (Berkeley: University of California Press, 1991).

[17] The controversial nature of these changes was also reflected in the fact that many of the women I interviewed wanted their mother or daughter (or daughters) to be present during the interview. In some cases, daughters also fetched their mother during the interview. The younger women then frequently directed their own questions at their mothers or grandmothers. See Inowlocki, "Collective Trajectory," 36–37.

[18] I have changed the names of the interviewed women.

[19] Instruction, lesson (Hebrew).

[20] On the situation of the Jewish population in Amsterdam after 1945, see the contribution "Amsterdam: The City of Conflicts" in this volume; Ido de Haan, "The Postwar Jewish Community and the Memory of the Persecution in the Netherlands," in *Dutch Jews as Perceived by Themselves and Others*, ed. Chaya Brasz and Yosef Kaplan (Leiden: Brill, 2001), 405–435.

[21] Modesty, discretion, decorousness.

[22] On the situation of the Jewish population in Frankfurt and Zeilsheim after 1945, see the contribution „Frankfurt and Zeilsheim: America in Germany" in this volume.

[23] Marie Syrkin, *The State of the Jews* (Washington D.C.: New Republic Books, 1980), 26–27. The yiddish comment in the quote can be roughly translated as „only a crooked shoe fits a crooked foot."

[24] On Frankfurt, see https://www.vielfalt-bewegt-frankfurt.de/de.

[25] Chabad has developed an extremely savvy global network engaged in the teaching, study, and practice of a form of Hasidic Judaism. Its activities are designed to lead Jews back to Judaism.

BIBLIOGRAPHY

Abicht, Ludo. *De Joden van Antwerpen.* Antwerpen-Baarn: Hadewijch, 1993. / *Ästhetik und Kommunikation* 14.51 (1983): *Deutsche, Linke, Juden.* / **Bönisch, Edgar.** "Das jüdisch geprägte Ostend und die jüdischen Institutionen im Röderbergweg." In *Das Gumpertz'sche Siechenhaus – ein „Jewish Place" in Frankfurt am Main. Geschichte und Geschichten einer jüdischen Wohlfahrtseinrichtung,* edited by Birgit Seemann and Edgar Bönisch. Frankfurt a. M.: Brandes und Apsel, 2019, 41–72. / **Brumlik, Micha.** *Kein Weg als Deutscher und Jude. Eine bundesrepublikanische Erfahrung.* Munich: Luchterhand, 1996. / **Daelen, Veerle Vanden.** "Returning: Jewish Life in Antwerp in the Aftermath of the Second World War (1944–45)." *European Judaism* 38.2 (2005), 26–42. / **Davidman, Lynn R.** *Tradition in a Rootless World: Women Turn to Orthodox Judaism.* Berkeley: University of California Press, 1991. / **Diner, Dan.** "Banished: Jews in Germany after the Holocaust." In *A History of Jews in Germany since 1945. Politics, Culture, and Society,* edited by Michael Brenner. Bloomington: Indiana University Press, 2019, 7–53. / **Feinstein, Margarete Myers.** *Holocaust Survivors in Postwar Germany, 1945–1957.* New York: Cambridge University Press, 2010. / **Freimüller, Tobias.** "Mehr als eine Religionsgemeinschaft. Jüdisches Leben in Frankfurt am Main nach 1945." *Zeithistorische Forschungen/Studies in Contemporary History* 7.3 (2010), 386–407. / **Haan, Ido de.** "The Postwar Jewish Community and the Memory of the Persecution in the Netherlands." In *Dutch Jews as Perceived by Themselves and Others,* edited by Chaya Brasz and Yosef Kaplan. Leiden: Brill, 2001, 405–435. / **Hyman, Paula E.** *Gender and Assimilation in Modern Jewish History. The Roles and Representations of Women.* Seattle: University of Washington Press, 1995. / **Inowlocki, Lena.** "Normalität als Kunstgriff. Zur Traditionsvermittlung jüdischer DP-Familien in Deutschland." In *Überlebt und unterwegs. Jüdische Displaced Persons im Nachkriegsdeutschland. Jahrbuch zur Geschichte und Wirkung des Holocaust,* edited by Fritz Bauer Institut. Frankfurt a. M.: Campus, 1997, 267–288. / **Inowlocki, Lena.** "Wenn Tradition auf einmal mehr bedeutet: Einige Beobachtungen zu biographischen Prozessen der Auseinandersetzung mit Religion." In *Migration und Traditionsbildung,* edited by Ursula Apitzsch. Opladen: Westdeutscher Verlag, 1999, 76–89. / **Inowlocki, Lena.** "Doing 'Being Jewish'. Constitution of 'Normality' in Families of Jewish Displaced Persons in Germany." In *Biographies and the Division of Europe. Experience, Action, and Change on the 'Eastern Side',* edited by Roswitha Breckner, Devorah Kalekin-Fishman, and Ingrid Miethe. Opladen: Leske + Budrich, 2000, 159–178. / **Inowlocki, Lena.** "Collective Trajectory and Generational Work in Families of Jewish Displaced Persons: Epistemological Processes in the Research Situation." In *Holocaust as Active Memory. The Past in the Present,* edited by Marie Louise Seeberg, Irene Levin, and Claudia Lenz. Farnham: Ashgate, 2013, 29–43. / **Kaplan, Marion A.** "Women and the Shaping of Modern Jewish Identity in Imperial Germany." In *Deutsche Juden und die Moderne,* edited by Shulamith Volkov. Munich: Oldenbourg, 1994, 57–74. / **Krohn, Helga.** *"Es war richtig, wieder anzufangen": Juden in Frankfurt am Main seit 1945.* Frankfurt a. M.: Brandes und Apsel, 2011. / **Mares, Andrei,** and **Cornelia Maimon-Levi,** "Bericht des Gemeinderats." *Jüdische Gemeindezeitung Frankfurt* 52.2 (2019), 12–13. / **Syrkin, Marie.** "The D.P. Schools." *Jewish Frontier* 15.3 (1948), 14–19. / **Syrkin, Marie.** *The State of the Jews.* Washington D.C.: New Republic Books, 1980. / **Trzebiner,**

Channah. *Die Enkelin oder wie ich zu Pessach die vier Fragen nicht wusste.* Frankfurt a. M.: Weissbooks, 2013. / **Volkov, Shulamit.** "Jüdische Assimilation und Eigenart im Kaiserreich." In *Antisemitismus als kultureller Code.* Munich: Beck, 2000, 257–270.

AUTHORS

NATALIA ALEKSIUN

is Professor of Modern Jewish History at the Touro College Graduate School of Jewish Studies in New York. She studied History and Modern Jewish History and received her two doctorates from Warsaw University and New York University. Her book *Dokad dalej? Ruch syjonistyczny w Polsce 1944–1950 (Where next? The Zionist Movement in Poland, 1944–1950)* was published in 2002.

MORITZ BAUERFEIND

is a doctoral student at the University of Bamberg. He studied History and Slavic Studies in Bamberg and Olomouc, Czech Republic. He worked at the Jewish Museum Franken, and between 2017 and 2019, he was a scientific trainee at the Jewish Museum Frankfurt, where he took part in the development of the exhibition *Our courage: Jews in Europe 1945–48.*

KATA BOHUS

is Curator at the Jewish Museum Frankfurt and Researcher at the Leibniz Institute for Jewish History and Culture–Simon Dubnow. She developed the new temporary Exhibition *Our courage: Jews in Europe 1945–48.* She specializes in modern Jewish history in Eastern Europe and received her doctorate from the Central European University in Budapest. Between 2014 and 2016, she was a Postdoctoral Fellow at the Georg-August-University/Lichtenberg Kolleg in Göttingen.

KATHARINA FRIEDLA

is a Postdoctoral Research Fellow at the Fondation pour la Mémoire de la Shoah Paris. She studied History, East European and Jewish Studies at the Free University Berlin and received her doctorate from the University of Basel. Her book *Juden in Breslau/Wrocław 1933–1949, Überlebensstrategien, Selbstbehauptung und Verfolgungserfahrungen (Jews in Breslau/Wrocław 1933–1949, Survival Strategies, Self-Assertion and Persecution Experiences)* was published in 2015.

ELISABETH GALLAS

works at the Leibniz Institute for Jewish History and Culture–Simon Dubnow as a Chief Research Associate where she is Head of the "Law"research unit. She specializes in Jewish History and Memory in the 20th Century as well as Jewish Legal History. Her monograph: *A Mortuary of Books. The Rescue of Jewish Culture after the Holocaust* won the 2020 JDC-Herbert Katzki Award for Writing Based on Archival Material, given by the Jewish Book Council. She studied Cultural and German studies and received her doctorate from the University of Leipzig.

PHILIPP GRAF

is Deputy Head of the "Law" research unit at the Leibniz Institute for Jewish History and Culture–Simon Dubnow. He is currently working on a political biography of the Jewish lawyer and communist Leo Zuckermann (1908–1985). His monograph *Die Bernheim-Petition 1933. Jüdische Politik in der Zwischenkriegszeit* (*The Bernheim petition 1933. Jewish Politics in the Interwar Years*) was published in 2008. He completed his doctorate at Leipzig University.

ATINA GROSSMANN

is Professor of Modern German and European History and Gender History in the Faculty of Humanities and Social Sciences at the The Cooper Union in New York City. She also taught at Mount Holyoke College, Massachusetts and New York's Columbia University. She is the author and editor of several books, among them the award-winning monograph *Jews, Germans, and Allies: Close Encounters in Occupied Germany*, which was published in 2007.

WERNER HANAK

is Deputy Director of the Jewish Museum Frankfurt and project leader of the temporary exhibition *Our courage: Jews in Europe 1945–48*. He studied Theater, Film and Media Studies and received his doctorate from the University of Vienna. As Chief Curator at the Jewish Museum Vienna, he curated numerous temporary exhibitions and the current permanent exhibition.

LAURA HOBSON-FAURE

is Professor of Modern Jewish History and member of the Center of Contemporary Social History at the Panthéon-Sorbonne University- Paris 1, Paris. She completed her doctorate in history at the *École des Hautes Études en Sciences* in Paris. Her monograph *Un Plan Marshall juif: la présence juive américaine en France après la Shoah, 1944–1954* (*A Jewish Marshall Plan: the American Jewish Presence in Post-Holocaust France, 1944–1954*) was published in 2013 and is forthcoming in English.

LENA INOWLOCKI

is a sociologist and Professor (retired) in the field of society and personality with a focus on family, young adults and migration biographies at Frankfurt University of Applied Sciences, where she continues to chair the Institute for Migration Studies and Intercultural Communication. She is Senior Professor (Associate) at the Department of Social Sciences at Goethe University Frankfurt. She completed her habilitation at Otto-von-Guericke-University Magdeburg.

KAMIL KIJEK

is Assistant Professor at the Jewish Studies Department at the University of Wrocław. His monograph *Dzieci modernizmu. Świadomość i socjalizacja polityczna młodzieży żydowskiej w Polsce międzywojennej (Children of Modernism. Political awareness and socialization of Jewish youth in interwar Poland)* was published in 2017. He received his doctorate from the Institute of History of the Polish Academy of Sciences in Warsaw.

TAMAR LEWINSKY

is Curator of Contemporary History at the Jewish Museum Berlin and one of the curators of the new permanent exhibition to be opened there in 2020. She studied Jewish Studies, Yiddish and Linguistics and received her doctorate from Munich University. Her monograph *Displaced Poets: Jiddische Schriftsteller im Nachkriegsdeutschland, 1945–1951 (Displaced Poets: Yiddish Writers in Postwar Germany, 1945–1951)* was published in 2008.

AVINOAM PATT

is Director of the Center for Judaic Studies and Contemporary Jewish Life at the University of Connecticut where he is also the Doris and Simon Konover Chair of Judaic Studies. He has been Professor of Modern Jewish History and Co-Director of the Maurice Greenberg Center for Judaic Studies at the University of Hartford. His edited volume *We Are Here: New Approaches to Jewish Displaced Persons in Postwar Germany* was published 2010 and his monograph *Finding Home and Homeland: Jewish Youth and Zionism in the Aftermath of the Holocaust* in 2009.

KATARZYNA PERSON

is Assistant Professor at the Jewish Historical Institute in Warsaw. She received her doctorate from the University of London and, as a historian of Eastern European Jewish history, held postdoctoral fellowships, among others, in Yad Vashem, the Center for Jewish History in New York and the Institute of Contemporary History in Munich. Her latest monograph *Dipisi. Żydzi polscy w amerykańskiej i brytyjskiej strefach okupacyjnych Niemiec, 1945–1948 (Dipisi: Polish Jews in the American and British occupation zones of Germany, 1945–1948)* was published in 2019.

ERIK RIEDEL

is an art historian, and supervises the exile art collection as well as the Ludwig Meidner Archive at the Jewish Museum Frankfurt. He studied at the Ruprecht-Karls-Universität Heidelberg and Goethe University Frankfurt, and curated numerous exhibitions on the art of the 19th and 20th centuries, focusing on artists like Moritz Daniel Oppenheim, Ludwig and Else Meidner, Charlotte Salomon and Arie Goral.

JOANNA TOKARSKA-BAKIR

is a cultural anthropologist, literary scholar, and religious studies scholar. She is Professor at the Institute of Slavic Studies at the Polish Academy of Sciences and published numerous books and articles on topics related to the anthropology of violence. Her latest monograph: *Pod klątwą. Społeczny portret pogromu kieleckiego* (*Cursed. A social portrait of the Kielce pogrom*) was published in 2018. Her previous book was published in 2015 under the title *Légendes du sang. Pour une anthropologie de l'antisémitisme chrétien* (*Legends of the blood. For an anthropology of Christian anti-Semitism*). She completed her habilitation at Warsaw University.

MIRJAM WENZEL

is the Director of the Jewish Museum Frankfurt since 2016. Previously, she was responsible for conveying Jewish history in digital and printed media at the Jewish Museum Berlin. She studied General and Comparative Literature, Theater, Film and Television Studies and Political Science in Berlin, Tel Aviv and Munich. Since 2019, she is Honorary Professor at the Goethe University in Frankfurt.

GLOSSARY OF TERMS

ALIYAH: Hebrew term (literally meaning "ascent") for the immigration of Jews from the diaspora to the Land of Israel.

ALIYAH BET: A codename given to the illegal immigration of Jews from Nazi-occupied and postwar Europe to Mandate Palestine between 1934 and the founding of the State of Israel in 1948.

ANGLO-AMERICAN COMMITTEE OF INQUIRY (AACI): A joint British-American task force established in January 1946 to examine the problem of Jewish immigration to British-ruled Mandate Palestine and make recommendations for its resolution. The British invited the Americans to form a joint inquiry in order to share responsibility for policy formation in Palestine because they feared Arab resistance in the area and hoped for American support. The report of the committee recommended the admission of 100,000 displaced Jews and that Palestine should be neither a Jewish nor an Arab state. The committee's recommendations were rejected by both Arabs and Jews, and Britain decided to refer the problem to the United Nations.

BEIT MIDRASH: Special premises for the study and interpretation of Jewish religious texts usually located in, or adjacent to, a synagogue.

BRICHA: Organized underground effort run by members of the Jewish resistance in Europe, the Jewish Brigade of the British Army, and Jews already living in Mandate Palestine (under British rule) during the Second World War and the early postwar years to help Holocaust survivors escape Europe and immigrate to Mandate Palestine.

CENTRAL COMMITTEE OF JEWS IN POLAND: The main political representative body of Polish Jews between 1944 and 1950. Its original name was Provisional Central Committee of Jews in Poland, which was changed in 1946 to Central Committee of Jews in Poland. It represented Jewish interests towards Polish authorities and supervised care and social assistance given to the survivors of the Holocaust.

CENTRAL COMMITTEE OF LIBERATED JEWS IN THE U.S. ZONE OF GERMANY (CCLJ): The official representative body of Jewish displaced persons in the American occupation zone between 1945 and 1950, with headquarters in Munich. The Central Committee was involved in every aspect of Jewish DP life.

CENTRAL JEWISH HISTORICAL COMMISSION (POLAND): A body established in 1944 under the auspices of the Central Committee of Jews in Poland to collect and record testimonies of Jewish survivors. The commission published many testimonies, memoirs, and diaries which documented Nazi crimes. It also worked on securing the remaining historical records of the Jewish population in Poland, especially from the war years. In addition, the commission aided Jewish honor courts and their lawyers in conducting their investigations. In 1947, the commission was transformed into the Jewish Historical Institute.

CHEDER: Jewish elementary school where young boys learn the Hebrew language and the basics of Judaism.

DEPORTÁLTAKAT GONDOZÓ ORSZÁGOS BIZOTTSÁG (DEGOB): The National Committee for Attending Deportees was the central organization established in the summer of 1945 by the postwar Jewish communities of Hungary, with the help of international Jewish aid organizations. Its tasks included helping with the repatriation of survivors to Hungary, providing them with social aid, and implementing documentation projects.

DISPLACED PERSONS (DPs): After the Second World War, the term referred to persons (Jews and non-Jews alike) who had been forcibly removed from their native countries during the war, consequently found themselves outside their home country at the end of the war, and could neither return there nor relocate elsewhere without help. Today, the term refers to anyone uprooted from their home, often as a result of violent coercion.

DOCTORS' PLOT: An antisemitic campaign organized by Joseph Stalin in 1952–53 during which a group of predominantly Jewish doctors was arrested, based on fabricated charges that they had intended to assassinate members of the Soviet leadership. After Stalin's death in 1953, the new Soviet leadership dismissed all charges related to the plot, and the imprisoned doctors were released.

HAGGADAH (plural: haggadot): Hebrew term (lit. telling or reporting) for the compilation of texts used during the Passover seder (evening meal) to guide the celebrations. It includes prayers, rituals, songs, and the biblical story of the Exodus from Egypt.

HAGANAH: Clandestine Jewish paramilitary organization in British Mandate Palestine between 1920 and 1948. It later formed the core of the Israel Defense Forces (IDF), the military of the State of Israel.

HAKHSHARAH (plural: Hakhsharot): The Hebrew term (literally meaning "preparation") referred to Zionist training programs and agricultural centers in postwar Europe where Jewish youth acquired the technical skills necessary for their emigration to Israel and subsequent life in agricultural settlements there.

HALAKHAH: The collective body of Jewish religious laws. It guides not only religious practices and beliefs, but also numerous aspects of Jewish everyday life.

HASHOMER HATZAIR: A secular socialist Zionist youth movement founded in 1913 in the Austro-Hungarian Monarchy.

HEBREW IMMIGRANT AID SOCIETY (HIAS): An aid organization founded in 1881 in New York to assist Jews fleeing pogroms in Russia and Eastern Europe by providing them with meals, jobs, and shelter after their arrival to the United States. During the Second World War the organization, which had by then several offices in Europe, helped Jews flee Nazi persecution. After the war, HIAS assisted survivors in finding their remaining family members and facilitated the emigration of Jewish displaced persons, mostly to North America.

HITAHDUT: A secular Zionist organization founded in Poland in the 1920s with the main aim of establishing a Jewish national center in Palestine based on socialist principles and a non-religious Hebrew-language culture.

HONOR COURT: Jewish honor courts were administrative tribunals set up after the Second World War by local Jewish communities to investigate fellow Jews whose behavior under Nazi occupation was called into question, and to condemn and sanction those whose actions were deemed reproachable. Most such courts operated in DP camps and in Poland, but ad-hoc tribunals were also set up elsewhere. The honor courts were dismantled by 1950.

IHUD: A small Zionist party in Mandate Palestine established in 1942 which proposed a bi-national solution, i.e. the establishment of an Arab-Jewish state with joint organs of government.

"INFILTREES": A term used in the DP camps of the postwar period for Jewish survivors from Poland who had spent the war years in the Soviet Union.

INTERNATIONAL REFUGEE ORGANIZATION (IRO): An intergovernmental organization established in 1946 to deal with the problem of displaced persons and refugees in Europe. In 1948, IRO officially became an agency of the United Nations and assumed most of the functions formally performed by the United Nations Relief and Rehabilitation Administration (UNRRA). In 1952, IRO was closed down and many of its responsibilities were taken over by the Office of the United Nations High Commissioner for Refugees (UNHCR).

JDC (AMERICAN JEWISH JOINT DISTRIBUTION COMMITTEE/ JOINT): A Jewish relief organization based in New York City that was founded in 1914 with the initial goal of providing funding for Jews living under Ottoman rule in Palestine. In the wake of the First World War, it also organized massive relief projects across Eastern Europe to support communities devastated by the war. After Hitler's rise to power in 1933, the JDC started to focus on helping Jews escape from Nazi Germany and, after the outbreak of the Second World War, from Nazi-occupied Europe. After the war, the JDC became a major aid provider for survivors, financing urgent necessities to prevent mass starvation, but also providing for the educational and cultural needs, and later the long-term rehabilitation of Jewish survivors in Europe.

JEWISH AGENCY FOR PALESTINE/ISRAEL: A Jewish non-profit organization which was established in 1908 in Jerusalem as the Palestine Office of the Zionist Organization in Palestine under Ottoman rule to represent the Jews living there at that time, aid Jewish immigration, and to buy land for the settlement of new Jewish immigrants. In 1929, it was officially renamed the Jewish Agency for Palestine and successfully negotiated with the British to expand Jewish immigration quotas to Mandate Palestine. After Hitler's rise to power in Germany in 1933, the Agency facilitated clandestine Jewish immigration from Europe to the area beyond the British quotas. After the war, it became a major diplomatic actor in the struggle for statehood while also continuing the organization of illegal immigration to Palestine. After the founding of the State of Israel, the Agency continued to deal with immigration and immigrant absorption.

JEWISH BRIGADE: A military formation in the British Army founded in 1944 which included more than 5,000 Jewish volunteers from Mandate Palestine.

JEWISH CULTURAL RECONSTRUCTION, INC. (JCR): An organization established in New York in 1947 to collect and redistribute heirless Jewish cultural property in the American occupation zone of Germany. Among the JCR's leaders were some of the most prominent American Jewish intellectuals of the time. By the time the organization finished its operations in 1952, it had redistributed hundreds of thousands of books and Jewish ritual objects, sending the great majority of them to Israel and the United States.

JEWISH LABOR BUND: Secular Jewish socialist party in the Russian Empire between 1897 and 1921. The Polish part of the Bund, which seceded from the Russian organization shortly before the birth of an independent Poland in 1917, continued to operate until 1948. The members of the Bund were called Bundists.

JUDENRAT (plural: Judenräte): Jewish representation or council set up in the ghettos in Nazi-occupied Europe on German orders. The task of a *Judenrat* was to provide basic community services for the Jewish populations, but also the implementation of Nazi policies.

KAPO: A prisoner in a concentration camp tasked by the SS guards with various roles including the guarding of barracks, leading and supervising forced labor units, and administrative functions. *Kapos* were usually spared hard labor and enjoyed some privileges.

KIBBUTZ (plural: kibbutzim): Collective communities in Israel that are traditionally based on agricultural production. In the postwar years, *kibbutzim* were also established in Europe in the framework of Zionist youth training programs preparing young survivors for emigration to Palestine/Israel. The member of a *kibbutz* is called a *kibbutznik*.

KIPPAH: The Hebrew word for a brimless cap worn by observant Jewish men.

MIKVEH: Jewish ritual bath.

NKVD (PEOPLE'S COMMISSARIAT FOR INTERNAL AFFAIRS): The Interior Ministry of Russia and (after its establishment in 1922) the Soviet Union between 1917 and 1946. The NKVD was notorious for its role in political repression which included, for example, an unknown number of executions and the administration of the forced-labor camp system known as the Gulag.

ORT (ORGANISATION–RECONSTRUCTION–TRAINING): Established in 1880 as the Society for the Promotion of Skilled Trades Among the Jews of Russia (*Obshchestvo remeslennogo i zemledel'cheskogo truda*) to provide education and training in practical occupations for needy Jews in the Russian Empire, ORT later moved its headquarters to Berlin, Paris, and eventually to Geneva while expanding its structure and creating local branches in various countries. After the Second World War, ORT established rehabilitation programs for survivors and, after the creation of the State of Israel in 1948, training programs there as well. Today, ORT is a global Jewish education network.

PESACH/PASSOVER: A Jewish holiday that celebrates the liberation of Jews from slavery in ancient Egypt. Traditionally, the holiday begins with an evening meal, the so-called *seder*, during which the biblical story is recounted. *Seder* customs also include eating only unleavened bread (*matzo* or *matzah*) as well as other symbolic foods, and drinking four cups of wine.

PEYES: The Hebrew word for sideburns or sidelocks worn by some Orthodox Jewish men.

POALE ZION: A Marxist-Zionist workers' movement which started in Poland and the Russian Empire in the late nineteenth and early twentieth centuries. The movement split in 1920 at its Congress in Vienna into two wings: the more Zionist right wing and the more communist-oriented Left Poale Zion.

PURIM: A holiday that commemorates Jewish deliverance from the hands of Haman, a main official of King Ahasuerus who wanted to kill all the Jews in the Persian Empire, as told in the Book of Esther.

REHABILITATION COMMISSION: A legal tribunal set up by the Central Committee of Liberated Jews in the American occupation zone of Germany in Munich in 1947. The Commission had jurisdiction over cases involving alleged Nazi collaborators.

SED, SOZIALISTISCHE EINHEITSPARTEI DEUTSCHLANDS (SOCIALIST UNITY PARTY): Established in 1946 by a forced merger of communists and social democrats, the SED was the governing communist party in the German Democratic Republic from its establishment in 1949 until its dissolution in 1989.

SHAMES: A member of a Jewish community who looks after the synagogue and the community cemetery.

SHE'ERIT HAPLETAH (SURVIVING REMNANT): A biblical term used by Jewish displaced persons after the Second World War to refer to themselves and their communities. The phrase indicated the hope of reconstruction stemming from those who remained alive.

SHLICHIM: Representatives of the Jewish Agency for Palestine and later, Israel.

SHOKHET: Ritual slaughterer certified under Jewish law to slaughter cattle and poultry.

SHTETL: A shtetl was a small town or village in Central Eastern Europe with a large Jewish population. During the Shoah, shtetls were completely eradicated.

SHUL: Synagogue in colloquial Yiddish.

SMAD, SOWJETISCHE MILITÄRADMINISTRATION IN DEUTSCH-LAND (SOVIET MILITARY ADMINISTRATION IN GERMANY): The SMAD ruled the Soviet occupation zone between 1945 and 1949. With the creation of the German Democratic Republic, the SMAD was abolished and its administrative responsibilities were turned over to the new GDR government.

TORAH: The five books of Moses. Traditionally, the Torah is written on a scroll in Hebrew and stored in the holiest spot in the synagogue (the Torah Ark or *Aron Kodesh* in Hebrew). It is used during the Torah reading rituals of Jewish services.

TZITZIT: Specially knotted textile fringes which are attached to the four corners of the prayer shawl (called *tallit*) worn by observant Jewish men.

UNITED ISRAEL APPEAL/KEREN HAYESOD: A fundraising organization for Israel which was established in 1920 to raise funds worldwide for the foundation of a Jewish homeland. During the Second World War, the organization launched emergency campaigns to help the Allied war effort. After the war, it supported the illegal immigration of Jews to Mandate Palestine.

UNITED NATIONS RELIEF AND REHABILITATION ADMINISTRATION (UNRRA): An international relief agency which operated between 1943 and 1947 (between 1945 and 1947 under the auspices of the United Nations) to administer and organize emergency aid (mostly food, clothes, and medications) for survivors of the war. UNRRA operated in postwar Germany, mostly in Displaced Persons' camps.

UNITED ZIONIST ORGANIZATION (UZO): An organization founded in Landsberg, Germany in 1945 by the Jewish Zionists of the DP camps. The main goal of the UZO was to prepare Jewish survivors for emigration to Israel and life there based on socialist ideals and the prioritization of work.

VVN, VEREINIGUNG DER VERFOLGTEN DES NAZIREGIMES (ASSO-CIATION OF PERSECUTEES OF THE NAZI REGIME): A union of many regional groups from the four Allied occupation zones of Germany and the city of Berlin founded in 1947 in Frankfurt am Main to represent political prisoners and those who had been persecuted by the Nazi system in Germany.

WORLD JEWISH CONGRESS: An international organization representing Jewish communities worldwide. It was established in 1936 in Geneva to act as "the diplomatic arm of the Jewish people" and fight for Jewish minority rights. However, during the Second World War, the organization focused on rescue efforts and, in the aftermath of the war, sought to secure civil rights, reparation payments, and property restitution for Jewish survivors in Europe.

YIDDISH: The traditional language of Central and East-European Jews. During the Shoah, the Jewish communities that used the language in their day-to-day life were largely destroyed, which led to a dramatic decline in the use of the language. Nevertheless, in the immediate postwar years, Yiddish emerged as the lowest common linguistic denominator within the heterogeneous Jewish DP community. Much of the extensive Jewish DP literature was therefore produced in Yiddish.

YISHUV: The Jewish community in Palestine before the establishment of the State of Israel.

YIVO: The Yiddish Scientific Institute (*Yidisher visnshaftlekher institut*) opened in 1925 in Wilno (today Vilnius), which then belonged to Poland, to study and document Jewish life, especially in the Yiddish-speaking parts of Eastern Europe. Though the institute was looted by the Nazis during the Second World War, some of its holdings were smuggled out and saved. The liberating American troops also found some of YIVO's collections in a former Nazi institute in Frankfurt am Main. The headquarters of YIVO had been moved to New York already during the war, and the remaining collections also transported there shortly after the war's end. The institute operates in New York up to this day.

PHOTO AND VIDEO SOURCES

American Jewish Historical Society, New York

American Jewish Joint Distribution Committee, New York

Amsterdam City Archives

Archive of the Taube Institute of Jewish Studies, University of Wroclaw, Polen

Beit Hatfutsot, Museum of the Jewish People, Tel Aviv, Israel – Simona Benyamini

Budapest City Archives

Bundesarchiv, Koblenz

Center for Traditional Music and Dance, New York

CHRONOS-MEDIA, Kleinmachnow

Deutsche Fotothek in der Sächsischen Landesbibliothek – Staats- und Universitätsbibliothek Dresden

dpa Picture-Alliance, Frankfurt am Main

Emanuel Ringelblum, Jewish Historical Institute, Warsaw

Fortepan, Budapest

Ghetto Fighters House Museum, Western Galilee, Israel

Heally Gross and the Natan and Yaakov Gross Archive, Israel

Dr. Hanna Herzig, Tel Aviv

Hungarian Telegraphic Agency (MTI), Budapest

Institut für Stadtgeschichte Frankfurt am Main

JDC Archives, New York City

Jüdische Gemeinde Frankfurt am Main

Andreas Kuba, Vienna

Landesarchiv Berlin

Library of Congress Geography and Map Division, Washington D.C., USA

Literatuurmuseum Den Haag

Magyar Nemzeti Filmlap, Budapest

Magyar Távirati Iroda, Budapest

MairDumont, Ostfildern

Mémorial de la Shoah, Paris

Muzeum Miejskie Dzierżoniowa, Polen

National Science and Media Museum, Bradford

Nederlands Fotomuseum, Rotterdam

Nederlands Instituut voor Beeld en Geluid, Hilversum

Shmuel Pelleg, Kfar Saba, Israel

Polish National Film Archive – Audiovisual Institute, Warschau

PROGRESS Filmverleih, Halle/Saale

Aviva Slesin, New York

Benjamin Soussan, Kirchzarten

Staatsbibliothek zu Berlin

Steven Spielberg Jewish Film Archive, Hebrew University of Jerusalem

Stiftung Stadtmuseum Berlin

Andrea Szapiro, Frankfurt am Main

The Joseph and Margit Hoffmann Judaica Postcard Collection at the Folklore Research Center of the Mandel Institute of Jewish Studies, The Hebrew University of Jerusalem, Israel

The Magnes Collection of Jewish Art and Life, University of California, Berkeley, USA

Unione Delle Comunità Ebraiche Italiane, Rom

United States Holocaust Memorial Museum, Washington, D.C.

University Archives and Special Collections, Paul V. Galvin Library, Illinois Institute of Technology, Chicago

Yad Vashem – The World Holocaust Remembrance Center, Jerusalem

YIVO Institute for Jewish Research, New York City

ACKNOWLEDGEMENTS

LENDERS

Akademie der Künste, Berlin
Arolsen Archives, Bad Arolsen
Abraham Ben, Frankfurt am Main
Binyamin Ben-Perach, Israel
Ewa Buszko, Warsaw
Rivka Cohen, Jerusalem
Dr. Helena Datner, Warsaw
Silvia Godelli, Bari
Deutsches Historisches Museum, Berlin
Kurt de Jong, Frankfurt am Main
Joods Historisch Museum, Amsterdam
Jewish Museum Berlin
Jewish Museum Munich
Jewish Museum Vienna
Keren Kajemet Leisrael – Jüdischer Nationalfonds,
  Düsseldorf
Efi Livnat, Timrat, Israel
Magyar Zsidó Múzeum és Levéltár, Budapest
Magyarországi Autonóm Orthodox Izraelita Hitközség,
  Budapest
Familie Julius Meyer, Campinas, Brasilien
Hannah und Rebecca Nieznanowski, Uppsala
Rosa Orlean, Frankfurt am Main
POLIN Museum of the History of Polish Jews, Warsaw
Lidia Robak, Warsaw
Familie Rozenberg, Frankfurt am Main
Dr. Hermann Simon, Berlin
Stiftung Neue Synagoge Berlin – Centrum Judaicum
Éva Szepesi, Frankfurt am Main
The Emanuel Ringelblum Jewish Historical Institute,
  Warsaw
United States Holocaust Memorial Museum,
  Washington, D.C.
Universitätsbibliothek Johann Christian Senckenberg,
Goethe-Universität, Frankfurt am Main
Vintage Galéria, Budapest
Yad Tabenkin Archives, Ramat Efal, Ramat Gan, Israel
Zentrum für verfolgte Künste, Solingen

SUPPORT

Esther Alexander-Ihme, Frankfurt am Main
Dr. Floriane Azoulay, Bad Arolsen
Sándor Bacskai, Budapest
Johannes Beermann-Schön, Frankfurt am Main
Michael Bernstein, Vienna
Viktória Bányai, Budapest
Eberhard Bätza, Frankfurt am Main
Monique Behr, Frankfurt am Main
Hetty Berg, Berlin
Jonathan Crossen, Frankfurt am Main and Tromsø
Gábor Dombi, Budapest
Dr. Axel Dossmann, Jena
Jutta Fleckenstein, Munich
Dr. Stefan Fricke, Frankfurt am Main
Katharina Friedla, Warsaw
Dr. Christian Groh, Bad Arolsen
Familie de Jong, Frankfurt am Main
Kamil Kijek, Wrocław
Prof. Dr. Salomon Korn, Frankfurt am Main
Katie Lanza, Washington D.C.
Linda Levy, New York
Tamás Lózsy, Budapest
Tobias Picard, Frankfurt am Main
Claudia Schüßler, Frankfurt am Main
Adam Strohm, Chicago
Bart Wallet, Amsterdam

SPONSORS

Bundeskulturstiftung der Republik Deutschland
Daimler
Hannelore Krempa Stiftung
Christiane Weickart und Nicolaus Weickart
Gesellschaft der Freunde und Förderer des Jüdischen
    Museums e.V.
Gemeinnützige Hertie-Stiftung
Stiftung Polytechnische Gesellschaft, Frankfurt am Main
European Association for Jewish Studies

PROJECT PARTNER

Leibniz-Institut für jüdische Geschichte und Kultur –
Simon-Dubnow

KULTURSTIFTUNG
DES
BUNDES

DAIMLER

hessische
kultur
stiftung

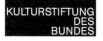
GESELLSCHAFT
DER FREUNDE UND FÖRDERER
DES JÜDISCHEN MUSEUMS E.V.

GEMEINNÜTZIGE
Hertie Stiftung

Stiftung
Polytechnische
Gesellschaft
Frankfurt am Main

EAJS
European Association for Jewish Studies

IMPRINT

This publication appears in conjunction with
the exhibition
Our Courage: Jews in Europe 1945–48
Jewish Museum Frankfurt
March 24 – August 22, 2021

EXHIBITION

DIRECTOR Prof. Dr. Mirjam Wenzel
PROJECT DIRECTOR Dr. Werner Hanak
CURATORS Dr. Kata Bohus, Erik Riedel
RESEARCH CONSULTANTS Prof. Dr. Atina Grossmann,
    New York, Dr. Elisabeth Gallas, Leipzig
RESEARCH INTERN Moritz Bauerfeind
RESEARCH ASSOCIATES Dr. Chiara Renzo (Research
    Italy), Franciszek Zakrzewski (Research Poland),
    Dennis Eiler (Yiddish literature and Pesach 1946),
PROJECT COORDINATOR AND REGISTRAR
    Sabine Paukner
EDUCATION Manfred Levy, Kathrin Schön
COMMUNICATION Sarah Mirjam Fischer,
    Korbinian Böck, Theresa Gehring
ADMINISTRATION Dorothea Spillmann, Michaela
    Dittrich, Jutta Keller

EXHIBITION AND GRAPHIC DESIGN, MEDIA
PRODUCTION gewerkdesign, Berlin: Jens Imig,
    Bianca Mohr, Birgit Schlegel, Franziska Schuh,
    Alexandra Zackiewicz, Jens Lohmann
MEDIA DEVELOPMENT Graphscape, Berlin,
    Michael Lorenz
SOUND DESIGN Peter Imig, Römstedt

PHOTOGRAPHY Studio für Fotografie Herbert Fischer,
    Frankfurt am Main
EXHIBITION FIT-OUT AND GRAPHIC PRODUCTION
    Messegraphik und Messebau Schreiber, Frankfurt
CONSERVATORS Atelier Carta, Martina Noehles,
    Frankfurt
LIGHTING Lightsolutions, Stephan Zimmermann,
    Oberursel
TRANSLATION Nick Somers, Vienna

CATALOG

EDITED by Kata Bohus, Atina Grossmann,
    Werner Hanak, and Mirjam Wenzel
EDITORIAL COORDINATION Sabine Paukner
    and Erik Riedel
PHOTO EDITOR Sabine Paukner
COPY EDITOR David Brenner
GRAPHIC DESIGN gewerkdesign Berlin, Birgit Schlegel

COVER ILLUSTRATION Survivors celebrate Pesach in
    Białystok, 1946. Emanuel Ringelblum Jewish Historical
    Institute, Warsaw

PUBLISHED AT WALTER DE GRUYTER
ISBN 978-3-11-064920-8
E-ISBN (PDF) 978-3-11-065307-6
LIBRARY OF CONGRESS CONTROL NUMBER
    2020943492
BIBLIOGRAPHIC INFORMATION PUBLISHED BY
THE DEUTSCHE NATIONALBIBLIOTHEK
    The Deutsche Nationalbibliothek lists this publication
    in the Deutsche Nationalbibliografie; detailed bib
    liographic data are available on the internet at
    http://dnb.dnb.de.

PRODUCTION EDITOR André Horn
PRINTING AND BINDING Beltz Grafische
    Betriebe GmbH, Bad Langensalza
www.degruyter.com

In spite of our efforts, we have not managed to identify
all holders of legal rights. We therefore ask you to
contact the Jewish Museum Frankfurt so that the
customary royalties can be paid.

Our/
Courage/ Jews
in Europe
1945–48